SAUDI ARABIA

Economic Trends,
Business Environment
and Investment Opportunities

with the compliments of

البنك الأهلي التجاري
THE NATIONAL COMMERCIAL BANK

SAUDI ARABIA

Economic Trends, Business Environment and Investment Opportunities

Henry T. Azzam
Chief Economist
The National Commercial Bank

Published by Euromoney Books
in association with
The National Commercial Bank, Jeddah, Saudi Arabia

To the People of Saudi Arabia

whose vision for the future is moulded by their rich culture, and the will to pursue development and modernisation while preserving traditional values.

Preface

This book is a guide to the Saudi Arabian economy, not an abstract theoretical work on economic development in the Kingdom. It is written as an introduction for businessmen, bankers, exporters, contractors, sales directors, industrial enterprises, joint venture partners, wholesalers, government trade officials, politicians, researchers, consultants and students, as well as all those keen on understanding the Saudi economy or who have business interests and/or financial exposure to the Kingdom.

I started working on this book after joining the National Commercial Bank (NCB) in February 1991. Without my association with NCB, and the support I received from the institution, the book would have never come to fruition. I should like to thank the General Management of NCB, and in particular Sheikh Khalid bin Mahfouz and Sheikh Mohamad bin Mahfouz for allowing me the opportunity to undertake such an endeavour.

The information and analysis contained within these pages draw heavily on the various issues of the *NCB Economist*, the bank's publication which I research and write every month. I should like to express my appreciation of the work done by the IMF staff on the Saudi economy which provided me with a lot of insight and on which I drew when building my data base on development trends in the Kingdom.

I am particularly grateful to Mr Abdulhadi Shayif, NCB's Deputy General Manager, for encouraging me to write this book during my tenure as Chief Economist of NCB. I sincerely appreciate as well his enthusiastic support for all that I have attempted to do and for taking time to read parts of the manuscript and give his comments on it. I am also grateful to Dr Abdulraouf Banaja, Assistant General Manager for introducing me to NCB and for his continuous moral support.

My thanks go as well to many people in the various government ministries and in the Saudi Arabian Monetary Agency who provided me with a lot of data used in this volume.

My appreciation and love to my wife Reem and my children Suhail, Ramzi and Marwan for sharing this experience with me and for suffering extra burdens during the preparation of this book without voicing any complaints. Mr Francisco Rubrico deserves much praise for making an excellent job of the typescript.

Henry T. Azzam
Jeddah, Saudi Arabia

Published by
Euromoney Books
Nestor House
Playhouse Yard
London EC4V 5EX

Telephone 071-779 8888

ISBN 1 85564 156 9

Typeset by Euromoney Books and PW Graphics
Printed in Singapore by Craft Print

Contents

Introduction

The Kingdom of Saudi Arabia, which was founded by King Abdel Aziz Al Saud in 1932, has been transformed beyond recognition over the past sixty years. The economy has grown to become the largest in the Middle East and one of the top non-OECD economies, with total GDP in 1991 of US$107 billion. It is the world's leading oil exporter, the Arab world's largest economy and the biggest consumer of foreign products between western Europe and Southeast Asia. In terms of imported goods and services it is a larger market than Portugal, Greece, Australia or Thailand. When the Kingdom decides to spend, save or invest, it is frequently on a scale much greater than in most other developing countries. Riyadh's voice is heard in the highest councils of world economic policy-makers. It plays a pivotal role in OPEC and other regional and international bodies and Saudi Arabia is the only country outside the group of seven (G7) with its own representative on the IMF's board of executive directors.

Throughout the past sixty years, Saudi governments and Saudi society have remained stable and true to their culture and beliefs. It is this attachment to traditional values and principles which has allowed the country, through six decades of rapid change, to come so far in so short a time. For the future, Saudi Arabia will no longer be content just to copy or to borrow western technology to further its development. Saudis are increasingly expressing a desire to mould western know-how and technology to Saudi needs and priorities, whether it is in the designing of buildings, the planning of cities or the building of new industries.

Many sceptics have often doubted the Kingdom's ability to build in such a short period of time a modern industrial society, given the constraints of limited infrastructure, the small pool of skilled labour and only a single exportable commodity. However, most of the dreams that inspired the first economic development plan in 1970 have been fulfilled. On every front, from standards of health and communications, to the higher number of students becoming university graduates to the eight-lane highways and sprawling modern urban centres, Saudi Arabia has risen up the economic development league to reach a position that is the envy of all but the world's most advanced economies. By 1991 *per capita* gross national product had surpassed every African and Latin American state and was exceeded in Southeast Asia only by Japan, Singapore and Hong Kong. According to the World Bank, Saudi Arabia is neither poor nor developing; it is classified as an upper middle income state, comparable with Portugal.

After laying the foundations of a modern economy in the 1970s, the planning emphasis shifted steadily in the 1980s towards creating productive activities. Electricity and drinkable water are available in most settlements of any size. There is free education and health care for all. Infrastructure work is continuing, some of it on a huge scale, but mostly involving adding to or improving what has already been built. At the end of 1991, there were more than 7,500 companies operating in the Kingdom with a total capital of SR90 bllion (US$24 billion). Of these, 85 were joint stock companies and 4,096 were limited liability parterships. A strong industrial base has been built, along with the related service back-up to encourage future industrial projects by the private sector. The further advancement of the industrial and services sectors is perceived as being the route to economic growth in the years ahead. The aim is to reduce the Kingdom's excessive dependence on oil and to create self-sustaining economic activities that are not directly affected by external shocks emanating from the world oil market.

The demand for goods and services in the Kingdom will change dramatically over the next ten years. This change will be largely driven by a growing national population, the changing demographic profile of expatriates living in the country, a shifting of tastes and preferences and the growth of local companies. As young nationals grow up, their needs will change and this will cause a shift in the balance of spending power. Europe and America saw the effects of this shift in spending power when the children of the post-1945 baby boom entered the market place as consumers and producers in the 1960s. In a similar way, Saudi Arabia will experience the fruits of its baby boom of the 1970s. It is projected that, by the turn of the century, more than 1 million new homes will be needed, as the majority of young nationals get married and establish their own dwellings, while the size of the non-national population will also be rising. The process of demographic settling, whereby dependents of expatriate workers move to the Kingdom, will become more entrenched in the coming years. All this will create many new opportunities in housing, building materials, home furnishings, consumer durables, foodstuffs and clothing. A wide range of services, particularly training, operating and maintenance, recreational and leisure activities will also have considerable growth potential.

Dealing with Saudi Arabia as simply a residual market for foreign goods and services is a less viable strategy now than it used to be. Foreign companies involved in exporting to Saudi Arabia are gradually realising that the best way to maintain, or expand, their share of the market is to establish a presence in the Kingdom. Saudi Arabia would like its trading partners to help in the process of economic diversification and become, in effect, the Kingdom's industrial partners. A greater share of the local market in the future will go to those exporters who establish a joint venture presence here, while those who do not join in the diversification drive may find themselves at a disadvantage. Protective tariffs are provided for selected commodities produced locally and other incentives greatly reduce the cost of establishing an industrial or a service-related joint venture in the Kingdom.

Historically, the economic system of Saudi Arabia has been based on the principles of free enterprise. The freedom to transact and to own property and assets unhindered by threats of nationalisation has been a fact of life in this society. There is a basic respect for the aspirations of the individual, a tradition for private property to exist as a right and a social recognition of private success. In countries where *laissez-faire* policies are encouraged, as in Saudi Arabia, entrepreneurs will continue to invest whenever they perceive an opportunity to make profits. The availability of capital, along with supportive government rules and regulations will increase such opportunities in the years ahead.

Socially, there is a retreat to traditional values, many of which were challenged in the boom years of the 1970s and 1980s. The extravagant consumer expenditure of that period has been tempered to a large extent. The future should see more conservative consumption habits and new attitudes towards savings and investment. Economically, a greater emphasis is being put on private initiatives, accompanied by a marked shift towards less government largesse. The public sector has given up its role as "employer of last resort", even though it continues to steer development trends in the country. The Saudi private sector has depended heavily in the past on government expenditure and any cutbacks invariably resulted in lower private sector output. There are signs that this linkage may have begun to weaken, possibly indicating a maturing private sector, and the trend is likely to continue in the years to come.

The road ahead remains long and challenging, not only because of the need to address fiscal imbalances and develop indigenous manpower and managerial skills that can man the restructured Saudi economy of the 1990s, but also because of a requirement to promote attitudes that are appropriate to industrial and financial development. The constraints on growth facing other developing countries, namely lack of capital, infrastructural bottlenecks and high external indebtedness, do not apply to Saudi Arabia. On the contrary, the huge oil and mineral resources and the abundance of capital would continue to facilitate the economic diversification process that is currently underway. Furthermore, unlike many developing countries, the Kingdom is internally stable, has in place a first class infrastructure and a private sector that is both dynamic and wealthy. The "take-off" stage is now completed and the rest of the 1990s will see a drive to maturity.

1 Development themes of the 1990s

Introduction

If economic adjustment to lower oil revenues and the uncertainty created by the Iran-Iraq war were the main constraints on growth in the 1980s, economic diversification, reduction of fiscal shortfalls and the creation of productive employment opportunities for a rapidly growing population are the main challenges of the 1990s. The efforts to diversify Saudi Arabia's economic structure have already started but these will be greatly intensified in the present decade. The advancement of the industrial and services sectors is now widely perceived as being the strategy most likely to lead to economic growth in the years ahead. The aim is to reduce the Kingdom's excessive dependence on oil and to create self-sustaining economic activities that are not directly affected by external shocks emanating from the world oil market.

The 1980s, promising at the outset, turned out to be a decade of missed opportunities. Rising oil revenues in the first half of the decade led to dramatic increases in imports of goods and services and excessive consumption in both public and private sectors. This put a lot of pressure on the country's finances and led to persistent current account and budget deficits. The seemingly limitless opportunities and easy access to wealth encouraged habits of conspicuous consumption that could not be sustained during the period from 1983 to 1988 when oil revenues plunged. Self-fulfilment was achieved for some to a large extent through purchasing power and the accumulation of wealth; and the relationship between productivity and reward was largely diluted. Others, however, were able to capitalise on these opportunities and build successful industrial and commercial enterprises.

A lot of money was allocated to human resource development programmes during the 1980s. This helped boost literacy rates in the Kingdom and a higher percentage of students became university graduates. However, the system did not succeed in producing sufficient people with the skills required to cope with continuing managerial, technological and financial progress. Private sector activities picked up considerably during the 1980s. The contribution to GDP of private sector output reached a peak of 46 per cent in 1988 before dropping to 37.6 per cent in 1990. However, government and public sector institutions continued to play a pivotal role in the process of growth and development. Value added in the oil sector maintained its supremacy over other economic sectors but the stage was set for economic diversification, with industry, agriculture and services contributing more to GDP.

At the start of the 1990s economic activity picked up once more and a new growth cycle started. The resurgence of private sector confidence, higher oil revenues and government expenditures, lower Saudi riyal interest rates and substantial flows of capital seeking domestic investment opportunities helped to place the Saudi economy on a growth path that is likely to continue over the coming few years. Saudis feel good about themselves and their country and are optimistic about the future. The resolution of the Gulf crisis reduced the risks of doing business in the Kingdom, boosted consumer confidence and encouraged more relaxed spending and investment patterns.

The manner in which the Gulf crisis was resolved demonstrated that the world is committed to the security, sovereignty and territorial integrity of the Gulf countries and to the free flow of oil from the region. Saudi Arabia has emerged from the crisis as a major regional power, capable of asserting itself in OPEC and in other regional and international bodies. The new world order and the end of communism, together with the ongoing Middle East peace negotiations, have contributed to a general improvement in the region's geopolitical atmosphere. A new consultative assembly (*Majlis al Shura*) is being set up in the Kingdom and this, together with the laying down of basic rules of government, demonstrates that social reform is intended to proceed alongside economic development and growth.

Development themes of the 1990s

By themes we mean ideas with continuity, trends running from the past into the future. The five themes presented here are not new or exhaustive but are selected because we believe that they will be instrumental in shaping Saudi Arabia's economic outlook in the years to come and because they overlap with the main goals of the current Five-Year Development Plan (1990 to 1995).

Diversification and economic restructuring

The contribution of the oil sector to GDP dropped from 38 per cent in 1983 to 25 per cent in 1988 but rose again to 36 per cent in 1992. Oil also contributes indirectly to GDP through other sectors, especially government expenditure, which is mostly financed by oil revenues, and oil-related activities such as petrochemicals and refining. The Kingdom is, therefore, still overdependent on its hydrocarbon resources for future growth and development. To reduce the impact of fluctuations in world oil prices on the domestic economy and to sustain an internal momentum of growth in the 1990s, various structural changes are expected to be pursued more forcefully. The most important of these is the progressive diversification of the country's productive base and a reorientation of the economy from growth based on the public sector to private sector initiative. Gradual privatisation of certain state enterprises and the mobilisation of private sector resources to reduce the burden on public funds are manifestations of this restructuring strategy.

The scope for new manufacturing activities is broadening all the time as new linkages are established and new technologies and services introduced (for example between basic industries and downstream products, between maintenance and spare parts manufacturing, between agriculture and food processing and between operations and other complementary services). The growing consumer markets offer unique opportunities to establish light industries and the population and labour force requirements of the forthcoming decade require a lot of supporting services. In general, any product or service which fills a local need (import substitution) or can be exported and does not require long-term subsidies and protection to become commercially viable may be considered. The comparative advantage of the Kingdom as a manufacturing base lies in the availability of cheap energy and the low price of local feedstock produced from petrochemical and natural gas plants. The presence of modern infrastructure, the wide range of industrial incentives, low utility prices, the availability of capital funding, internal stability and the freedom of capital movement are all added advantages.

Saudi Arabia would like its trading partners to help in the process of economic diversification by producing part of their exports in the country and becoming, in effect, the Kingdom's industrial partners. A greater share of the local market in the future will go to those exporters who establish a presence in the Kingdom, while those who do not join in the diversification drive may find themselves at a disadvantage. Protective tariffs reaching 20 per cent, together with various other incentives, are provided for selected, locally produced commodities.

There are also promising opportunities for investment in the services sector, which accounts for around 22 per cent of the Kingdom's GDP. Saudi Arabia is a major consumer of foreign services, with roughly US$18 billion spent annually. Operations and maintenance undoubtedly form the biggest growth area, with the market in the 1990s estimated to be worth more than US$8 billion annually. Other promising opportunities include health care, telecommunications, computers and data processing, technology transfer, human resources development, consulting, marketing, research, entertainment, information and general support services.

Privatisation of some public sector enterprises is likely to be a major policy directive of this decade. The government is expected to maintain its ownership of the country's heavy industries, such as oil production and refining, as these require a long time for the return on investments to materialise and marketing and capital structure are beyond the present abilities of the private sector. Commercially viable public sector establishments whose assets can be assessed to give estimates of share values are prime candidates for privatisation. These include various petrochemical plants, telecommunications, grain silos and the airline and railway companies among others. There are public projects that can be privatised through operation and maintenance contracts (lease contracts). These include airports and ports (excluding customs and security), public hospitals, sewage projects, irrigation and maintenance work carried out by municipalities.

Employment and human resources development

The need to create employment opportunities for its growing population is one of the most pressing issues facing the Kingdom. The baby boom generation of the 1970s will enter the labour force in the 1990s, with the percentage of the national population in the age bracket 15 to 59 reaching 50 per cent by the year 2000, compared to around 46 per cent in 1990. The preliminary results of the first Saudi census since 1974 puts the total population of Saudi Arabia in 1992 at 16.9 million, 12.3 million or 73 percent of the total were nationals and 4.6 million or 27 percent were non-nationals. The male population among the Saudi nationals was 6.2 million or 50.4 percent of the total number of Saudis while Saudi females constituted around 49.6 percent of the total or 6.09 million. Males accounted for 70.4 percent of the total expatriate population compared to only 29.6 percent for females. More than 50 per cent of Saudi nationals (or 6.15 million) are aged under 15 years, with the annual population growth rate of around 3.5 per cent being among the highest in the world. During the remaining part of the decade growth is expected to slow, reflecting higher levels of education and larger female participation in the labour force. However, the population is forecast to double over the next 20 years.

Some 150,000 young Saudis enter the job market each year but this figure will soon increase. Government estimates in the Fifth Development Plan are for 575,000 Saudi nationals, with varying levels of education, to enter the labour market over the five-year period. They will fill about 294,000 new jobs, while a total of 281,000 existing positions will be "Saudised"; the private sector is expected to provide most of these jobs. These new arrivals in the labour market will in general have greater educational attainments and higher aspirations than their parents. Their expectations have been moulded by the exceptional period of growth in the 1970s and early 1980s.

More than one-third of the Saudi population is currently in education at primary and secondary schools, girls' colleges, the country's seven universities and some 60 vocational and technical colleges. As the number of school and university graduates increases, while job preferences remain narrow, unemployment among youth will become more visible, or at least long periods of searching for jobs will become common. Such unemployment appears paradoxical in the face of a large expatriate workforce. However, its roots lie in the artificially high expectations of Saudi nationals entering the labour market, the availability of lowly paid expatriate labour, attempts to limit the expansion of public sector employment and a mismatch between the educational qualifications of labour force entrants and the skill requirements of existing jobs.

The idea that Saudis do not, or will not, work is a popular misconception. In the oil and petrochemical sectors there have been Saudis in blue-collar jobs for years and many have moved up the management ladder. The government sector has been "Saudised" to the maximum extent possible, while aviation, banking and utility companies are on the way towards achieving maximum "Saudisation" of employees. In other sectors it may take more time for Saudis to achieve the skills and experience necessary. The government could help in this respect by addressing both the educational system and the labour laws that govern the hiring and firing of Saudis. In the past five years the government has already begun to adjust its education policies away from university degrees towards more technical training. Employers would also like to work more closely with the government to improve the educational curricula and would welcome government financial support for on-the-job training.

Eventually, large numbers of national workforce entrants, denied their first choice of public sector employment or a management job, will seek other opportunities in the manufacturing sector. Larger indigenous labour force participation in certain occupations will be achieved when economic pressures dictate it. Rising budget deficits will limit the ability of the government to create more public sector jobs for new graduates as has been done in the past. The earlier policies have resulted in enormous overstaffing of government institutions. The new realities dominating the Kingdom's labour market in the 1990s will lead nationals to seek whatever opportunities are available, namely technical jobs and the more remunerative, albeit more demanding, openings in the private sector.

Women are an under-utilised human resource which will be drawn upon in the 1990s to help in the process of growth and development. Not only would a larger female labour force reduce the level of dependence on expatriate labour, it would also help to save on the cost of social services incurred, eg medical care, utilities and transport. Many young women are getting education today at all levels from school to university and this will inevitably result in more of them joining the labour force, especially in occupations such as teaching, nursing and other public services. In sectors where a single sex environment is possible (eg banking, health, education and social work), women may become a significant addition to the domestic labour force.

The process of "Saudisation" of the labour force will, therefore, be given added impetus during the current growth cycle. Expatriates are often looked upon by manpower planners as a "sponge" to be squeezed when employment opportunities for the national workforce need to be generated. However, planning and reality are not necessarily identical. The challenge is to devise a system of recruitment, selection, training and placement for nationals, whereby the dependence on expatriate labour is progressively reduced without producing a serious drop in efficiency or a loss of economic competitiveness. This can be done only by well planned and skilfully implemented schemes.

Only when nationals are trained to a level of industrial competence that meets the actual needs of industry and commands its respect will the private sector employer become more responsive to the policy of "Saudisation" of the labour force. The recent tightness of conditions in the Kingdom's labour market, especially for Arabic-speaking expatriates, in the aftermath of the Gulf crisis will undoubtedly facilitate this process.

Oil price and production strategy

The Gulf War brought about important structural changes in the oil industry and the power structure of OPEC. Saudi Arabia emerged as the dominant power in the organisation and a major influence on the world oil market. In future, if strong demand raises the calls on OPEC oil or if the situation in Algeria or Venezuela worsens and leads to a disruption of oil and gas flows, Saudi Arabia's response to tightening markets will be of crucial importance. If and when Iraq re-enters oil markets or the position of the oil industry in the former USSR improves, markets will carefully monitor Saudi policy response to such developments as being the most important factor affecting oil prices.

The Kingdom is essentially a one-resource country with huge oil reserves (30 per cent of the world's total) that would allow it to maintain current levels of production for over 100 years. Its strategy is to preserve the long-term competitiveness of oil *vis-à-vis* alternative energy resources and to foster the increase of the past few years in world demand for oil. To achieve this, a policy of oil price stability and predictability has been pursued and attempts by other OPEC members to engineer any oil shortage have been resisted.

Stability does not preclude a gentle upward adjustment of prices with time. However, in order to stabilise prices at reasonable levels, say within striking distance of the current reference price of US$21 a barrel in nominal terms for the OPEC basket of seven crudes, Saudi Arabia would be ready to boost production in the event of a sudden increase in world demand or such an unforeseen drop in supply as happened following the Gulf crisis. This is not an easy task and would require a sizeable investment of capital resources to be made in advance to prepare idle production capacity for emergency use. The Kingdom has already started a US$16 billion programme to expand its production capacity to 10 million barrels a day (b/d) by 1995, in order to guarantee security of supply to the world oil market.

Saudi Arabia would like to encourage oil producers, both inside and outside OPEC, to work together to prevent excessive volatility and market disequilibrium. It has been made clear by Saudi officials at the highest level that the Kingdom will never again play the role of swing producer. Maintaining market stability is perceived as a common task of all oil producers and Saudi Arabia will contribute only its fair and proportionate share to this task.

A problem at present is that most oil-producing countries are overspending to raise oil production capacity to ensure security of supplies to consumers, while European governments are considering new taxes on oil, over and above the existing ones (the average EC tax in 1991 was US$56 per barrel), that will greatly curtail demand for refined oil products in the European Community. The European countries, staunch advocates of free market principles when it comes to their own industrial exports, are implementing energy policies that are discriminatory and contrary to efficient resource allocation. Such measures could tax away the benefits to consumers of stable oil prices, curtail energy demand and increase inflationary pressures worldwide.

These moves may encourage oil producers to reconsider their long-term investment plans to boost production capacity and additional taxes on oil may be countered by reciprocal measures on imports from the European Community. If the objective of the EC is to reduce oil and energy consumption by putting up prices to the end-users through taxation, then oil producers can do this by cutting production and allowing oil prices to rise.

On the refining side, the Kingdom's strategy is to become the world's largest producer of unleaded petrol and a major exporter of environmentally friendly refined products such as reformulated petrol. Environmental constraints will feature prominently in future Saudi oil and refining strategy. The Kingdom has developed its refining and marketing capacity and plans to expand further, both domestically and by acquiring downstream outlets overseas. If all its current plans come to fruition, Saudi Arabia will have created by the turn of the century a global network from the oil well to the petrol station that is unrivalled by any other producing nation. The long-term goal is to acquire a capacity to refine up to 3 million b/d outside the Kingdom and 2.8 million b/d domestically.

The world oil market is therefore experiencing a major transition back to a fully integrated industry, much as it was in the 1950s and 1960s when the major oil companies (the "Seven Sisters") managed the oil market from the well-head to the retail outlet. This time the principal oil-producing countries, motivated by a desire to gain guaranteed marketing outlets for oil products and to share in the refining and marketing profits, are joining the other major players. Downstream integration will also contribute to market stability and will prove beneficial to oil consumers. The Gulf crisis of 1990 and the oil embargo on Iraq brought home to consumers the advantage of securing long-term oil supplies through direct ties with an oil producer.

Financial policies

The government's fiscal policies in the 1990s will obviously affect the Kingdom's future growth. Saudi Arabia's budget deficits averaged 17.5 per cent of GDP during the period from 1984 to 1991 but the IMF expects this figure to drop to 8 per cent in the first half of the decade. Even this improved level, however, is not sustainable; unless the fiscal imbalance is reduced significantly. The increase in the Kingdom's debt service bill will greatly reduce room for fiscal manoeuvre in the second half of the decade. However, Saudi Arabia is set apart from other countries experiencing rising internal debt by the high level of personal savings (around 30 per cent of disposable income) and by excess liquidity in the hands of the private sector. This will allow additional government borrowing without necessarily crowding out private investment. Furthermore, the Saudi Arabian Monetary Agency (SAMA) is prohibited by law from "monetising" the budget deficit, ie financing it by printing money, and this greatly reduces the inflationary pressures associated with deficit financing.

Debt service will become an important feature of Saudi financial policy in the mid-1990s as repayments start to fall due on some US$15 billion of medium-term loans taken out between 1990 and 1992. However, the Kingdom is not expected to face any difficulty in servicing these debts. Saudi Arabia's debt service ratio remains low (less than 10 per cent) and its underlying balance of payments position is stable.

External borrowing and the issuing of domestic treasury instruments are regular features of public finance in the developed economies and there is no reason why analysts should be alarmed to see Saudi Arabia using them now, simply because it has funded investment and deficits in the past from its foreign reserves. Much of the recent medium-term borrowing has been either exceptional in nature (covering, for example, Desert Storm obligations) or project related. There is no evidence that the Kingdom's year-on-year financial shortfall is out of control. Furthermore, about 60 per cent of the country's total debt obligations have been taken up by autonomous public sector institutions (eg the General Organisation for Social Insurance, the Public Investment Fund and so on). This gives the government the option of writing off the debt if the need arises.

The primary goal during the rest of the decade is to keep fiscal deficits in check through appropriate action. However, there is relatively limited scope for action on the revenue side. The value of Saudi Arabia's oil exports is forecast to remain between US$40 billion and US$45 billion until 1995, increasing only gradually thereafter. This is based on the assumptions of oil prices averaging US$19 a barrel for Brent Crude from 1993 to 1995 and average Saudi crude oil output of 8 million b/d. The anticipated rise in world demand for OPEC oil will be more than fully absorbed by the restoration of oil production in Iraq and Kuwait through 1995. No major tax initiatives are being contemplated for the time being in the Kingdom and there is limited scope for increasing fees and charges for government services and/or reducing subsidies following the sweeping price cuts on such services announced on 24 March 1992. The package of price cuts is estimated to cost the government around SR4.87 billion (US$1.3 billion) a year.

Reduction of government expenditures, the search for further efficiency and productivity in the public sector and a gradual privatisation of state enterprises are the likely avenues for action to generate budgetary savings. While defence spending is expected to remain high, more public sector institutions will be encouraged to meet their funding requirements by raising money directly from the local and international markets. Privatisation of selective public enterprises and the mobilisation of private sector resources will go a long way towards strengthening the country's capital markets, besides generating additional revenues for the government. The most likely form of privatisation, initially at least, is the sale of a proportion of government shares in profitable public sector companies. This will increase the supply of shares available to the public, which currently falls far short of demand. Full divestiture of government shareholdings is likely to be spread over several years.

Attention will also be paid to the need to ensure that adequate financing mechanisms are in place to tap private sector resources effectively. Although the government bond scheme is regarded as having worked well, it is recognised that the heavy reliance on the autonomous government bodies to place the bonds in the past few years cannot continue indefinitely. Accordingly, the authorities have taken a number of steps to enhance the attractiveness of government bonds to the private sector (both banks and non-banks) and to diversify the range of financing instruments available to the government. The recent introduction of treasury bills and repurchase facilities, the development of secondary market operations for government bonds and bills and a reduction in minimum purchase requirements will contribute further to a deepening of the Kingdom's financial markets.

The viability of public sector borrowing has already been tested and the secondary markets for these instruments will follow in years to come. The 1990s should see an increase in the volume of various government bonds and bills issued, the fine-tuning of flows into the primary and secondary markets and a refinement of prices. As the Kingdom's financial markets gain depth, and once a pricing benchmark has been established by the government sector, corporations and banks may be encouraged to issue their own debt instruments.

The next decade will also witness the rise of intermediate institutions to act as underwriters, stockbrokers, fund managers and investment banking advisers and to carry out periodic credit analysis of local companies in order to provide investors with reliable business information. More stringent reporting practices will be implemented and a more adequate legal system to govern the financial sector will evolve. This will eventually offer greater scope for foreign investors to participate in the capital markets of the Kingdom. Expatriates may also be allowed to invest locally, if not directly, possibly through investment funds managed by financial institutions in the Kingdom. Capital markets cannot be created or superimposed on the country; they evolve from a need. At present there is a need for diversified financial services, for developed stock and bond markets that will attract domestic capital which otherwise might be invested abroad and for intermediaries who can facilitate the overall investment process.

Regional integration

With the preparatory work being almost completed, regional cooperation and integration among the six Gulf states is expected to proceed at a quicker pace during the 1990s. Since its establishment in 1981, the Gulf Cooperation Council (GCC) has managed to achieve the free flow of people and capital across boundaries and to streamline certain economic policies at a joint level. A Gulf common market will now evolve that will eliminate completely any remaining barriers and introduce common external tariffs on imports from outside the region.

Even though full monetary union remains a long-term objective (it is expected by the turn of the century), a common exchange rate system is in place *de facto*, since all the Gulf currencies are in effect pegged to the US dollar and there are no restrictions on transferring money from one Gulf state to another. The next step is the successive harmonisation of the countries' laws and regulations and the implementation of greater economic and monetary cooperation and coordination. There are both internal and external forces motivating the move towards a Gulf common market. As the world at large evolves into inward-looking economic groupings, the Gulf countries will find it necessary to shake off any remaining nationalistic idiosyncrasies, in order to emerge as one solid, economic, if not political, entity. This will be capable of dealing on an equal footing with the emerging regional groupings worldwide (post-1992 Europe, the North American cooperation zone, the Asia-Pacific Region and the Indian sub-continent).

Although inter-Gulf trade constitutes less than 10 per cent of the region's foreign trade, the flow of services (banking, insurance, communications, transport, tourism and so on) between GCC member states is rising. Regional trade is also likely to grow in the next few years as the Gulf countries diversify their economies away from oil. Capital flows will be further liberalised by encouraging GCC nationals to own shares, real estate and financial instruments and to establish joint venture firms in the Gulf states.

With the full implementation of the Unified Economic Agreement among the six GCC states, a large number of manufacturing projects become viable on a regional basis. The Agreement specifies that local manufacturing within the GCC will be protected by a common tariff applied by all member states once reasonable capacity has been reached. Exporters to the region should, therefore, prepare now for the opportunities that will arise once the cooperative schemes are finally in place.

Concluding remarks

Forecasting the future is not an exact science; indeed it is not a science at all. One may exaggerate or underestimate particular factors and there is the problem of entirely unforeseen variables (eg the Gulf crisis) which can alter the whole economic outlook. However, the general picture that should be formed is that the Saudi economy is fundamentally healthy. With oil revenues above US$40 billion a year, and given the wealth and dynamism of the Saudi private sector, the problems that the Kingdom face are clearly not insurmountable. In addition, it has been enjoying internal stability unmatched elsewhere in the developing world.

While the current strong growth cycle is expected to prevail for the next few years, possibly reaching a peak in 1994, the second half of the decade may see generally less buoyant growth conditions. World demand for oil will continue to grow, albeit at lower rates than in the first half of the decade, and will be tempered by the new energy taxes being considered. By 1995 most of the large projects to expand oil production, refining, petrochemicals and other manufacturing activities in the Kingdom will have been completed. The surge in public infrastructure investment (in defence, communications, water and municipal services among other areas), initiated after the end of the Gulf crisis to make up for the retrenchment in spending in the previous years, will return to more normal levels. Once the pent-up consumer demand that the Kingdom's markets have been witnessing is satisfied, business investment may also slow. Tighter budgetary controls, higher US dollar and Saudi riyal interest rates, slower population growth and more normal productivity growth rates will contribute further to the postulated slower growth scenario during the second half of the 1990s. The 6 per cent to 8 per cent nominal GDP growth forecast for 1993 to 1995 is expected to give way to growth rates of only 3 per cent to 5 per cent in the years to follow.

2 Economic trends and structure

Economic trends

The Saudi economy was originally based on subsistence agriculture, the livestock of the nomadic tribes and funds brought in by the annual pilgrimage to Makkah and Madinah. The discovery of oil irrevocably changed the situation, with oil revenues becoming the chief source of government finance and oil production the dominant component of GDP. It was not until 1962 that the Saudi government started using the ever-increasing oil revenues to modernise the country's agricultural, industrial and infrastructural base. During the late 1960s and throughout the 1970s the Kingdom experienced substantial economic growth and development, building a modern physical and social infrastructure virtually from scratch.

The oil sector has dictated the course of economic development in Saudi Arabia over the past 30 years. The fall in oil revenues during the 1980s from a peak of US$101 billion in 1981 to US$21 billion in 1989 brought with it a corresponding drop in government expenditure and a deep recession lasting from 1983 to 1986. This was followed by a period of very slow growth in 1987 and 1988 before a general recovery started in 1989. Nominal GDP fell by over 10 per cent in each of 1983, 1985 and 1986, in marked contrast to the boom years of the 1970s. Growth averaged around 1.7 per cent in 1987 and 1988 before surging ahead once more (see Exhibit 2.1).

Exhibit 2.1

GDP growth rates, 1983 - 90 (%)

	1983	*1984*	*1985*	*1986*	*1987*	*1988*	*1989*	*1990*
Changes in total GDP:								
In current prices	-17.8	-6.0	-10.8	-13.6	1.6	1.8	9.8	21.6
Oil sector	-36.6	-15.1	-26.9	-30.4	4.4	-1.9	31.3	53.1
Non-oil sector	5.2	0.4	-0.8	-6.0	0.6	3.1	2.7	8.2
Private sector	(10.7)	(2.7)	(0.8)	(-5.6)	(-0.6)	(3.1)	(2.5)	(6.9)
Government	(-2.0)	(-3.0)	(-3.3)	(-6.6)	(2.5)	(3.0)	(2.9)	(10.2)
In constant (1970) prices	-4.1	-2.8	-4.1	5.7	-1.4	6.6	0.5	8.8
Oil sector	-20.7	-9.7	-18.9	40.3	-11.6	20.9	-2.2	21.6
Non-oil sector	4.3	-0.3	0.7	-3.3	2.4	1.9	1.5	3.9
Private sector	(7.0)	(1.2)	(1.1)	(-3.5)	(0.9)	(2.4)	(1.4)	(3.8)
Government	(-109)	(-4.6)	(-0.4)	(-2.5)	(7.0)	(0.7)	(1.9)	(4.5)

Source: IMF *Saudi Arabia Staff Report*, January 1992.

The Five-Year Development Plans

Economic development in Saudi Arabia has been set out since 1970 in a series of Five-Year Development Plans, which set target growth rates and provide an overall spending framework. The targeted rates of growth in real, non-oil GDP were exceeded in the first three plans but actual growth fell short of the target in 1985 to 1990, owing to the decline in oil receipts (see Exhibit 2.2). The second plan (1975 to 1980) had the following goals: to assure the defence and internal security of the Kingdom; to maintain a high rate of economic growth; to reduce dependence on oil; to develop indigenous human resources; to raise the standard of living; and to develop the physical infrastructure. The third and fourth plans maintained these central goals but elaborated on certain specifics. The third plan (1980 to 1985), for instance, placed particular emphasis on restraining growth of the expatriate labour force and on promoting growth in agriculture, industry and mining.

The fourth plan (1985 to 1990) introduced the theme of efficiency and productivity more strongly than previously, promoted economic and social integration within the GCC, reinforced the desirability of reducing the foreign labour force, underlined the importance of the private sector in all sectors of the economy and stressed the need for a return to fiscal

Exhibit 2.2

Average annual sectoral growth rates under the five development plans, 1970/71 - 1995 in constant 1970 prices (%)

	First Five-Year Plan 1970/71-1974/75		*Second Five-Year Plan 1975/76-1979/80*		*Third Five-Year Plan 1980/81-1984/85*		*Fourth Five-Year Plan 1985/86-1989/90*		*Fifth Five-Year Plan 1990-1995*	
	Target	*Actual*	*Target*	*Actual*	*Target*	*Actual*	*Target*	*Actual*	*Target*	*Actual*[1]
Non-oil sectors										
Producing sector										
Agriculture	4.6	3.6	4.9	6.9	5.4	8.1	6.0	13.4	7.0	7.0
Other mining	...	21.1	15.0	9.6	9.8	7.3	3.0	-1.9	4.0	3.3
Other manufacturing	14.0	11.4	14.0	15.2	18.8	12.4	15.5	1.1	7.8	5.5
Utilities	...	10.9	15.0	21.9	29.5	18.6	5.0	5.6	6.9	5.0
Construction	10.4	18.6	15.0	15.8	-2.5	-0.9	-2.8	-8.5	3.8	...
Service sector										
Trade	...	13.9	15.0	22.8	8.4	8.7	2.5	-1.5	3.0	2.0
Transport	12.9	17.0	15.0	19.3	12.9	7.1	5.0	-1.2	3.2	3.5
Finance	...	8.2	9.7	14.0	8.3	4.4	9.0	-4.8	6.6	2.6
Other services	...	7.1	14.0	11.8	3.0	4.4	3.5	2.3	2.3	3.0
Government	7.0	7.8	12.9	6.5	7.2	6.4	...	2.2	0.8	6.0
Total non-oil sector	10.5	11.7	13.3	14.8	6.2	6.4	2.9	0.6	3.6	3.9
Government	(7.0)	(12.7)	(12.9)	(14.6)	(...)	(3.0)	(...)	(1.2)	(...)	(4.5)
Private	(12.0)	(11.1)	(13.4)	(14.9)	(...)	(7.9)	(...)	(0.4)	(...)	(3.8)
Oil sector	9.1	14.8	9.7	4.8	1.3	-14.2	5.6	3.6	2.2	21.6
Total GDP	9.8	13.4	10.0	9.2	3.3	-1.5	4.0	1.4	3.2	8.8

[1]Preliminary data for 1990.

Sources: Ministry of Planning, the Five-Year Development Plans and IMF statistics, January 1992.

balance. Because of the anticipated greater involvement of the private sector in economic development during the fourth plan, and because the Kingdom's basic infrastructure was substantially complete, the plan adopted a new methodology that concentrated on programmes and policies rather than specific projects and targets.

The current plan (1990 to 1995) follows a similar pattern, setting a limited number of broad targets for all sectors. These include expansion of education and health services, development of new roads, telephone lines and municipal water networks, expansion of electricity generating capacity by 25 per cent and growth in agricultural production and the number of factories. The plan aims at annual GDP growth of 3.2 per cent, with the non-oil sector expanding at 3.6 per cent annually. This is to be realised through a growth rate of 7 per cent in the agricultural sector, 6.5 per cent in manufacturing, 3.8 per cent in construction and 3.5 per cent in the service sector.

In order to achieve these objectives, overall government expenditure of SR753 billion (US$200 billion) is envisaged over the five years. Expenditure on civil development, which is set at SR395 billion (US$105.3 billion) for the period, is about 16 per cent higher than the level of the previous five years. In addition, government-owned companies are expected to invest SR56 billion (US$14.9 billion) and the private sector SR144 billion (US$38.4 billion) during the period. The specialised credit institutions are projected to provide SR35 billion (US$9.3 billion) in loans for investment. The largest share (SR140 billion) has been allocated for human resources development, followed by infrastructure (SR116 billion), economic resources (SR73 billion) and health and social services (SR66 billion). These figures are set out in Exhibit 2.3.

Financial effects of the Gulf crisis

By the end of the last decade, when the Kingdom was within reach of a complete recovery from the recession of the mid-1980s, it found itself facing another testing event. This was the 1990 Gulf crisis, which is estimated to have cost Saudi Arabia over US$55 billion (the equivalent of 56 per cent of GDP). In addition to its own army mobilisation costs, the

Exhibit 2.3

Target government development expenditure under the third, fourth and fifth plans

	Level of development expenditure (SR billions)			*Structure of development expenditure (%)*		
	Third	*Fourth*	*Fifth*	*Third*	*Fourth*	*Fifth*
Economic resources	190.7	130.7	73.0	31.3	26.1	18.5
Human resources	129.6	135.3	139.9	21.3	27.1	35.4
Health & social services	61.2	89.7	66.1	10.0	17.9	16.8
Transport & communications	138.6	76.9	52.6	22.7	15.4	13.3
Municipality & housing	89.3	67.4	63.2	14.7	13.5	16.0
Total	**609.4**	**500.0**	**394.8**	**100.0**	**100.0**	**100.0**

Source: Ministry of Planning.

Kingdom absorbed the local costs of the allied forces (fuel, food, accommodation and so on). Economic aid was given to supportive countries, while some debt owed to Saudi Arabia was forgiven. Furthermore, the Saudi government reimbursed the US, the UK and France for a substantial part of their war-related expenses and boosted defence spending. The heavy financial burden caused by the crisis forced Saudi Arabia to draw heavily on its foreign liquid assets and reserves.

The Saudi economy withstood the shock of the crisis very well and this can be attributed to a number of factors. In addition to the underlying strength and resilience of the economy, the impact of the crisis was alleviated by a surge in oil revenues and by skilful financial management on the part of the authorities. Oil earnings benefited from higher prices and from increased production levels aimed at stabilising conditions in the world oil market. In the final quarter of 1990 Saudi Arabia was able to make up for around two-thirds of oil production lost by Iraq and Kuwait. This was accomplished through an acceleration of the programme to expand domestic oil production capacity and involved considerable additional cost.

Composition and structure of Gross Domestic Product

Growth in total GDP in Saudi Arabia is dominated by developments in the oil market. Oil provides the bulk of the Kingdom's export earnings and budgetary revenues and accounts for around 37 per cent of GDP (see Exhibit 2.4). Most government expenditure is financed by oil revenues and related activities include refining and petrochemical production. Double digit declines in oil GDP from 1983 to 1986 pulled down total GDP

Exhibit 2.4

Composition of GDP 1983 - 90

	1983	*1984*	*1985*	*1986*	*1987*	*1988*	*1989*	*1990*
	(Composition in current prices as percentage of total)							
Oil sector	42.4	38.8	31.3	25.2	25.9	25.0	29.8	37.6
Non-oil sectors	57.6	61.8	68.7	74.8	74.1	75.0	70.2	62.4
Private sector	(34.4)	(37.4)	(42.2)	(46.2)	(45.2)	(45.8)	(42.8)	(37.6)
Government	(23.2)	(24.4)	(26.5)	(28.6)	(28.9)	(29.2)	(27.4)	(24.8)
Total	100.0	100.0	100.0	100.0	100.0	100.0	100.0	100.0
Gross fixed investment	25.4	29.3	19.4	17.9	17.7	20.1	21.8	19.6
Final consumption	74.6	70.7	80.6	82.1	82.3	79.9	78.2	80.4
Private consumption	(41.7)	(40.2)	(46.8)	(46.7)	(45.9)	(47.0)	(47.0)	(44.8)
Government	(32.9)	(30.5)	(33.8)	(35.4)	(36.4)	(32.9)	(31.3)	(35.6)
Domestic demand	100.0	100.0	100.0	100.0	100.0	100.0	100.0	100.0
	(Value in current prices)							
Total GDP (SR billions)	374.0	347.4	310.0	267.8	272.0	276.9	304.1	369.8

Source: IMF *Saudi Arabia Staff Report*, January 1992.

Exhibit 2.5

Gross Domestic Product by economic activity at current prices, 1983 - 91 (SR billions)

	1983	*1984*	*1985*	*1986*	*1987*	*1988*	*1989*	*1990*	*1991*[1]
Agriculture, forestry & Fishing	9,642	11,620	13,789	15,861	18,312	20,895	22,650	25,142	26,900
Mining & quarrying	145,714	122,169	90,098	63,020	65,113	63,471	85,659	132,613	151,274
Crude petroleum & natural gas	(143,865)	(120,305)	(88,286)	(61,262)	(63,390)	(61,711)	(83,847)	(130,801)	(149,374)
Other	(1,849)	(1,864)	(1,812)	(1,758)	(1,723)	(1,760)	(1,812)	(1,812)	(1,900)
Manufacturing	26,887	27,421	24,499	19,722	23,852	24,462	25,227	29,819	32,500
Petroleum refining	(14,742)	(13,824)	(10,200)	(5,894)	(9,902)	(9,675)	(9,405)	(12,415)	(13,800)
Other	(12,145)	(13,597)	(14,299)	(13,828)	(13,950)	(14,787)	(15,822)	(17,404)	(18,700)
Electricity, gas & water	-295	-586	301	523	681	722	750	780	819
Construction	52,889	44,964	38,745	33,989	33,250	32,027	32,475	34,099	37,000
Wholesale & retail trade, restaurants & hotels	29,243	30,386	30,222	29,072	27,797	26,802	26,078	27,382	28,203
Transport, storage & communications	23,746	23,845	23,719	22,783	22,087	22,807	23,121	24,739	25,481
Finance, insurance, real estate & business services	32,938	30,500	27,184	22,458	21,472	22,412	23,069	24,162	26,095
Ownership of dwellings	(14,030)	(13,117)	(10,648)	(7,934)	(6,528)	(6,093)	(6,071)	(6,314)	(6,882)
Other	(18,908)	(17,383)	(16,536)	(14,524)	(14,944)	(16,319)	(16,998)	(17,848)	(19,213)
Community, social & personal services	9,266	9,704	11,033	10,584	10,507	11,107	11,414	11,985	12,344
Government services	48,519	52,072	54,971	54,138	53,061	56,308	57,840	63,400	79,584
Public administration & defence	(24,950)	(26,417)	(27,757)	(27,336)	(26,792)	(28,432)	(29,206)	(32,013)	(43,489)
Other	(23,569)	(25,655)	(26,214)	(26,802)	(26,269)	(27,876)	(28,634)	(31,387)	(36,095)
Less: imputed bank service charges	-4,526	-4,670	-4,529	-4,304	-4,132	-4,104	-4,200	-4,326	-5,000
Sub–total	374,023	347,424	310,031	267,846	272,000	276,910	304,083	369,795	415,200
Import duties	3,677	3,973	3,910	3,245	3,453	8,236	6,740	6,740	8,000
GDP in purchasers' values	377,699	351,397	313,941	271,091	275,453	285,146	310,823	376,535	423,200

[1]Estimates.

Sources: Central Department of Statistics, Ministry of Finance and National Economy and IMF statistics.

(in current prices) by between 6 per cent and 17 per cent. In the following years, as oil GDP started recovering, total GDP also moved up, albeit more slowly than the oil sector. In 1990 oil sector output rose by 53 per cent, pulling nominal GDP up by nearly 21.6 per cent. Real GDP growth in 1991 is estimated at around 6.6 per cent.

GDP by economic activity is given in Exhibit 2.5. Oil sector GDP dropped from SR145.7 billion (US$39.9 billion) in 1983 (34 per cent of the total) to SR63 billion (US$16.8 billion) in 1986 (23 per cent of the total). From 1986 to 1989 the oil sector accounted for a fairly stable proportion

Exhibit 2.6

Contribution of major sectors to GDP (%)

	1984	*1985*	*1986*	*1987*	*1988*	*1989*	*1990*	*1991*[1]
Agriculture	3.3	4.4	5.9	6.7	7.4	7.3	6.7	6.4
Oil & mining	34.8	28.7	23.3	23.7	22.3	27.6	35.6	35.8
Manufacturing	7.8	7.8	7.3	8.6	8.6	8.1	7.9	7.7
Utilities	–	0.1	0.2	0.3	0.3	0.3	0.2	0.2
Construction	12.8	11.0	12.5	12.1	11.2	10.5	9.1	8.7
Finance & real estate	8.7	8.7	8.3	7.8	7.9	7.4	6.4	6.2
Government & defence	14.8	17.5	19.9	19.3	19.8	18.6	16.8	18.8
Other services	17.8	21.8	22.6	21.5	22.5	20.2	17.6	16.2
Total	**100.0**	**100.0**	**100.0**	**100.0**	**100.0**	**100.0**	**100.0**	**100.0**

[1]Estimates.

of GDP, before surging in the following years as a consequence of the Gulf crisis. Exhibit 2.6, which is derived from Exhibit 2.4, shows this. Growth targets for the current Five-Year Development Plan were set at an annual 2.7 per cent for the oil sector. However, the increase in oil production in the second half of 1990, sustained through 1991 and 1992, suggests that the oil sector could overshoot its target by a considerable margin.

Performance in the non-oil sectors

Agricultural output rose in the later 1980s, with the share of the agricultural sector in total GDP increasing from 3.3 per cent in 1984 to 7.4 per cent in 1988. GDP generated in the agricultural sector reached SR26.9 billion (US$7.2 billion) in 1991, up from SR9.6 billion (US$2.7 billion) in 1983. However, the sector's annual rate of growth, which had averaged around 17 per cent from 1984 to 1987, slowed to 11 per cent in 1989, 10 per cent in 1990 and 7 per cent in 1991, bringing contribution to GDP down to 6.4 per cent in that year. The growth in agricultural output has been due mainly to the price support policy and other incentives provided by the government, as well as to the adoption of modern farming techniques. The government's objectives are to reduce the Kingdom's dependence on imported food, to improve the welfare of the rural population and to limit migration into urban areas. The fifth Five-Year Development Plan aims at achieving an annual growth rate of 7 per cent in the agricultural sector.

After increasing at a rapid pace in the early 1980s, the growth of manufacturing slowed in 1984 and turned negative in 1985 and 1986, in response largely to the contraction in domestic economic activity. Value added in manufacturing rose at an average rate of 20.8 per cent in 1987, 2.9 per cent in 1988 and 1989 and 18.3 per cent in 1990. The upturn resulted from a sharp rise in petrochemical production and a turnaround in domestic demand. The trend continued in 1991 with a growth rate of around 9.1 per cent to SR32.5 billion (US$8.7 billion), up from SR26.9 billion (US$7.2 billion) in 1983, while the contribution of manufacturing to total GDP rose from 7.1 per cent in 1983 to 8.6 per cent in 1988 and 1989, before dropping to 7.7 per cent in 1991. The fifth plan aims at a growth rate of 7.8 per cent in manufacturing, to be achieved mainly through increased private sector investment.

After peaking at SR53 billion (US$14.2 billion) in 1983, GDP in the construction sector declined, reaching a low of SR32 billion (US$8.5 billion) in 1988, before rising to SR34 billion (US$9 billion) in 1990 and an estimated SR37 billion (US$9.8 billion) in 1991. The contribution of the sector to total GDP dropped from 14 per cent in 1983 to 9.1 per cent in 1990 and an estimated 8.7 per cent in 1991. Negative growth was recorded in the value added by this sector throughout most of the 1980s. Growth turned positive in 1989 and surged from 1.6 per cent in that year to 8.5 per cent in 1991, with strong growth also expected in 1992. The construction sector is projected to record an annual growth rate of 3.8 per cent during the period 1990 to 1995, helped by the ongoing expansion in the oil and manufacturing sectors and by contracts won by Saudi contractors abroad. The government is estimated to have been a client in approximately 67 per cent of all construction activities during the first three development plans. However, a lower percentage is forecast for the current plan.

The diversification of, and growth in, the economy since the mid-1970s and the subsidised utility rates, which continue to be below the cost of production and delivery, have contributed to an increasing consumption of electricity, water and gas in Saudi Arabia. The annual average growth rate of these utilities amounted to 5.6 per cent from 1984 to 1990. The utilities sector has accounted for only 0.2 per cent to 0.3 per cent of total GDP over the past few years, with a target growth rate of 6.9 per cent forecast for the current plan period.

The Government and defence sector constituted the second largest contributor to GDP after oil, accounting for around 19 per cent of total GDP in 1991. Value added in the finance, insurance, real estate and business services sector rose from SR21.5 billion (US$5.7 billion) in 1987 to SR26.1 billion (US$6.7 billion) in 1991 but the sector's contribution to total GDP dropped from 7.9 per cent to 6.7 per cent. Other services, including wholesale and retail trade, transport and communication, hotels and restaurants, community, social and personal services, have accounted for around 20 per cent of GDP on average over the last eight years.

Employment and inflation

Employment

Total employment in Saudi Arabia increased by a total of 1,420,000 (an average annual rate of 8 per cent) between 1980 and 1985, far exceeding the planned annual growth rate of 1.2 per cent. At the end of 1985 the civilian workforce was 4,446,000, of whom 2,660,000 were non-Saudis, with 1,649,200 Saudi men and 136,800 Saudi women. The proportion of Saudis in the total labour force declined during the period from 49.4 per cent to 40.2 per cent. During the fourth plan period (1985 to 1990) the civilian workforce grew at an average 5.4 per cent a year to reach

5,771,800, despite projections of a net decline (see Exhibit 2.7). Growth in services sector employment was particularly high during this period and, despite output gains in the agricultural sector, the number of people employed on the land fell to below 10 per cent of the total workforce.

The fifth plan aims at increasing total civilian employment to 5.98 million in 1995, representing an annual growth rate of 0.7 per cent over the plan period. Most of the growth in employment (96 per cent) is expected to be generated by the private sector, reflecting both the leading role accorded to the private sector in the plan and the emphasis on greater restraint in government expenditure. The part of the labour force composed of Saudi nationals is projected to grow by more than 400,000, while a reduction of more than 200,000 is expected in the non-Saudi labour force. The government intends to double or triple Saudi military manpower during the current decade.

Some unemployment is reported to have emerged among nationals in recent years, especially among university graduates seeking high wages and managerial jobs. Student enrolment within the education system as a whole has increased from 547,000 in 1969 to around 3 million 1990. Enrolment at Saudi colleges and universities rose from 48,000 in 1979 to around 140,000 by 1990. The unemployment problem has been addressed by the government through a wider dissemination of information on vacancies, increased efforts aimed at matching job seekers with available vacancies, the provision of training facilities and calls on the private sector

Exhibit 2.7

Distribution of employment by economic activity (thousands)

	1985		*1990*		*Average annual growth rate*
	Workers	*% of total*	*Workers*	*% of total*	*1985-90 (%)*
Producing sectors	**2,067.2**	**46.5**	**2,018.6**	**35.0**	**-0.5**
Agriculture	617.4	13.9	569.2	9.9	-1.6
Mining[1]	5.1	0.1	3.5	0.1	-7.3
Manufacturing	411.4	9.3	374.9	6.5	-1.8
Utilities	147.4	3.3	126.9	2.2	-3.0
Construction	885.9	19.9	944.1	16.4	1.3
Service sectors	**1,844.6**	**41.5**	**3,081.6**	**53.4**	**10.8**
Trade	556.1	12.5	898.3	15.6	10.1
Transport	303.4	6.8	262.3	4.5	-2.9
Finance	136.3	3.1	99.0	1.7	-6.2
Other services	848.8	19.1	1,822.0	31.6	16.5
Government[2]	**469.1**	**10.6**	**624.8**	**10.8**	**5.9**
Sub-total:					
non–oil sectors	4,380.9	98.5	5,725.0	99.2	5.5
oil sectors	65.1	1.5	46.8	0.8	-6.4
Total	**4,446.0**	**100.0**	**5,771.8**	**100.0**	**5.4**

[1]Excluding oil sector.

[2]Excludes non-civilian employment and includes daily wage workers not classified as civil servants.

Source: Ministry of Planning, summary of the fifth development plan.

to replace expatriate workers with Saudi nationals wherever possible.

In order to encourage the employment of Saudi nationals, changes were introduced in December 1985 in the rules governing the employment of expatriates. These changes include a curb on the transfer of employment sponsorships to foreign companies operating on temporary licences. Only workers with specialised degrees or graduates from technical institutes are allowed to hold transferable work permits. In a related decision, private sector companies have to prove conclusively the absence of adequately trained indigenous workers before being permitted to hire foreign workers. The government is pushing local firms to "Saudise" their companies by hiring and training more nationals. "Saudisation" is occurring to some degree but the general attitudes of new Saudi entrants to the workforce towards many areas of the labour market must change considerably to facilitate a significant displacement of expatriates. One negative aspect of "Saudisation", from a competitiveness perspective, is the higher wages Saudis typically enjoy compared to those received by expatriates.

Inflation

Until 1973 official retail and wholesale prices rose by less than 1.5 per cent annually. However, during the boom years that followed, inflationary forces, both generated domestically and imported, resulted in annual price rises in excess of 10%. The third Five-Year Development Plan recognised the dangers of rising inflationary pressures and introduced a policy of subsidising consumer prices of basic commodities and services. This brought inflation back under control, with the rise in the cost of living index dropping to 4.39 per cent in 1980. Inflation declined in the early 1980s and was negative every year from 1984 to 1987, registering a cumulative decline of 9 per cent, as shown in Exhibit 2.8. Although import prices rose by a total of 23 per cent during this period, their influence was more than offset by declines in housing and transport costs in line with the contraction in GDP. Rents and utility prices dropped by 29 per cent, reflecting the emergence of excess supply in residential and commercial accommodation.

In 1988, 1989 and 1990 there was minimal inflation but prices rose more rapidly in 1991, reflecting the extra costs relating to the Gulf crisis, especially the higher cost of transporting imported products and higher rents. The consumer price index ended 1991 at 107.8, a rise of 4.6 per cent on the year before. Inflation continued to be subdued in 1992, following the sweeping price cuts introduced by the Saudi government early in the year. The domestic price of petrol was cut by 38 per cent, electricity by 29 per cent, water by 77 per cent and registration fees for businessmen and traders by up to 87 per cent (see Exhibit 2.9). The aim is to boost people's purchasing power and to take pressure off employers to give wage increases, thereby contributing to the abatement of inflation. In the first quarter of 1992 inflation was 3 per cent but it dropped in the second quarter.

Exhibit 2.8

Cost of living index for 10 cities combined (1988=100)

	% change in overall index	*Overall index*	*All food*	*Housing*	*Fabric & Apparel*	*House furnishings*	*Medical care*	*Transport & communications*	*Entertainment & education*	*Other expenditure*
1979	–	100.4	93.2	151.4	91.3	104.7	86.7	67.9	115.9	98.5
1980	4.39	104.8	99.7	151.8	102.9	104.1	87.6	71.6	113.6	101.5
1981	2.77	107.7	104.5	151.9	109.1	106.9	87.3	75.0	113.7	98.9
1982	1.03	108.8	106.3	148.7	112.7	106.9	93.8	78.0	112.2	93.5
1983	0.19	109.0	106.5	151.0	113.3	105.7	97.7	76.0	111.0	98.3
1984	-1.56	107.3	105.8	146.6	113.4	104.6	97.5	74.7	104.5	98.2
1985	-3.07	104.0	102.9	142.2	108.2	98.4	98.3	74.6	99.5	92.7
1986	-3.17	100.7	101.4	124.9	105.1	95.1	96.2	80.0	97.0	94.4
1987	-1.58	99.1	99.9	107.5	102.9	96.0	97.3	90.4	99.3	97.8
1988	0.91	100.0	100.0	100.0	100.0	100.0	100.0	100.0	100.0	100.0
1989	1.00	101.0	102.3	97.7	98.1	98.9	102.0	104.9	101.1	97.9
1990	2.08	103.1	104.0	97.6	98.2	98.6	100.7	121.1	99.8	93.5
1991	4.56	107.8	111.9	102.1	98.0	101.4	100.2	126.8	102.8	94.2
1992[1]	3.00	111.1	117.6	105.9	–	102.5	101.2	128.5	105.2	94.3

[1]First quarter.

Source: Saudi Arabian Monetary Agency, Research and Statistics Department, Quarterly Bulletins.

Exhibit 2.9

New fees and prices for selected government items, from March 1992 (SR)

	New price	*Old price*	*% change*
Electricity (total of following consumption)			
3,000 kwh	150	210	-29
4,000 kwh	200	310	-35
6,000 kwh	360	610	-41
Water			
First 100 litres consumption	7	30	-77
Petrol (litre)	0.33	0.53	-38
LPG (per 25 lb)	7	10	-30
Telephone			
Installation	300	600	-50
Annual subscription	150	360	-58
Local calls (a minute)	–	0.05	-100
Passport fees	200	300	-33
Final exit visa	–	100	-100
Commercial registration			
Share company	1,600	10,000	-84
Limited liability company	1,200	8,000	-85
Other company	800	6,000	-87
Sole trader	200	500	-60

Budgetary developments

The fiscal year in Saudi Arabia begins on 31 December and ends on 30 December. Until 1985/86 the fiscal year corresponded to the *Hijri* year and ended in the middle of the Gregorian year. The government budget covers the financial operations of the central government and includes transfers to and from several public sector entities. These include five specialised credit institutions, the Saudi Development Fund (which provides project loans to developing countries) and numerous semi-autonomous entities, including the Royal Commission for Jubail and Yanbu', several universities and educational institutions, public utilities, the Ports Authority and municipalities. The specialised credit institutions provide concessionary loans to the private sector for the development of industrial, agricultural, utility and real estate projects.

From 1984 to 1988 fiscal developments in Saudi Arabia were characterised by a sharp decline in revenues, a contraction in expenditure and large budget deficits. The trend changed in 1989, with total expenditure rising once again, supported by higher oil revenues (see Exhibit 2.10). Total oil receipts, which constitute the major source of revenues, fell from SR119 billion (US$31.7 billion) in 1984/85 to SR77 billion (US$20.5 billion) in 1987 and to SR48 billion (US$12.8 billion) in 1988. In response to this sharp decline, the authorities cut total government spending from SR216 billion (US$57.6 billion) in 1984/85 to SR135 billion (US$36 billion) in 1988. The major part of the cutback was in project expenditure; this was made possible by the completion of major infrastructural facilities during the period. Transfers to the specialised credit institutions were discontinued in 1989, owing to reduced demand for credit and an increasing reliance by these institutions on their own resources.

Exhibit 2.10

Budgetary development, actual revenues and expenditures, 1984/85 - 1991 (SR millions)

	1984/85	*1985/86*	*1986*	*1987*	*1988*	*1989*	*1990*	*1991**
Revenues	**171,510**	**133,565**	**80,098**	**117,189**	**84,600**	**121,400**	**154,721**	**172,400**
Oil revenues	103,880	61,195	39,636	60,157	48,400	78,850	118,142	135,300
Other receipts[1]	15,120	25,977	6,426	17,250	–		–	–
Returns on investments	32,000	23,000	17,500	18,000	12,000	15,130	10,000	9,50
Other revenues	20,510	23,393	16,536	21,782	24,200	27,420	26,579	27,600
Income taxes	(2,346)	(1,253)	(848)	(902)	(905)	(1,160)	–	–
Other taxes & fees[2]	(6,567)	(8,937)	(6,212)	–	(8,220)	(10,225)	–	–
Customs duties	(3,916)	(3,943)	(2,953)	(3,946)	(7,500)	(7,150)	–	–
Miscellaneous[3]	(7,681)	(9,260)	(6,523)	(8,210)	(7,575)	(8,885)	–	–
Expenditure	**216,363**	**184,004**	**141,022**	**185,317**	**134,850**	**150,048**	**210,430**	**261,570**
Current expenditure	87,699	88,419	74,417	90,315	82,641	94,865	96,000	103,700
Salaries & wages	(53,913)	(55,221)	(46,788)	(54,400)	(56,141)	(59,900)	(61,000)	(63,100)
Supplies & services	(23,131)	(22,691)	(15,754)	(25,565)	(21,385)	(23,538)	(20,000)	(20,700)
Subsidies	(10,655)	(10,507)	(11,875)	(10,350)	(5,115)	(6,413)	(7,000)	(7,700)
Interest payments	(–)	(–)	(–)	(–)	(–)	(5,014)	(8,000)	(12,200)
Foreign aid	10,451	10,890	8,150	11,500	7,423	6,435	10,200	16,500
Operations & maintenance	25,746	24,255	18,727	22,797	18,876	21,418	18,200	19,500
Project expenditure	79,736	53,490	36,398	57,632	25,405	27,330	21,100	22,800
Transfers to specialised credit institutions	12,731	6,950	3,330	3,073	505	–	–	–
Emergency expenditures	–	–	–	–	–	–	64,930	99,070
Budgetary surplus/deficit	**-44,853**	**-50,439**	**-60,924**	**-68,128**	**-50,250**	**-28,648**	**-55,709**	**-89,170**
Financing	44,853	50,439	60,924	68,128	50,250	28,648	55,709	89,170
Drawdown of deposits with SAMA	36,853	37,238	60,450	65,307	12,000	–	–	–
Bond sales (net)	–	–	–	–	42,250	28,648	55,709	62,920
Foreign exchange loans	–	–	–	–	–	–	–	26,250
Discrepancy[4]	8,000	13,201	474	2,821	-4,000	–	–	–

[1]Transfers from the petroleum sector.
[2]Includes Zakat and various fees and charges.
[3]Includes revenue from the sale and rental of property, operational surpluses of public corporations and revenues generated from sale of goods and services.
[4]Mainly timing differences between budgetary and monetary accounts.
*Estimates.

Source: Ministry of Finance and National Economy and IMF *Saudi Arabia Staff Report*, 1992.

The budget deficit increased from SR45 billion (US$12 billion) in 1984/85 to SR68 billion (US$18.1 billion) in 1987, despite the marked decline in expenditure. In an effort to strengthen the budgetary position and to contain the loss of official foreign assets, expenditure was reduced by 27 per cent in 1988. Although revenues also fell substantially, the budget deficit declined to SR50 billion (US$13.3 billion) in that year, constituting around 18 per cent of GDP. For the first time the deficit was financed through the sale of government bonds to commercial banks and autonomous government institutions.

In 1989 total oil revenues rose by 63 per cent to SR78.8 billion (US$21 billion), reflecting the recovery in oil prices. The price per barrel of the OPEC basket of seven crudes averaged US$17.31 in 1989, against US$14.24 the previous year. This caused a decline of 43 per cent in the fiscal deficit to SR28.6 billion (US$7.6 billion), constituting around 10 per cent of GDP. The deficit was wholly financed by the sale of government bonds.

The broad components of government revenues in Saudi Arabia are oil receipts, investment income and domestic revenues. Oil receipts are by far the major source, accounting for about two-thirds of total revenues in the period from 1984/85 to 1989 and 77 per cent in 1990 and 1991. From 1984/85 to 1987 regular oil receipts were supplemented by transfers from the petroleum sector of funds previously retained by this sector and earmarked for capital investments. The fall in investment income from SR32 billion (US$8.5 billion) in 1984/85 to SR15 billion (US$4 billion) in 1989 reflected mainly the large reduction in the government's foreign assets in the period and, to a lesser extent, the decline in international interest rates after 1984. As a proportion of total government revenue, investment income declined from 19 per cent in 1984/85 to 12.6 per cent in 1989.

Saudi Arabia's domestic revenues consist mainly of income tax receipts, *Zakat* receipts (an Islamic tax), income from various fees, licences and charges, income generated from the rental or sale of property, operating surpluses of revenue-generating public corporations and receipts from customs duties. Income taxes are payable only on personal and business income of self-employed expatriates, foreign companies and non-Saudi shareholders in Saudi Arabian companies. For the self-employed expatriates, the rate ranges from 5 per cent on annual income of SR16,000 (US$4,266) to 30 per cent for income above SR66,000 (US$17,600). For foreign companies, tax rates range from 25 per cent on profits up to SR100,000 (US$26,666) to a maximum of 45 per cent on profits over SR1 million (US$266,666). *Zakat* has been payable by Saudis and Muslim residents at the flat rate of 2.5 per cent of income since 1985/86.

Despite the limited revenue base, total domestic revenues increased by 30 per cent from SR21 billion (US$5.6 billion) in 1984/85 to about SR27.6 billion (US$7.4 billion) in 1991. Most of the increase occurred in 1988 and 1989 and reflected the impact of higher fees and charges, improved collection, higher operating surpluses in certain government corporations and increases in import duty rates. The decline in oil and investment income caused a relative increase in domestic revenue as a proportion of total government revenue from 12 per cent in 1984/85 to 23 per cent in 1989 but its share dropped to 16 per cent in 1991.

In 1990, before the Gulf crisis loomed, the government projected a budget deficit of SR25 billion (US$6.66 billion) and had planned to cover this by the sale of government bonds. However, according to the Saudi Arabian Monetary Agency (SAMA) annual report for 1990/91, the actual 1990 budget deficit was SR55.7 billion (US$14.8 billion), more than double the pre-crisis estimate. The government's actual figures for 1991 also show a major deficit, as the second tranche of payments for the Gulf crisis was due in that year. The IMF puts the 1991 budget deficit at SR77.1 billion (US$20.6 billion). The 1990 figures give actual expenditure of SR210.4 billion (US$56.1 billion), which is SR67.4 billion (US$18 billion) higher than the level projected in the budget. Actual revenues were SR154.7 billion (US$41.3 billion), compared with the budget forecast of SR118 billion (US$31.5 billion), with oil revenues at SR118.1 billion (US$31.5 billion).

The 1992 budget statement said that government spending in 1990 and 1991 totalled SR472 billion (US$125.8 billion), of which SR186 billion (US$49.6 billion) was additional spending relating to the Gulf crisis. This implies that SR261.6 billion (US$69.8 billion) was spent in 1991. The estimated total revenues for that year are put at SR172.4 billion (US$46 billion), implying a deficit of around SR89.2 billion (US$23.8 billion). This deficit was financed partly through borrowing SR16.87 billion (US$4.5 billion) from the international markets and SR9.37 billion (US$2.5 billion) from the domestic Saudi banks. The balance of SR62.9 billion (US$18.5 billion) is believed to have been covered by the sale of government bonds and Treasury bills.

Financial developments

The financial system

The financial system in the Kingdom comprises the Saudi Arabian Monetary Agency (SAMA), the commercial banks, autonomous government institutions (AGIs) and five specialised credit institutions, as well as a variety of other non-monetary institutions, such as money changers and insurance companies. The AGIs include the pension and social security organisations and the Saudi Development Fund. The commercial banking system comprises 12 banks, with a total of just over 1,100 branches throughout the country. The number of branches has increased by more than 400 in recent years, reflecting both the addition of a large new bank (Al Rajhi Banking and Investment Corporation, which became a fully-fledged financial institution in 1988) and the continuing process of monetisation in the economy. Three commercial banks are wholly owned by Saudis and the remaining nine are joint ventures with foreign banks; these hold a combined market share of 45 per cent. One of the wholly-owned Saudi banks, the National Commercial Bank, dominates the banking scene, accounting for more than one-third of total Saudi banking assets.

Commercial banks concentrate primarily on retail activities, with branch networks extending throughout the Kingdom. Approximately two-thirds of the liability base is drawn from retail sources. Further growth in retail activity is anticipated, given that only a small percentage of the population currently uses the domestic banking system. The banking community is becoming increasingly active on a wholesale level, supplanting international competitors in trade finance, project finance and capital formation. Financial market activity is concentrated across a range of traditional treasury products, with initiatives in recent years focusing on the development of capital markets and derivative products. It should be noted that broking operations are not licensed to operate directly in the Kingdom. Brokers are present in Bahrain and London, operating in an intermediary capacity for the domestic banks and the offshore market.

SAMA, based in Riyadh, was established in 1952 and functions as the Kingdom's central bank. In this capacity, SAMA attends to a wide range of functions. It monitors the money supply (M1, M2 and M3 following conventional definitions), issues and controls the currency, oversees the national clearing house system and manages the Kingdom's international reserves. SAMA also serves as the government's fiscal agent and, in recent years, has assumed the responsibility of funding the government's budget deficit. From a market perspective, the two principal objectives of SAMA's mandate are to stabilise the value of the currency and to regulate the domestic banks. It acts directly through an extensive range of open market tools and operations and indirectly through moral suasion. All new domestic market activity must be formally sanctioned by SAMA, with approval forthcoming only after a rigorous review to ensure its appropriateness to domestic requirements. The domestic banks are regulated under the Banking Control Law of 1966. Reserves (maintained at SAMA) are determined on a liability ratio basis: 7 per cent of demand deposits plus 2 per cent of savings/time deposits.

The Saudi Arabian financial system operates in an environment of openness with respect to exchange transactions and capital flows. The official exchange policy is aimed at effectively linking the Saudi riyal to the US dollar. The rate has been SR3.75 to US$1 since 1 June 1986. Consequently, interest rates on financial instruments denominated in Saudi riyals have generally remained quite close to rates on comparable dollar instruments. In these circumstances, the role of monetary policy is limited primarily to maintaining the liquidity of the system at an appropriate level and to assisting in meeting objectives relating to the level of foreign exchange reserves and the overall net foreign asset position.

Evolution of the government bond market

The most important financial development in the Kingdom in the late 1980s was the issuance of debt instruments by the government. The aims were to help finance budget deficits, to generate an effective tool of monetary policy and to create new investment channels for the private sector. In December 1987 it was announced as part of the Kingdom's budget that up to SR30 billion (US$8 billion) of the projected deficit of SR38 billion (US$10 billion) in fiscal 1988 would be financed through domestic borrowing. This was an event of major significance, as it ended a period of three decades during which the Kingdom had not borrowed. SAMA was given the responsibility of managing the debt issues on behalf of the Ministry of Finance and National Economy. The debt instruments, known as "development bonds", were offered in one- to five-year maturities and were officially linked to the profits on unspecified development projects. The yields on the bonds offer a small margin (30 to 50 basis points) over US Treasury notes with similar maturities. Other market conditions are taken into consideration when setting the yields.

The instruments were initially offered only to Saudi banks and autonomous government institutions (AGIs) but banks were later permitted to resell them to local investors. The banks have demonstrated a preference for shorter maturities, mostly of two years (the one-year bonds were discontinued after a few months), while the AGIs take the longer maturities. Every two weeks SAMA offers government bonds of various maturities totalling SR1.5 billion; yields are fixed and coupons are paid semi-annually.

SAMA's ability to manage domestic liquidity was greatly enhanced by the introduction of short-term Treasury bills in November 1991. The facility was a welcome development for Saudi banks, which are flush with liquidity but lack attractive domestic instruments to absorb their mostly short-term deposits. SAMA sells the Treasury bills on a discount basis at set prices. One particularly attractive feature of the Treasury bills is SAMA's willingness to repurchase and then resell them on a very short-term basis, providing domestic banks with a new channel to manage their liquidity without having to go into the foreign currency markets. The Treasury bills, which are fully negotiable, are currently available to Saudi and other GCC entities only and carry four-, 13- , 26- and 52-week maturities.

The private financial sector still has large holdings of foreign assets but domestic financial developments and borrowing needs are likely to draw some of these assets back into the Kingdom. According to the Bank of International Settlements (BIS), the combined foreign deposits of the 12 domestic banks at the end of the first quarter of 1992 stood at US$46.38 billion. If SAMA continues to offer attractive rates on Treasury bills, the banks are likely to draw down some of their foreign currency assets to purchase them. Furthermore, the expansion programmes of the Saudi Arabian Oil Company (ARAMCO), the Saudi Arabian Marketing and Refining Company (SAMAREC) and the Saudi Basic Industries Corporation (SABIC) also need large amounts of direct local financing and are likely to prompt a return of some foreign assets.

Commercial banking

The consolidated loan portfolio of the Saudi commercial banks has shown strong growth since the end of the Gulf crisis. Total loans grew by 26 per cent in 1991 and continued their uptrend in 1992, in contrast with the period of stagnation in 1984 to 1986 when banks concentrated on cleaning up their portfolios and building strong provisions against non-performing loans (see Exhibit 2.11). After dropping in 1985 and 1986, banks' profits and total loans recovered gradually through the later 1980s. In 1990 loans contracted by 9.6 per cent as funds were channelled to the foreign interbank market following the Iraqi invasion of Kuwait. The 1990 Gulf crisis shook the banking system and caused temporary operational and liquidity difficulties. However, with strong support form SAMA, most banks came out of the crisis better organised and stronger.

Although investment opportunities abroad have been reduced as a result of the worldwide reduction in interest rates and the economic slowdown, local economic vitality and the funding needs of the AGIs have provided ample business opportunities for the banks. The 59 per cent increase in miscellaneous loans from 1990 to 1991 is also partly accounted for by the US$2.5 billion loan to the government, which carries a spread of 0.25 per cent over LIBOR and is to be amortized in 1995 (US$0.5 billion) and in 1996 (US$2 billion). Miscellaneous loans accounted for 28 per cent of total commercial bank credit in 1991, compared to only 19.6 per cent in 1984. Construction-related business, trade finance and

Exhibit 2.11

Commercial bank credit by economic activity, excluding investments and including loans to government departments and agencies (SR millions)

End of period	*1984*	*Distribution (%)*	*1985*	*1986*	*1987*	*1988*	*1989*	*1990*	*1991*	*Distribution (%)*
Agriculture & fishing	1,073	1.74	1,045	990	967	1,019	1,124	1,193	1,604	1.89
Industry & manufacturing	6,099	9.90	5,452	5,452	4,749	4,126	4,083	5,138	6,324	7.46
Mining & quarrying	437	0.71	663	310	322	549	382	253	449	0.53
Electricity, water & other utilities	1,011	1.64	1,413	1,260	690	986	542	664	945	1.12
Building & construction	13,217	21.45	14,062	11,231	11,138	12,835	10,721	10,986	10,744	12.67
Commerce	19,072	30.94	20,018	20,032	19,608	18,950	20,643	14,705	14,829	17.48
Transportation & communication	4,170	6.77	4,040	3,786	4,338	5,391	4,856	5,353	5,758	6.76
Finance	1,779	2.89	2,216	2,450	4,401	8,648	4,710	9,525	13,103	15.45
Services	2,703	4.39	3,261	3,388	2,994	4,051	3,980	4,302	7,252	8.55
Miscellaneous	12,079	19.60	9,090	9,604	14,363	14,422	23,237	15,000	23,847	28.09
Total	**61,640**	**100.00**	**61,235**	**58,503**	**63,570**	**70,077**	**74,278**	**67,119**	**84,855**	**100.00**

Source: Saudi Arabian Monetary Agency, Money and Banking Statistics, *Quarterly Bulletin*, 1st Quarter 1992.

selected consumer financing have also risen. Dollar-denominated loans have increased, raising the importance of maintaining a stable exchange rate for the riyal against the dollar. There is intense competition to offer better packaged and more sophisticated products and services to corporate and retail clients. Banks have reported strong business growth in 1992 and the outlook for 1993 and 1994 is quite optimistic.

Commercial banks in Saudi Arabia also serve as brokers and market makers for equity trading, since there is no central stock exchange in the country. A trading floor was established briefly in 1987 but it was decided that a decentralised system, operating mainly through banks, would be more efficient. Some 80 companies are now listed for public trading, with a combined capital of SR60 billion (US$16 billion). Share prices soared by 92 per cent in 1991 and were up by another 20 per cent in the first half of 1992 before correcting downwards in the second half of the year. The strong performance of the Saudi Stock market reflects healthy economic growth, lower riyal interest rates, a sizeable increase in the earnings of Saudi companies and an abundance of private liquidity chasing a limited number of shares, as well as the release of pent-up demand following the end of the Gulf crisis.

Exports and imports

Saudi Arabia does not impose exchange control or trade restrictions on imports, nor are there any restrictions on exports, other than a prohibition on re-exporting imported items benefiting from government subsidies. Certain measures have been applied to encourage domestic industry and agriculture, including protective tariffs, government procurement practices, sub-contracting requirements and regional and bilateral trade arrangements. Most imports are subject to tariffs at the rate of 12 per cent, with a 20 per cent protective tariff imposed on a limited number of imports where a similar product is manufactured domestically. The government is planning to apply for full membership of GATT upon conclusion of the present round of multilateral trade negotiations.

For many years Saudi Arabia has maintained a surplus on merchandise trade and a deficit on services and private transfers. Both the trade surplus and the deficit on invisible transactions have, however, been reduced sharply since the early 1980s, mainly in response to declines in oil export earnings and service payments. The trade surplus fell to a low of US$3 billion in 1986 but recovered over the following years to US$22.1 billion in 1991 (see Exhibit 2.12). The deficit on services and private transfers, having declined from US$35 billion in 1981 to US$11.9 billion in 1988, reached around US$48 billion in 1991. The current account shifted into deficit after 1982 due to the sharp drop in oil exports. After peaking at around US$18.4 billion in 1984, the current account deficit fell to US$9.2 billion in 1989 and US$4.4 billion in 1990. The IMF balance of payments estimates for 1991 reveal an increase of about 50 per cent in invisible payments, to some US$59 billion, reflecting additional Gulf War-related expenses, a further increase in transfers by foreign workers and a rise in foreign aid disbursements. Despite a modest increase in the trade surplus (due to a further rise in oil earnings), the current account deficit is estimated to have reached US$25.7 billion in 1991. The generally firm oil prices in 1992 and the drop in imports from the inflated levels reached during the Gulf War suggest a much larger trade surplus and a smaller current account deficit for 1992.

The value of Saudi Arabia's oil exports fell steeply from a peak of US$111 billion in 1981 to a low of US$18 billion in 1986, before recovering to about US$20 billion in 1987 and 1988, US$24 billion in 1989 and over US$40 billion in 1990 and 1991. The major markets for Saudi Arabia's oil exports are Asia (mainly Japan), western Europe and North America. Having remained virtually unchanged at a low level in the early 1980s, the value of non-oil exports increased substantially from US$1 billion in 1983 to over US$4 billion a year from 1989 onwards. With the sharp fall in oil exports, the contribution of non-oil exports to the total rose from less than 1 per cent in 1981 to an average of about 15 per cent in 1988 and 1989, before slipping to around 10 per cent in 1990 and 1991. The strong growth in non-oil exports after 1983 was associated with the commencement of exports of petrochemical products from the plants constructed at Jubail and Yanbu. Other non-oil exports (mainly wheat and light manufactured goods) remained low up to 1986 but then increased substantially in response to various export promotion measures.

Following a rapid growth from the mid-1970s through 1982, merchandise imports dropped considerably during the recession of 1983 to 1986, with imports of capital goods, construction materials and transport equipment particularly affected. Imports reached a low of US$17.1 billion in 1986, before rising again to US$26.1 billion in 1991 as economic activity gradually picked up. While the US and Japan remain the two largest individual suppliers to the Kingdom, western Europe

Exhibit 2.12

Balance of payments, 1984 - 91 (US$ billions)

	1984	*1985*	*1986*	*1987*	*1988*	*1989*	*1990*	*1991*
1. Merchandise trade, fob	**8.9**	**7.0**	**3.1**	**4.9**	**4.5**	**9.1**	**22.8**	**22.1**
Oil exports	36.2	25.8	18.0	20.4	20.1	24.0	40.0	43.7
Other exports	1.3	1.5	2.1	2.8	4.2	4.3	4.3	4.5
Imports	-28.6	-20.4	-17.1	-18.3	-19.8	-19.2	-21.5	-26.1
2. Services & transfers	**-27.3**	**-19.9**	**-14.9**	**-14.6**	**-11.9**	**-18.3**	**-27.2**	**-47.8**
Receipts	17.6	16.1	13.9	13.1	12.8	13.0	12.1	10.9
Investment income	(13.4)	(12.4)	(11.3)	(10.5)	(10.5)	(10.4)	(9.2)	(8.0)
Oil sector (bunkers)	(0.1)	(0.1)	(0.1)	(0.1)	(0.1)	(0.1)	(0.1)	(0.1)
Other	(4.1)	(3.6)	(2.6)	(2.5)	(2.3)	(2.5)	(2.8)	(2.8)
Payments	-44.9	-36.0	-28.8	-27.7	-24.7	-31.3	-39.3	-58.7
Freight & insurance	(-5.1)	(-3.3)	(-2.0)	(-1.8	(-2.0)	(-1.9)	(-2.6)	(-2.3)
Oil sector investment income & services	(-3.1)	(-1.7)	(-0.7	(-0.7)	(-0.7)	(-0.7)	(-0.9)	(-0.9)
Other private services	(-9.1)	(-10.6)	(-7.9)	(-7.2)	(-5.6)	(-7.4)	(-10.2)	(-11.0)
Government services	(-19.0)	(-12.2)	(-10.7)	(-10.0)	(-7.9)	(-11.2)	(-11.1)	(-24.4)
Private transfers	(-5.3)	(-5.2)	(-4.8)	(-4.9)	(-6.5)	(-8.3)	(-11.6)	(-13.6)
Official transfers[1]	(-3.3)	(-3.0)	(-2.7)	(-3.1)	(-2.0)	(-1.7)	(-3.0)	(-6.5)
3. Current account balance (1+2)	**-18.4**	**-12.9**	**-11.8**	**-9.8**	**-7.4**	**-9.2**	**-4.4**	**-25.7**
4. Capital movements	**2.3**	**3.5**	**2.4**	**6.2**	**2.7**	**7.4**	**3.5**	**15.7**
Official borrowing	–	–	–	–	–	–	–	4.5
Private capital & errors & omissions	3.4	4.4	5.1	7.6	4.8	6.9	5.9	8.7
Commercial banks[2]	-1.1	-0.9	-2.7	-1.4	-2.2	0.5	-2.4	2.5
5. Overall balance (3+4)	**-16.1**	**-9.4**	**-9.4**	**-3.6**	**-4.7**	**-1.8**	**-0.9**	**-10.0**
6. Financing	**16.1**	**9.4**	**9.4**	**3.6**	**4.7**	**1.8**	**0.9**	**10.0**
Foreign assets of:								
Autonomous government institutions[2]	-0.9	-2.7	-1.9	-1.8	4.8	4	1.7	–
SAMA[2]	17.0	12.1	11.3	5.4	-0.1	-2.2	-0.8	–

[1]Foreign aid as shown in budgetary accounts. Excluding loans to developing countries extended on concessional terms by the Saudi Development Fund. Data for 1990-91 are somewhat higher than budgetary foreign aid because of the inclusion of grant-in-kind and cancellation of debts.
[2]Increase in foreign assets denoted by minus sign.

Sources: Saudi Arabian Monetary Agency, Ministry of Finance and National Economy and IMF country reports on Saudi Arabia, January 1992 and International Financial Statistics, October 1992.

continues to account for around 40 per cent of total imports.

The deficit on the balance of services and transfers dropped from US$27.3 billion in 1984 to US$11.9 billion in 1988, before surging to US$27.2 billion in 1990 and an estimated US$47.8 billion in 1991. Receipts remained relatively stable at around US$12 billion to US$13 billion, while a large increase in service payments was recorded as economic activity accelerated. There appears to have been a shift from foreign to domestic provision of services in recent years. However, government expenditure on foreign services more than doubled in 1991 because of the Gulf crisis. Remittances by expatriate workers (private transfers) declined only slightly from 1982 to 1987 and increased significantly in the following years. They jumped to US$11.6 billion in 1990 and US$13.6 billion in 1991 as the uncertainty associated with the Gulf crisis induced some to repatriate accumulated savings abroad. After declining from the high levels of earlier years, foreign aid disbursements (official transfers) rose again in 1990 and 1991, due mainly to the additional aid extended to friendly countries during the Gulf crisis.

Current account deficits throughout the 1980s and early 1990s were financed by capital inflows from the private sector and Saudi commercial banks, as well as by the drawdown of foreign reserves by SAMA and the AGIs. The US$2.4 billion capital outflow recorded by the commercial banks in 1990 following Iraq's invasion of Kuwait was reversed in 1991 and 1992. Banks drew down some of their foreign assets to purchase Treasury bills and to finance development projects by parastatal institutions. The end of the Gulf crisis and the buoyant business conditions in the Kingdom encouraged huge inflows of private sector capital seeking domestic investment opportunities in equities, real estate and business in general. The large capital account receipts in 1991 reflect external borrowing by the government from foreign commercial banks (US$4.5 billion) and from local banks (US$2.5 billion).

Substantial sales of foreign assets were made by SAMA and the AGIs to help finance the remaining gap in the Kingdom's balance of payments. According to the IMF's *International Financial Statistics*, SAMA's foreign assets stood at about US$56.6 billion at the end of 1990, the equivalent of more than two years of merchandise imports at the 1990 level. Total reserves minus gold stood at US$10.4 billion by the end of August 1992. Around one-third of SAMA's foreign assets are held as statutory cover for the riyal and a further one-third is held against letters of credit, mainly for public sector imports.

Conclusion

The current and projected developments in the Saudi economy mean that the market for imported goods and services (currently worth over US$40 billion) will continue to expand, although not at the rate seen in the last two years. The broad framework for further development and diversification of the economy is presented in the fifth Five-Year Development Plan (1990 to 1995). The goal is to attain a 3.6 per cent annual growth in the non-oil sectors within a framework of prudent fiscal policy, greater private sector participation and continued economic integration among the six GCC states. Efforts are underway to strengthen and diversify the Kingdom's financial markets, in order to help mobilise private sector resources more efficiently. Continued strength in the trade account is forecast, based largely on the expectation of stable or higher oil revenues during the 1990s. At the same time the deficit on invisibles is expected to fall as the shift from foreign to domestic provision of services continues. This implies that the current account deficit will remain modest over the medium term, offset mainly by net inflows of capital seeking buoyant business conditions in the Kingdom. SAMA's foreign reserves are unlikely to be drawn down further. On the contrary, as net capital inflows from commercial banks and other private sector entities continue, this should help boost SAMA's foreign assets besides financing the country's current account deficit.

3 The oil and refining sectors

Introduction

As already mentioned in Chapter 1, Saudi Arabia has emerged as the dominant power in OPEC, overtaking the role of the organisation as a whole in balancing supply and demand and hence influencing oil prices. The Kingdom's strategy is to maintain its current market share, to discourage a shift towards alternative energy resources and to secure a steady growth in world oil demand. To achieve these aims, a policy of oil price stability has been pursued and attempts by other OPEC members to engineer shortages have been resisted. The Kingdom is spending close to US$16 billion in order to expand its production capacity to 10 million b/d by 1995 and thus guarantee security of supply to the world oil market.

During the past few years it has become evident that oil prices are determined by those OPEC members selling marginal barrels and with the lowest price tolerance. In other words, prices reflect the lowest amount acceptable to a country with spare production capacity. During the period from 1987 to 1990 both the UAE and Kuwait had spare capacity and would tolerate prices as low as US$15 a barrel for Brent crude (the average in 1988). Kuwait is striving to regain output and the UAE is producing at close to maximum capacity and neither has much influence on prices. Oil prices are largely determined by Saudi Arabia, the only country with enough excess capacity to have an influence on the market. The 1990s will fall into two phases. First, an extension of short-term market conditions will leave little scope for sustained real increases in prices before the middle of the decade. Then, from 1995 to 2000, growth in oil demand will absorb some of OPEC's spare capacity, providing scope for real oil prices to move into a new stable range of US$19 to US$23 a barrel in real 1992 prices. In nominal terms, this implies an average barrel price of US$26 in the late 1990s.

There may be a general convergence between Saudi Arabia's objectives regarding future oil prices and those of the industrialised countries. The Kingdom has reserves that would allow the current levels of production to be maintained for between 80 and 150 years. Preserving the long-term competitiveness of oil with alternative energy sources and continuing the increase of the past three years in world demand for oil requires stable and reasonable oil prices but stability does not preclude a gentle upward adjustment of prices with time. This may turn out to be the optimum price path for oil consumers as well, ensuring that oil prices are not high enough to accentuate inflationary pressures and damage growth prospects but not so low as to threaten the domestic oil industry, increase oil imports and adversely affect the environment.

Saudi Arabia has also developed its domestic refining and marketing capacity in order to meet local demand and avoid reliance on overseas interests. The Kingdom is the largest refiner in OPEC, with a capacity of 1.58 million b/d, constituting around 2.2 per cent of the world total. Its exports of around 765,000 b/d in 1991 accounted for about 10 per cent of total free world trade in oil products. Current refinery expansion plans will make the Kingdom the world's largest producer of unleaded petrol and a major exporter of refined products. The aim is not only to acquire a share of the profit margin taken by refineries, which in the past has accounted for about one-third of the net earnings of the international oil companies, but also to develop local technical skills, expand employment opportunities and add value to the crude oil produced domestically.

Over the past few years Saudi Arabia has started acquiring refining and marketing interests abroad in the search for downstream outlets and enhanced investment opportunities. Apart from securing overseas markets, it may make more sense for the Kingdom to sell more of its oil in product form out of its refineries abroad than to export petroleum products from local plants. The main reason is that the freight costs for crude and fuel oil are very low relative to those for light and middle distillates and the exporter would be in a better position to manage the market for refined products out of its overseas outlets. Furthermore, profit margins for major refineries have been improving and it is still cheaper to buy an operating refinery in any of the main OECD markets than to build a new one in the Gulf.

Saudi Arabia is setting the pace for the downstream trend. The Kingdom now has ventures up and running in the US and in South Korea, as well as a preliminary agreement to start one in Japan; it is also holding talks on developing a European presence. The long-term goal of refining up to 3 million b/d overseas compares with the current refining capacity of Royal Dutch/Shell Group, the world's largest oil company, of 3.3 million b/d.

The essential premises of Saudi oil policy, as set by the Custodian of the Two Holy Mosques, King Fahd bin Abdulaziz, and implemented by the oil Minister, Hisham Nazer are:

- stability and predictability in the oil market to ensure Saudi and global economic growth;
- promotion of transparency in the market mechanism so that prices are freely determined by market fundamentals. Any artificial shortage or oversupply must be avoided and oil's position in the energy mix must be protected to assure the revenues of oil producers. This also means that Saudi Arabia has no objection to an increase in the price of oil, provided the increase comes as a result of the working of the market mechanism;
- discouragement of discriminatory taxation against oil under whatever pretext, including the carbon tax;

• encouragement of large oil producers, within and outside OPEC, to contribute their share of balancing the market in order to prevent volatility and market disequilibrium;

• ensuring that Saudi Arabia is never again made a swing producer. Market stability is to be a common task of all oil producers and Saudi Arabia will contribute only its fair and proportionate share to this task; and

• the promotion of the concept of "reciprocal security" among producers and consumers. This means that the consumers must be assured a steady and uninterrupted supply of oil at market prices and producers must be given open and free access to markets to facilitate a commercially profitable global integration of the oil industry.

This chapter will review the structure and organisation of the Kingdom's oil sector and the outlook for the world oil market, giving forecasts for oil prices, demand and supply, as well as future production capacity of the oil-producing countries. The issue of energy taxes will be analysed and an overview of the Saudi refining sector and the Kingdom's downstream refining and marketing outlets abroad will be presented. The conclusion will point towards new trends in the world oil market, both on the production (upstream) side and on the refining (downstream) side.

Structure and organisation of the oil industry

Crude oil

Saudi Arabia is a major player in world oil markets. Its proven oil reserves amount to approximately 260 billion barrels, by far the largest for any individual country in the world and the equivalent of about 25 per cent of total world reserves. It is also the world's largest exporter and second largest producer of crude oil, accounting in 1992 for about 13 per cent of world output and almost 25 per cent of world trade. Moreover, Saudi Arabia's strong position in world oil markets will almost certainly expand over the next 10 years. If output reaches the target of 10 million b/d during the 1990s, this will account by the year 2000 for as much as 15 per cent of world production and 30 per cent of world trade.

Internally, the oil industry remains the mainspring of the Saudi economy. While its contribution to GDP has declined somewhat over the past nine years, the oil sector still accounted for 37 per cent in 1991. More importantly, oil revenues accounted for 80 per cent of government revenues and 90 per cent of the country's export earnings that year. Only in regard to employment has the industry's contribution been relatively small. In 1991 employment in the oil industry totalled approximately 60,000, less than 2 per cent of the workforce in Saudi Arabia. Of this total, about 50,000 (83 per cent) were Saudis.

There are two key points regarding the structure and organisation of the Saudi oil industry. First, the entire industry is dominated by the government, which retains title to all mineral resources in the country, sets basic policy and makes all major decisions regarding production, investment and domestic energy pricing. The government also holds a sole or majority ownership interest in most major operating companies in the Kingdom, including ARAMCO, SAMAREC, the Petromin Lubricating Oil Refining Company (LUBEREF) and the Petromin Lubricating Oil Company (PETROLUBE). Only the two small foreign companies operating in the Neutral Zone between Kuwait and Saudi Arabia, Getty Oil Company and the Arabian Oil Company of Japan (AOC), are exceptions to this rule.

Secondly, company responsibilities are generally parcelled out along product lines, with individual public companies dominating individual product lines. ARAMCO, for instance, has sole responsibility within the Kingdom for the production and export of crude oil and natural gas. Originally founded by four US companies (Chevron, Texaco, Exxon and Mobil), ARAMCO was purchased by the government in 1976 and converted into an entirely Saudi company in 1988. It now manages the oilfields, pipelines, crude oil export facilities, crude oil tankers and the Master Gas System throughout the country.

SAMAREC operates as a wholly government-owned service company responsible for the government's interests in the production and marketing of refined products in Saudi Arabia. Established in 1988, it now manages three wholly-owned Saudi refineries at Riyadh, Jeddah and Yanbu', controls the government's 50 per cent interest in three joint venture export refineries at Jubail, Yanbu' and Rabigh and coordinates with ARAMCO on refinery runs at ARAMCO's Ras Tanura refinery. It also holds a monopoly on domestic distribution of refined products and manages the bulk plants, loading terminals, tanker fleet and product pipelines used in Saudi Arabia's internal product distribution system.

ARAMCO responded to the Gulf crisis and the loss of Iraqi and Kuwaiti production by boosting output and accelerating plans to raise the country's production capacity to 10 million b/d. Originally scheduled for

Exhibit 3.1

Saudi oilfield expansion, costs (US$ millions) and capacity (b/d thousands), 1991 - 95

Name of field	*Budgeted cost*	*1992 capacity*	*1995 capacity*	*API gravity (in degrees)*	*% sulphur*
Ghawar Fields	2,500	4,700	5,300	34	1.91-2.15
Manifa	2,500	200	300	28	2.97-3.66
Safaniya	2,090	1,300	1,500	27	2.93-2.96
Qatif	1,500	100	200	33-34	2.45-2.92
Najd fields	1,500	–	300	45+	0.06
Zuluf	1,000	500	700	32	2.41
Marjan	500	100	570	33	2.42
Berri	500	700	700	32-34	1.14-2.00
Khurais	300	75	150	33-36	1.89
Khursaniya	235	75	150	31	2.63
Abu Hadriya	195	50	75	35	1.51-2.40
Harmaliya	120	50	75	35	1.65
Abqaiq	100	850	850	37	1.32-2.80
Shaybah	2,000	–	–	40-42	N/A
Total	**16,000**	**8,700**	**10,870**	**–**	**–**

Sources: APS Review, 27 April 1992 and *Saudi Arabia Monitor*, May 1990.

Exhibit 3.2

Saudi Arabian crude oil statistics (b/d millions)

	1979	*1980*	*1981*	*1982*	*1983*	*1984*	*1985*	*1986*	*1987*	*1988*	*1989*	*1990*	*1991*
Productive capacity	10.00	10.20	10.40	10.20	9.60	8.80	8.50	8.00	7.80	7.50	7.50	8.50	8.70
Saudi production ceiling[1]	–	–	–	7.15	5.00	4.35	4.35	4.35	4.35	4.52	5.38	N/A	8.03
OPEC production ceiling[1]	–	–	–	17.50	17.50	16.00	16.00	15.04	15.04	18.50	22.09	N/A	22.30
Crude oil production	9.53	9.90	9.81	6.48	4.54	4.08	3.24	4.88	4.19	5.09	5.06	6.41	8.21
ARAMCO	9.25	9.63	9.62	6.33	4.37	3.92	3.04	4.69	3.99	4.93	4.86	6.26	8.15
AOC	0.20	0.19	0.11	0.09	0.11	0.09	0.13	0.12	0.13	0.09	0.13	0.12	0.06
Getty	0.08	0.08	0.07	0.06	0.05	0.07	0.07	0.07	0.07	0.07	0.07	0.04	0.00
Domestic consumption	–	0.51	0.60	0.67	0.75	0.80	0.73	0.72	0.72	0.79	0.82	0.90	0.94
Direct crude consumption	–	0.05	0.05	0.06	0.08	0.08	0.09	0.09	0.09	0.10	0.10	0.10	0.10
Refined product consumption	0.29	0.46	0.56	0.61	0.67	0.72	0.63	0.62	0.63	0.69	0.72	0.80	0.84
Crude oil exports	8.82	9.22	9.02	5.64	3.92	3.19	2.15	3.27	2.42	3.03	3.34	4.82	6.74
Refined product exports	–	0.06	0.04	0.08	0.07	0.09	0.29	0.46	0.72	0.82	0.76	0.73	0.76
Discrepancy[2]	–	0.11	0.14	0.10	-0.21	0.00	0.08	0.44	0.33	0.46	0.15	0.00	0.00

[1]year-end.
[2]production not accounted for.

Sources: OPEC Statistical Bulletin for 1991, and a survey of the Saudi Arabian oil industry, US Embassy in Riyadh, July 1992.

completion in 1998 at an overall capital cost of US$13 billion, this programme will now be completed in 1995 at an overall cost of US$16 billion (see Exhibit 3.1). ARAMCO also added plans for the development of its new light crude oil finds in the Central Region. According to current plans, US$500 million will be invested over the five years from 1991 to 1996 to produce 150,000 b/d of Arab Super Light from the Hawtah field and to connect that field with both the PETROLINE crude oil pipeline (to allow export through Yanbu') and ARAMCO's pipeline system in the Eastern Province (to allow export through the Gulf).

Five prime contractors have been selected to handle these major expansion and development projects under ARAMCO's overall management. Fluor Daniel has received a five-year contract to manage the expansion of capacity in the Northern Producing Areas; Ralph Parsons received a similar contract for the Southern Producing Areas; ABB Lummus Crest received a five-year contract to "maintain potential" in the offshore oilfields; John Brown Engineers and Contractors was selected for the development of the Central Region; and Stone & Webster was chosen to supervise pipeline work throughout both the Central Region and the Eastern Province.

In the Neutral Zone two major field development projects were under consideration in the days before the Iraqi invasion of Kuwait. The first was a US$400 million gas-gathering project in AOC's Khafji field, which was to be entirely paid for by the governments of Kuwait and Saudi Arabia. On completion (now postponed until 1993), the project will have a capacity of 140 million standard cubic feet per day (cf/d), with output split equally between Saudi Arabia and Kuwait.

As a result of the de-mothballing and expansion programmes already executed, Saudi Arabia's maximum sustainable production capacity was put at about 8.7 million b/d in 1991 (see Exhibit 3.2). ARAMCO accounted for about 8.5 million b/d of this capacity, broken down between 5 million b/d of Arab Light, 1.3 million b/d of Arab Medium, 1.6 million b/d of Arab Heavy and 700,000 b/d of Arab Extra Light. The AOC, for its part, retains the capacity to produce about 400,000 b/d of heavy, sour crudes, of which 200,000 b/d would fall to Saudi Arabia's account as its half share. Getty Oil Company's capacity was entirely disabled during the Gulf War and it is currently undergoing massive reconstruction.

Natural gas and natural gas liquids

Saudi Arabia does not have the dominant position in natural gas that it has in oil, despite reserves of 186.5 trillion cubic feet (the fifth largest total in the world). Natural gas, however, has played a major role in the industrialisation of Saudi Arabia, particularly since the completion of the Master Gas System, which was designed, built and is now operated by ARAMCO. That system has also made Saudi Arabia the world's largest exporter of natural gas liquids.

Overall, ARAMCO produced about 2.2 billion cf/d of fuel gas and 310 million cf/d of ethane in 1991, barely enough to meet demand. By 1995, with current facilities, it may be able to produce 2.5 billion cf/d to 2.7 billion cf/d of fuel gas. Demand from current customers alone, however, is forecast to be in the range of 3 billion to 3.2 billion cf/d, opening up a potential deficit of 500 million cf/d if steps are not taken to add facilities, raise prices or otherwise restrict demand.

Saudi Arabia is a major player in the world liquefied petroleum gas (LPG) markets. It accounts for 7 to 10 per cent of annual world output of natural gas liquids or NGLs (propane, butane and natural gasoline) and 30 per cent of the world seaborne trade in LPGs (propane and butane). It is the world's largest exporter of LPGs. ARAMCO has the capacity to produce about 600,000 b/d of NGLs. Included in this total is approximately 315,000 b/d of propane, 165,000 b/d of butane and 120,000 b/d of natural gasoline. In addition, Saudi Arabia's refineries can contribute up to 40,000 b/d of LPGs when operating at full capacity.

Domestic consumption in 1991 accounted for a small proportion (5 per cent to 8 per cent) of Saudi LPG production, with most going either as fuel and feedstock for petrochemical industries in Jubail and Yanbu' or as bottled gas for distribution to household consumers and small industries by the National Gas Company. Looking ahead, however, domestic consumption will almost certainly increase rapidly over the next five years as a series of second generation, LPG-based petrochemical plants comes onstream. Included here are two flexible feedstock ethylene crackers with a combined capacity in excess of 1 million tons a year, a series of MTBE (methyl tertiary butyl ether) plants with a combined capacity in excess of 1.7 million tons a year and, possibly, one or two propane-based propylene plants.

The refining sector

The world picture

The move downstream by various oil-producing countries is taking a variety of forms, ranging from full ownership and operation of integrated refining and marketing systems, as seen in Kuwait's overseas acquisitions, through the joint venture approach adopted by Saudi Arabia to the minority equity position of Abu Dhabi and Oman. Kuwait has already penetrated the European market by acquiring three refineries with a capacity of 235,000 b/d and around 6,800 petrol stations. Abu Dhabi has embarked on a similar path with its acquisition of a 10 per cent stake in Spain's largest private oil refiner Cia Española de Petróleos (CEPSA) and a 10 per cent stake in the French company Total. Oman recently took a 20 per cent stake in Caltex's planned 120,000 b/d refinery in Thailand that will run on Omani crude. As for Qatar and Bahrain, a different pattern of downstream integration may unfold, involving tie-ups with more significant regional oil producers.

The distribution of the world's refining capacity by region at the end of 1991 is given in Exhibit 3.3. North America and western Europe account for 42 per cent of existing capacity, the Commonwealth of Independent States (CIS) for 16.4 per cent, Japan for 6 per cent, Latin America and the Caribbean for 10 per cent and the Asia-Pacific region (other than Japan) for 8.2 per cent. The combined refining capacity of the GCC countries does not exceed 2,477,000 b/d, or 3.3 per cent of the total, while the other Arab countries account for another 3.8 per cent. Kuwait saw its refining capacity drop from 820,000 b/d before the Gulf crisis to 270,000 b/d. The 195,000 b/d refinery at Mina Shuaiba suffered extensive damage, while production at the Mina Abdulla refinery is down to 100,000 b/d from 235,000 b/d before the crisis and at Mina al Ahmadi to 170,000 b/d from 390,000 b/d. The Gulf countries have been consuming around 1.24 million b/d of oil products, with their average to the year 2000 not likely to exceed 1.8 million b/d and current capacity is adequate for their future oil needs.

Exhibit 3.3

World refining capacity, 1991

	B/d thousands	*% of total*
US & Canada	17.400	23.3
Western Europe	14.000	18.8
GCC countries	2.477	3.3
Other arab countries	2.844	3.8
Other Middle East[1]	1.380	1.8
Other Africa	1.200	1.6
Latin America & Caribbean	7.500	10.1
Russia & CIS states[2]	12.260	16.4
China	2.200	2.9
Other eastern European countries	2.650	3.6
Asia – Pacific (except Japan)	6.150	8.2
Japan	4.570	6.1
Total	**74.631**	**100.0**

[1]Includes Turkey and Iran.
[2]Former USSR.

Source: Petroleum Economist, September 1991 and national plans to expand refineries in the various Gulf countries.

After 15 years of closures and under-utilisation, there is now concern that not enough new refining capacity is being built. *Petroleum Economist's* construction survey for 1991 has identified only one substantial new refinery in the US due for completion within the next few years, together with only four relatively small expansions of distillation capacity. Nothing is planned in western Europe and capacity added by the US projects amount to only 200,000 b/d. The reasons for this are partly environmental: it is reckoned to be virtually impossible now to secure consents to construct a new refinery at a US or western European location with good market access. Further, specifications for refinery air, water and noise emissions are being made progressively more stringent, adding to capital and running costs. Labour costs and taxes are also generally high in areas near markets.

Even OPEC producers are apparently reluctant to build additional refineries at home. Exhibit 3.4 identifies five new refineries in the Middle East either under construction or expected to come onstream by 1995. Three refineries are in Iran (Bandar Abas, Bandar Taheri and Arak), one in Iraq (this may not go forward because of cash limitations following the Gulf crisis) and there is to be a new export refinery in Jabal Ali, Dubai with a capacity of 120,000 b/d. There are also nine refinery expansion projects in the region, one in Bahrain, two in the UAE, two in Kuwait and four in Saudi Arabia. The Far East is attracting 23 of the world's 55 refining projects, with additional refining capacity of 3 million b/d and the Middle East has 14 projects and 1.5 million b/d of additional capacity. There is roughly 200,000 b/d being added in each of North America, Africa and South America. The additional world refining capacity of 5,487,000 b/d by 1995 represents only a 7.4 per cent increase on the 1992 level of 74,631,000 b/d.

The amendments to the US Clean Air Act of 1990 will have far-reaching effects on the market for refined products worldwide. The single most significant is the requirement to sell reformulated petrol by 1995 in the nine US cities with the worst air pollution. Starting in October 1992 the bill requires the 41 cities with the worst smog (ozone) problems to

Exhibit 3.4

Distribution of new refining capacity due by 1995 (b/d thousands)

	New refineries		***Refinery expansions***		***Total projects***	
	Number	*Capacity*	*Number*	*Capacity*	*Number*	*Capacity*
Western Europe	0	0	0	0	0	0
Africa[1]	0	0	5	215	5	215
Middle East	5	690	9	835	14	1525
Far East	16	1745	7	345	23	3090
North America	1	120	4	78	5	198
Caribbean/South America[2]	2	225	3	34	5	259
Former USSR & eastern Europe	1	120	2	80	3	200
Total	**25**	**2900**	**30**	**1587**	**55**	**5487**

[1]Including Egypt.
[2]Including Mexico.

Sources: IEA/OECD *Note on Saudi Arabia,* ARAMCO annual reports, and a survey of the Saudi Arabian oil industry, US Embassy in Riyadh, July 1992.

use a better quality petrol containing 2.7 per cent oxygenates. There will, therefore, have to be radical changes in refining operations, requiring heavy investment in new plant and research into new processes. Estimates of costs for the industry as a whole vary between US$20 billion and US$30 billion over the next four years. In particular there will have to be a quick increase in MTBE capacity. MTBE is the industry's major oxygen-containing additive; it boosts the octane rating of fuels, as well as reducing carbon monoxide emissions from vehicles.

The new legislation in the US means that the outlook for refiners and the likely future levels of petrol supply and demand in the American market are less clear. It seems probable that there will be shortages of new specification petrols, while supplies of today's conventional formulation will run into surplus. During the next two to five years industry profitability will become progressively more dependent upon the ability to supply reformulated petrols. It is estimated that 330,000 b/d of the product will be needed by 1995, by which time some 30 per cent of US sales will be of reformulated petrol. Demand growth between 1992 and 1995 should therefore average 27 per cent annually. On the supply side, US capacity at end-1991 was close to 120,000 b/d from 26 MTBE plants. Some 29 new plants are planned, providing an additional 106,000 b/d by 1995. This implies that there will still be a growing shortage of MTBE in the US during the 1990s, which may be alleviated by higher prices and by imports.

Saudi Arabia's position

Saudi Arabia is emerging as the preferred site for MTBE plants, building on its advantage of existing methanol production. The Kingdom's first MTBE plant was built by the Saudi European Petrochemical Company (Ibn Zahr), an affiliate of the state-controlled petrochemicals giant SABIC, in Jubail and has been in production since 1988. Five more are under construction or consideration. If they all go ahead, Saudi MTBE output will rise to 3.7 million tons a year by the mid-1990s. Projects realised so far have been dominated by SABIC, which has built up a network of heavy industrial plants since the late 1970s. Ibn Sina (another affiliate of SABIC) and Ibn Zahr awarded contracts for two new MTBE plants in mid-1991. The local private sector is also showing keen interest. Two groups of local investors, Saudi Chemical Investments (Chemvest) and the National Industrial Petrochemical Company (Teldene), are putting together plans with international companies to build two MTBE factories to come onstream by mid-1995.

Saudi Arabia operates eight refineries, three of these (the Riyadh Oil Refining Company, the Jeddah Oil Refining Company and the Petromin/Yanbu' refinery) either wholly- or majority-owned by SAMAREC and orientated towards the domestic market. Three others are large, export-orientated refineries in which SAMAREC is joint venture partner with Shell (at Jubail), Mobil (at Yanbu') and the Greek company Petrola (at Rabigh). A seventh, at Ras Tanura, is owned by ARAMCO but operated according to a product call dictated by SAMAREC, with its output split between exports and the domestic market. There is also a small refinery in the Neutral Zone, the AOC refinery at Khafji.

Exhibit 3.5

Saudi Arabia's refined product capacity, 1983 - 91 (b/d millions)

Location	*Owner*	*1983*	*1984*	*1985*	*1986*	*1987*	*1988*	*1989*	*1990*	*1991*
Ras Tanura	Saudi ARAMCO	0.450	0.450	0.450	0.500	0.530	0.530	0.530	0.530	0.300
Jeddah	Jeddah Oil Refinery Company (SAMAREC)	0.090	0.090	0.090	0.090	0.090	0.090	0.090	0.090	0.090
Riyadh	Riyadh Oil Refinery Company (SAMAREC)	0.135	0.135	0.135	0.135	0.135	0.135	0.135	0.135	0.135
Mina Saud	Getty Oil (Texaco)[1]	0.050	0.050	0.050	0.050	0.050	0.050	0.070	0.070	0.000
Khafji	Arabian Oil Company	0.030	0.030	0.030	0.030	0.030	0.030	0.030	0.030	0.030
Yanbu'	SAMAREC	0.170	0.170	0.170	0.170	0.170	0.170	0.170	0.170	0.170
Yanbu'	Petromin/Mobil	0.250	0.250	0.250	0.250	0.250	0.250	0.280	0.280	0.280
Jubail	Petromin/Shell	–	0.250	0.250	0.250	0.250	0.250	0.250	0.250	0.250
Rabigh	Petromin/Petrola	–	–	–	–	–	–	0.325	0.325	0.325
	Total	**0.925**	**1.175**	**1.425**	**1.475**	**1.505**	**1.505**	**1.880**	**1.880**	**1.580**

[1]Entirely destroyed during the Gulf War.

Source: A survey of the Saudi Arabian oil industry, US Embassy in Riyadh, July 1992.

During the early 1980s Saudi Arabia more than doubled its refining capacity with the construction of four new refineries (the two at Yanbu' and those at Jubail and Rabigh), the expansion of the one at Riyadh and the modernisation and upgrading of that at Ras Tanura. As a result, Saudi Arabia had nine refineries in operation by 1990, with a combined nameplate capacity of 1.88 million b/d (see Exhibit 3.5). During the Gulf War about 300,000 b/d of this capacity was lost. The 70,000 b/d Getty Oil refinery at Mina al Saud in the Neutral Zone was destroyed and in late November 1990 a fire at the Ras Tanura refinery took down one of that refinery's two crude distillation towers, reducing capacity from 530,000 b/d to approximately 300,000 b/d. This reduced the overall refining capacity of the Kingdom to about 1.58 million b/d in 1991. Refinery output has been heavily slanted towards heavy products, with heavy fuel oil accounting for 30 per cent of total output, diesel for 28.8 per cent and petrol for 15 per cent (see Exhibit 3.6).

Saudi Arabian domestic consumption of oil products quadrupled between 1971 and 1984, before levelling off in the late 1980s at around 700,000 b/d. During the Gulf crisis, military demand, reaching at one point around 200,000 b/d, added to this figure. In 1991 demand in the domestic market averaged 840,000 b/d. All petroleum product prices in the Kingdom are controlled by the government and products are sold at very low levels compared to international prices. Petrol prices were reduced by 38 per cent in March 1992 to SR0.33 (8.7 US cents) a litre. Low prices have encouraged high levels of domestic product consumption at the expense of exports. Each of the 12 million residents of Saudi Arabia now consumes about three gallons of oil products a day (a ratio comparable to those prevailing in industrialised societies), despite Saudi Arabia's lower level of industrialisation. Furthermore, this price structure has distorted consumption, encouraging, for example, the use of higher valued diesel in place of heavy fuel oil.

Exhibit 3.6

Saudi Arabia's 1992 refinery capacity by product (b/d thousands)

Location	*Owner*	*LPG*	*Naphtha*	*Benzene*	*Petrol*	*Jet fuel kerosene*	*Diesel*	*Fuel oil*	*Asphalt*	*Base oil*	*Loss*	*Total nameplate capacity*	*Maximum sustainable output*
Ras Tanura	Saudi ARAMCO	5.0	7.0	0.0	48.0	22.0	95.0	110.0	5.0	0.0	8.0	300.0	300
Jeddah	Jeddah Oil Refinery Company (SAMAREC)	2.5	12.9	0.0	8.3	0.0	25.2	25.9	7.3	4.1	4.8	91.0	100
Riyadh	Riyadh Oil Refinery Company (SAMAREC)	6.1	0.0	0.0	39.6	14.5	48.4	0.0	12.5	0.0	12.9	134.0	140
Khafji	Arabian Oil Company	0.0	8.0	0.0	0.0	0.0	0.0	22.0	0.0	0.0	0.0	30.0	30
Yanbu'	SAMAREC	4.3	0.0	0.0	33.5	0.0	46.4	80.2	0.0	0.0	5.6	170.0	220
Yanbu'	Petromin/Mobil	3.0	0.0	0.0	107.0	40.0	85.0	45.0	0.0	0.0	0.0	280.0	310
Jubail	Petromin/Shell	4.2	70.0	5.4	0.0	27.0	80.0	56.0	0.0	0.0	7.4	250.0	300
Rabigh	Petromin/Petrola	5.2	66.5	0.0	0.0	32.4	74.4	135.5	0.0	0.0	11.1	325.0	325
	Total	**30.3**	**164.4**	**5.4**	**236.4**	**135.9**	**454.4**	**474.6**	**24.8**	**4.1**	**49.8**	**1580.0**	**1725**

Source: OPEC Statistical Bulletin for 1991, a survey of the Saudi Arabian oil industry, US Embassy in Riyadh, July 1992 and IEA/OECD *Note on Saudi Arabia*.

Saudi petroleum product exports (not including LPGs) peaked in 1988 at about 819,000 b/d and have since declined in response to the rationalisation of SAMAREC's refinery operations (cutting production from the least sophisticated refineries), surging military demand during 1990 and 1991 and a recovering national economy, which should itself add 50,000 b/d to domestic demand in 1992 and 1993. As a result, exports appear to have totalled no more than 765,000 b/d in 1991, down by 6.6 per cent from 1988. Middle distillates in particular were cut from exports, with most being of petrol, naphtha or heavy fuel oil. Around 45 per cent of these export sales have traditionally been directed to the Asia-Pacific market, with Japan alone accounting for one-third of SAMAREC's total sales. As for other exporters, Mobil's sales (from its half share of the output of the Yanbu' refinery) were primarily directed to the US and western Europe; Rabigh's sales were split between Europe and the Far East; and Shell's sales were almost exclusively to the Far East.

SAMAREC has a 10-year programme to upgrade as well as expand its three domestic refineries and the three joint venture export refineries. The total cost of this programme is estimated at US$5 billion and it will be executed in three phases. The final goal is a cleaner, lighter product, featuring higher octane unleaded petrol that meets the stringent requirements of the export market. Under the first phase to 1995 the three domestic refineries will be expanded, with new upgrading units to increase their output of light products. Petrol production will be raised from 93,000 b/d to 208,000 b/d, mostly to consist of reformulated and unleaded products in line with European and US specifications. The new facilities will include boosting the capacity of the Yanbu' plant by 70,000 b/d to 240,000 b/d, with a large vacuum gas oil conversion unit, a catalytic reforming system and units for isomerisation, alkylation and MTBE production (see Exhibit 3.7). The Riyadh refinery will be expanded by 15,000 b/d to 150,000 b/d and, together with the Jeddah refinery, will be

Exhibit 3.7

Saudi refining capacity expansion plans, 1992 - 2000 (b/d)

Location	*Owner*	*Nameplate capacity*	*1995 capacity*	*2000 capacity*
Ras Tanura	Saudi ARAMCO	300,000	500,000	1,000,000
Jeddah	Jeddah Oil Refinery Company (SAMAREC)	90,000	110,000	110,000
Riyadh	Riyadh Oil Refinery Company (SAMAREC)	135,000	150,000	150,000
Mina Saud	Getty Oil (Texaco)[1]	(50,000)	(50,000)	(50,000)
Khafji	Arabian Oil Company	30,000	30,000	180,000
Yanbu'	SAMAREC	170,000	240,000	240,000
Yanbu'	Petromin/Mobil	280,000	280,000	350,000
Jubail	Petromin/Shell	250,000	250,000	350,000
Rabigh	Petromin/Petrola	325,000	325,000	400,000
	Total	**1,630,000**	**1,905,000**	**2,830,000**
	Total excluding Mina Saud	**1,580,000**	**1,855,000**	**2,780,000**

[1]Entirely destroyed during the Gulf War and it is not clear whether or not it will be rebuilt.

Sources: SAMAREC *Newsletters* and APS *Review*, 20 April 1992.

upgraded for products similar to those of Yanbu'. A total of 11 new units will be installed at Yanbu', three at Riyadh and six at Jeddah.

Under the second and third phases to the year 2000 another US$2 billion will be spent to upgrade the 325,000 b/d refinery at Rabigh. The third phase will also involve expanding the other two export plants, the Petromin/Shell refinery at Jubail and the Petromin/Mobil refinery at Yanbu'. Each of these plants has a nameplate capacity of 250,000 b/d, expected to reach 350,000 at the end of the expansion. The AOC, which owns the Al Khafji refinery, is a partner in a proposed Saudi-Japanese refining venture proposing expansion of plants in Japan and the Saudi Arabia. Under these plans the capacity of the Al Khafji refinery could be boosted to 180,000 b/d by the year 2000. At Ras Tanura Saudi ARAMCO has a US$1.7 billion programme to rebuild the refinery's damaged distillation tower and to add fluid catalytic cracking, hydrocracking, continuous catalytic reforming, isomerisation, alkylation and diesel desulphurisation units. The project started in 1991 and should be completed by 1995, returning Ras Tanura to its prewar capacity of 500,000 b/d. Finally, a small project worth noting at the Petromin/Mobil refinery in Yanbu' is the US$60 million olefin upgrading announced in 1991, which involves the installation of a new MTBE production unit.

Saudi overseas refining and distribution ventures

The oversupplied crude oil markets and volatile prices of the 1980s encouraged major crude oil buyers to shift from one supplier to another and the market for long-term contracts at fixed prices shrank dramatically. Exporting refined products at market prices and selling crude on the basis of netback deals with major companies helped to offset, at least partially, this loss of marketing and pricing flexibility. However, exporting has proved to be commercially less desirable than ownership of downstream assets in consuming countries. Not only is it much more expensive to transport refined products than crude oil but, without direct access to distribution networks, the products have to be sold wholesale. The netback deals also proved less efficient and Saudi strategists realised it made more sense to acquire, rather than hire the services of, local refineries. Thus the emphasis shifted towards integrating crude oil production with existing overseas downstream operations.

Oil consumers are becoming more accommodating to the downstream trend of the major oil producers. They realise the importance of having a secure source of oil in the event of any supply shortage. Indeed, jointly-owned refineries have first call on oil in the event of supply restrictions, as was clearly demonstrated during the Gulf crisis. With expensive overseas refineries and petrol stations to feed, oil producers who own these outlets will give priority of supply to their joint ventures abroad. They will also have a greater interest in the wellbeing of the oil-importing countries and will not jeopardise their own investments. Inflows of equity investment are always a gesture of trust, first that the assets will produce a dividend and secondly trust in the jurisdiction in which those assets are located. Such investments also benefit the host countries by providing employment.

From the refiners' perspective, there is also a strong motivation to enter joint ventures with crude oil suppliers. Overcapacity and the competitive nature of the refining industry, along with highly volatile crude oil prices, have made it imperative for a refiner to have access to guaranteed supplies of crude on a long-term basis to maintain production rates at or near optimum capacity. Allowing foreign producers to buy equity in domestic refineries also encourages capital inflows to the country concerned and provides companies with an opportunity to sell their excess capacity to oil producers instead of shutting it down completely.

For any investment to make sense, whether in the stock market, the oil industry or anywhere else, it must be economically attractive and must generate sufficient returns to cover its costs. If future demand for refined oil products drops below the levels currently anticipated, there will once more be a surplus of refining capacity. This will inevitably force margins down, as downstream players try to protect their market shares by cutting prices, thus repeating the events of the early and mid-1980s. Those who cannot compete in such times will not earn an adequate rate of return and will ultimately shut down. However, companies that have integrated with foreign producers will be at an advantage, as they may be able to draw on discounted crude oil from their upstream partners.

The first downstream investment by Saudi Arabia was with Texaco in the US. The deal, initiated in 1988, gives the Kingdom a guaranteed market in the US for 615,000 b/d of crude oil exports. This is the biggest export deal for any OPEC country (Venezuela is next at about 450,000 b/d, followed by Kuwait at less than 250,000 b/d). Saudi Arabia paid Texaco US$812 million in crude oil for 50 per cent ownership of three refineries in the US (one in Texas with 250,000 b/d capacity, one in Louisiana with 225,000 b/d capacity and one in Delaware with 140,000 b/d capacity). The partnership also includes 49 terminals, a distribution network of around 11,450 petrol stations and the right to use the Texaco trademark in 23 states. Texaco was one of the four original partners in ARAMCO and shared in the production and marketing of Saudi Arabia's oil until 1976.

In July 1991 Saudi ARAMCO paid US$470 million for a 35 per cent stake in South Korea's Ssangyong refining company, gaining a foothold in the rapidly growing Korean and Far Eastern markets. The new joint venture, known as the Han-Saudi Oil Refining Company Ltd, will acquire, own and operate new refining facilities, with a capacity of around 175,000 b/d, adjacent to Ssangyong's existing 90,000 b/d refinery at Onsan in South Korea. When upgrading plans are completed, the joint venture will have sophisticated, deep conversion capacity capable of handling 100 per cent heavy, high-sulphur crudes. Saudi ARAMCO will guarantee the supply of all the venture's crude oil requirements under a long-term agreement. The venture's output of refined products will be supplied to the domestic Korean market or exported.

There has been an agreement in principle for a third major deal with Japan. Saudi ARAMCO, Nippon Oil Co (Japan's largest distributor of petroleum products), Nippon Mining Co, AOC and Caltex Petroleum are undertaking feasibility studies for investment in a joint venture project that could include several refineries in Japan with a total capacity of 450,000 b/d and one or more refineries in Saudi Arabia with a total capacity of 300,000 b/d. Shareholdings in the projected venture have not yet been determined, though there is an understanding that Saudi ARAMCO will have a 50 per cent interest, Nippon Oil will have 20 per cent, Nippon Mining 15 per cent, Caltex 10 per cent and AOC 5 per cent. The total investment for the plants in Japan is put at US$8 billion, of which US$3.6 billion would be for the acquisition of existing capacity by the joint venture and the balance for expansion projects.

Saudi officials are also keen to purchase downstream operations in Europe but discussions have not to date yielded any agreements or immediate prospects. It was reported that the Italian energy giant ENI offered ARAMCO a 15 per cent share of the Italian refined products market. There have also been talks with France's Total and Elf Aquitaine but the focus seems to have moved recently to the European operations of Exxon, the US company whose seven refineries in Europe produce 13 per cent of the continent's needs.

The expansion into overseas downstream operations has not only been pursued by the state-owned ARAMCO. In February 1992 a group of private Saudi investors (coming together to form the Arabian Petroleum Co, whose main shareholder is the Jeddah-based investment group Delta International) signed a letter of intent to buy half of the refining and marketing operations of Fina, the Dallas-based subsidiary of the Belgian oil company Petrofina. The deal, estimated to be worth more than US$1 billion, includes two refineries in Texas and 3,000 service stations. It would thus represent a major expansion of the Saudi presence in the US oil market.

The deals with Texaco, Ssangyong and Nippon oil seem to set the pattern for Saudi Arabia's overseas partnerships. The aim is to acquire additional refining and distribution facilities in the major oil-consuming countries that will provide secure outlets for a sizeable part of Saudi Arabia's crude oil production (up to 3 million b/d by the turn of the century). The preference is for buying equity, paid for mostly in crude oil, and forming partnerships, rather than taking full ownership as is the case with Kuwait. This strategy should enable the Saudi Arabian national oil company to become one of the largest integrated companies in the world by the year 2000.

The outlook for the world oil market

Recent events

The Gulf crisis coincided with a growing dependence by western economies on oil from the region. This growing importance of Gulf oil to the world, and especially the US, is due to OPEC's low price strategy, which has been maintained since the early 1980s. From 1973 to 1981, when oil prices were firming, the growth in petrol consumption in the OECD countries first slowed then went into reverse, while non-OPEC supply continued to

Exhibit 3.8

Regional oil production (b/d millions)

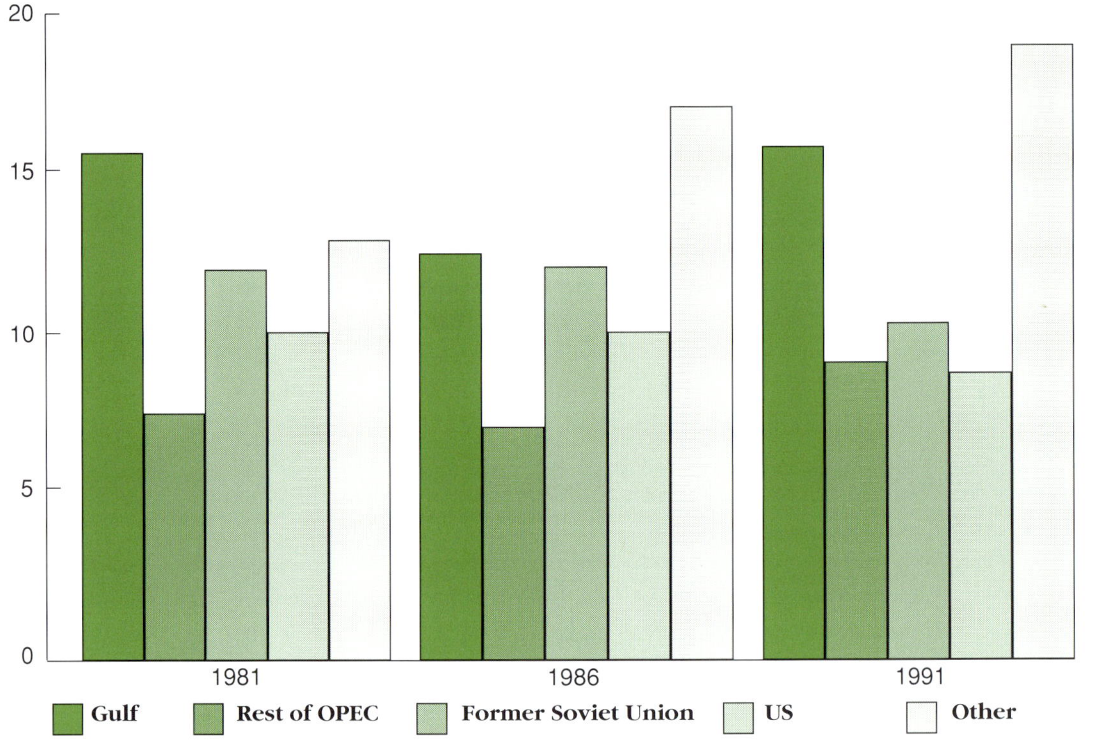

increase. OPEC countries, which account for 77 per cent of the world's proven oil reserves, saw their market share dropping from 61 per cent of the world total in 1979 to 34 per cent in 1985, before rising once again thereafter.

The downward trend in the demand for oil, which started in 1979, bottomed out in 1986 and then reversed once more. The call on OPEC oil rose from 15.5 million b/d in 1985 to 23.3 million b/d in 1990. It is true that part of the increase in oil consumption during the past few years has been due to the "income effect", with higher world growth rates translating into higher world demand for oil. However, the "price effect" may also have contributed. Changes in price have little immediate effect on demand but low sustained prices have a significant impact over time. World demand for OPEC oil rose to 24 million b/d in 1992, while oil prices edged slightly higher, reflecting tighter supply conditions with Iraq's output of 3.5 million b/d remaining outside the market.

OPEC's price and production strategies of the last few years have reversed the growth in non-OPEC supply (see Exhibit 3.8). More than 1 million b/d of high cost US production has been shut down, perhaps permanently, and production in the former USSR (CIS) dropped by 11 per cent from 1988 to 1991. Total output in the CIS for 1992 is expected to be only 9.2 million b/d, down from 12.4 million b/d in 1986. Other non-OPEC producers were also hurt, putting added pressure on OPEC's excess capacity.

Oil is likely to continue to play at least as important a role in the world economy as it has done so far. Perhaps less obvious, however, is the growing dependence on oil from the Gulf. In the US, oil imports rose from 8 per cent of total imports in 1985 to 26 per cent in 1990. The US Energy Information Agency estimates that, by the year 2000, almost 60 per cent of US oil consumption will be imported, most of it from the Gulf (7 million b/d, against 2 million b/d in 1990). Europe continues to get 41 per cent of its oil imports from the region, while Japan's dependence on Gulf oil exceeded 68 per cent in 1990 (see Exhibit 3.9)

Energy use per unit of real GDP has been falling in the OECD countries since the early 1970s. However, the decline appears to have been slowing down since 1986. The reduction is due to structural changes in economies from heavy, energy-intensive industries to services and is helped by steady improvements in the efficiency of energy use, stimulated by increasing fuel prices caused by higher taxes. This trend should continue during the 1990s, driven by competition to reduce manufacturing costs and also perhaps by growing environmental pressures. In the developing countries rates of energy use per unit of GDP have been rising and we expect them to continue upwards throughout the 1990s. Oil is the preferred fuel for industrial expansion, as it does not require the same fixed delivery infrastructure as gas. There are also fewer environmental objections in developing countries. Projections of oil demand by region are illustrated in Exhibit 3.10.

Exhibit 3.9

Percentage share of Middle Eastern oil in total oil imports

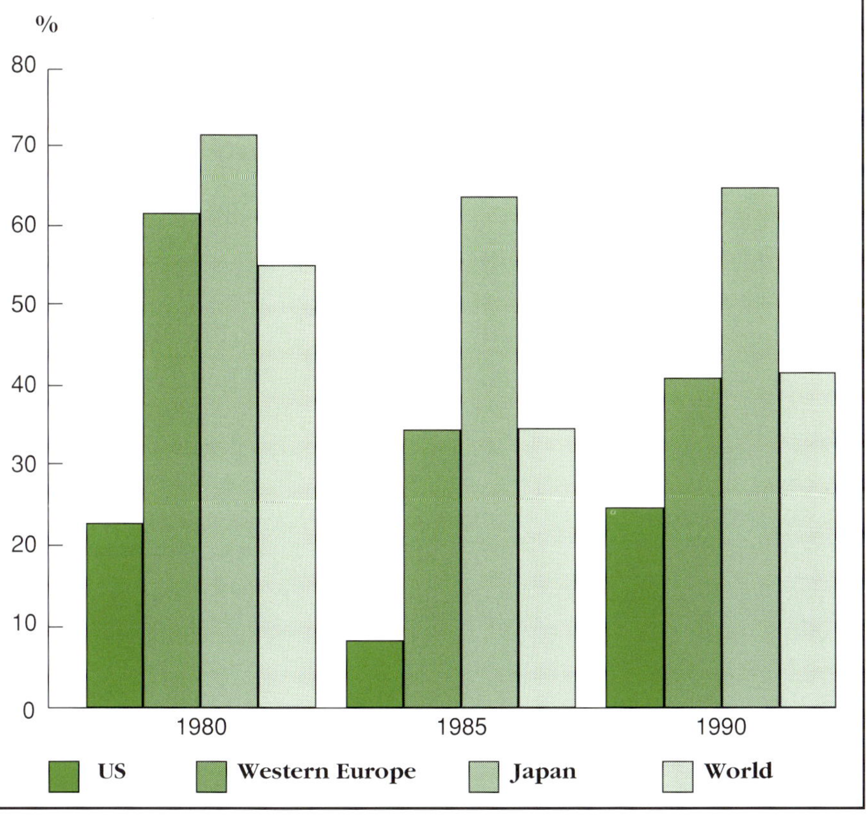

Exhibit 3.10
Oil demand by region (b/d millions)

	1985	*1990*	*1991*	*1992*	*1995*[1]	*2000*[1]	*% change 1985-90*	*% change 1990-95*	*% change 1995-2000*
US	15.71	16.97	16.73	17.01	16.78	16.45	1.5	-0.2	-0.4
Western Europe	12.15	13.00	13.37	13.54	13.74	12.91	1.2	1.0	-1.2
Japan	4.40	5.25	5.34	5.48	5.99	6.44	3.5	2.6	1.4
Rest of OECD	2.14	2.36	2.29	2.28	2.56	2.72	2.2	1.7	1.3
Central Europe	1.77	1.61	1.34	1.33	1.30	1.70	-1.9	-4.2	5.6
LDCs	10.41	12.02	12.72	13.62	16.60	19.72	3.1	5.6	3.7
CIS *(former USSR)*	11.35	12.30	12.00	11.00	9.40	10.00	1.6	-4.7	1.3
China	1.82	2.28	2.38	2.47	2.92	4.03	4.7	5.0	6.6
Oother Regions	0.37	0.45	0.45	0.45	0.48	0.51	3.6	1.4	1.2
World	60.10	66.20	66.60	67.08	69.77	74.45	1.8	1.1	1.4
(OECD)	34.40	37.57	37.72	38.31	39.07	38.52	1.7	0.7	-0.3

[1]Forecasts.

Sources: UBS Phillips & Drew *Macro Oil Special Edition*, April 1992 and our estimates.

Projections for the non-OPEC countries

Excluding the CIS and China, non-OPEC production should rise by 1.48 million b/d from 1991 to 1995. A steady fall in the US will be more than offset by increases from elsewhere during the first half of the 1990s. By 1995 US production will be some 870,000 b/d lower than in 1991. The major offsetting increments are UK (up 700,000 b/d), Norway (400,000 b/d), Colombia (400,000 b/d) and an additional 400,000 b/d should also be available from India, Yemen and Brazil. Exhibit 3.11 shows likely production levels until the turn of the century.

In the second half of the 1990s a further decline in US production of around 800,000 b/d is expected, to be offset by higher output from Yemen (200,000 b/d or more) and Colombia (250,000 b/d or more). Norwegian production should remain at 2.3 million b/d from 1995 on but the UK may drop some 150,000 b/d below its mid-1990s peak. Chinese production should increase by a modest 150,000 b/d during the 1990s, with over 70 per cent of the increment coming from offshore.

Oil production in the CIS is expected to recover from 1994 onwards to reach 9 million b/d in 1995 and 10 million b/d by the turn of the century. The introduction of real economic incentives to boost oil production, good management practices and adequate investment should help lift output. On the other hand, the continuing economic depression and the slow transition towards a more economical use of energy are likely to reduce further the domestic demand for oil products. This decline in oil use may, however, be tempered somewhat because of problems in other primary energy industries, most notably with coal production and the generation of electricity from nuclear power stations. As a result, domestic demand for oil in the CIS is forecast to reach 9.4 million b/d in 1995 and 10 million b/d in the year 2000.

Exhibit 3.11

Non-OPEC production, 1990 - 2000 (b/d millions)

	1990	*1991*	*1992*	*1993*[1]	*1995*[1]	*2000*[1]
Canada	1.62	1.59	1.57	1.55	1.44	1.20
US	7.36	7.39	7.19	6.98	6.52	5.72
North America	**8.98**	**8.98**	**8.76**	**8.53**	**7.96**	**6.92**
Argentina	0.47	0.49	0.52	0.53	0.55	0.55
Brazil	0.66	0.64	0.66	0.74	0.95	1.20
Colombia	0.44	0.44	0.48	0.50	0.75	1.10
Peru	0.12	0.12	0.11	0.11	0.10	0.10
Mexico	2.51	2.64	2.65	2.69	2.75	3.00
Others	0.27	0.27	0.28	0.29	0.24	0.13
Latin America	**4.47**	**4.59**	**4.70**	**4.86**	**5.34**	**6.08**
Angola	0.48	0.50	0.52	0.53	0.66	0.70
Cameroon	0.17	0.16	0.17	0.17	0.13	0.05
Congo	0.16	0.16	0.16	0.19	0.21	0.21
Egypt	0.91	0.92	0.89	0.90	0.80	0.65
Other Africa	0.19	0.19	0.19	0.20	0.23	0.28
Africa	**1.91**	**1.92**	**1.93**	**1.99**	**2.03**	**1.89**
Australia	0.56	0.53	0.51	0.48	0.50	0.50
Malaysia	0.61	0.67	0.65	0.63	0.60	0.50
India	0.68	0.65	0.66	0.75	0.95	1.03
Others	0.45	0.52	0.56	0.58	0.61	0.56
Southeast Asia	**2.30**	**2.37**	**2.38**	**2.45**	**2.66**	**2.59**
Norway	1.60	1.89	2.05	2.20	2.30	2.30
UK	1.75	1.72	2.02	2.18	2.45	2.20
Rest of Europe	0.58	0.61	0.62	0.66	0.68	0.64
Western Europe	**3.93**	**4.22**	**4.69**	**5.04**	**5.43**	**5.14**
Oman	0.67	0.72	0.73	0.73	0.73	0.70
Other Middle East	0.08	0.08	0.08	0.08	0.08	0.08
Syria	0.38	0.48	0.50	0.48	0.40	0.40
Yemen	0.19	0.20	0.20	0.22	0.40	0.60
Middle East Non-OPEC	**1.32**	**1.47**	**1.51**	**1.51**	**1.61**	**1.78**
CIS (former USSR)	11.40	10.60	9.20	8.50	9.00	10.00
China	2.80	2.80	2.80	2.80	2.85	2.95
Others	4.69	4.55	4.73	4.30	3.60	2.00
Total Non-OPEC	**41.80**	**41.50**	**40.70**	**40.00**	**40.48**	**39.35**

[1]Forecasts.

Sources: UBS Phillips & Drew *Macro Oil Special Edition*, April 1992 and our estimates.

Likely developments in OPEC

The sustainable OPEC production capacity (defined as the highest percentage of installed capacity that could be produced and maintained over a period of 12 months) was put at around 27.9 million b/d at the end of 1989, ie before the Iraqi invasion of Kuwait. Exhibit 3.12 shows forecasts for OPEC output to the year 2000. The decline in OPEC's production capacity compared to the heyday of the late 1970s and early 1980s, when the organisation's production reached 34 million b/d, is due mainly to the neglect of oilfields and the drop in investment during the oil glut period of the mid-1980s. The biggest capacity losses were

Exhibit 3.12

OPEC production capacity, 1989 - 2000 (b/d thousands)

	1989	*1990*	*1991*	*1992*	*1993*[1]	*1994*[1]	*1995*[1]	*2000*[1]
Saudi Arabia	7,500	8,500	8,700	9,000	9,250	9,500	10,000	12,000
UAE	2,210	2,400	2,500	2,500	2,600	2,700	2,700	3,000
Venezuela	2,400	2,450	2,500	2,500	2,800	2,900	3,000	3,500
Kuwait	2,200	25	200	1,500	2,000	2,200	2,500	2,700
Iraq	3,500	300	1,000	2,300	3,000	3,500	3,500	4,000
Iran	3,000	3,300	3,500	3,500	4,000	4,350	4,500	6,000
Neutral Zone	600	50	300	400	450	500	500	600
Algeria	800	800	800	800	800	820	850	1,000
Ecuador	315	315	315	315	400	400	400	400
Gabon	300	300	310	310	315	320	330	370
Indonesia	1,300	1,300	1,300	1,500	1,500	1,500	1,450	1,300
Libya	1,600	1,600	1,625	1,650	1,700	1,800	2,000	2,000
Nigeria	1,700	1,700	1,900	1,900	2,100	2,200	2,400	2,500
Qatar	450	450	450	450	500	550	600	650
Total	**27,875**	**23,490**	**25,400**	**28,625**	**31,415**	**33,240**	**34,730**	**40,020**

[1]Forecasts.

Source: Middle East Economic Survey, various issues.

recorded in Saudi Arabia (3 million b/d) and Iran (2.8 million b/d). In 1990 OPEC capacity dropped further to 23.5 million b/d after the loss of output from Kuwait and Iraq, before rising to 28.6 million b/d in 1992.

Non-OPEC oil output will continue to decline in the second half of the 1990s, meaning that any increase in world demand will have to be met by additional OPEC production. Assuming that a safety margin of 10 per cent in production capacity over and above net demand for OPEC production is required for long-term price stability, then around 15 million b/d of additional capacity will be needed during the 1990s. It is believed that, by 1995, Iraq and Kuwait will resume their prewar production levels of 3.5 million b/d and 2.5 million b/d respectively, leaving 8 million b/d of additional capacity to be built by 1995, boosting OPEC's capacity to 3.5 million b/d. Production capacity will increase further in the second half of the decade to 40 million b/d, provided a better investment climate prevails. The expansion plans include developing entirely new oilfields, drilling new wells in existing fields and restoring pipelines and other equipment that deteriorated during the oil glut of the early 1980s.

Saudi Arabia has started implementing its programme to raise sustainable crude oil production capacity from 8.5 million b/d in 1990 to 10 million b/d by 1995 and 12 million b/d in the year 2000. The UAE has plans to boost capacity from 2.5 million b/d in 1992 to 3 million b/d in 2000, while Venezuela's capacity is projected to reach 3 million b/d by the mid-1990s and 3.5 million b/d by the turn of the century. Iran, with a production capacity of 3.5 million b/d in 1992, would like to increase this to 6 million b/d by the year 2000. Kuwait's capacity expansion planned prior to the crisis has presumably been pushed down the list of priorities, in view of the more urgent goal of regaining prewar production levels by 1995. Iraq's oil sector requirements have certainly increased and the country's aim would at best be to get back to the 1989 production level of 3.5 million b/d in 1995 and possibly raise this to 4 million b/d by the year 2000.

Iraq's re-entry into the market during the next few years is the single biggest risk to oil prices. So far as possible, Saudi Arabia will try to retain its market share (35 per cent of the OPEC total) built up during the Gulf crisis and will resist any quota below 8 million b/d unless other OPEC members also reduce production to accommodate Iraqi exports. Accordingly, the Kingdom may tolerate temporary prices as low as US$16 a barrel for Brent crude if this is necessary to protect long-term market share.

Assuming gradual resumption of Iraqi crude oil exports in 1994, reaching prewar levels in 1995, oil prices would be likely to ease from an estimated average of US$19.3 a barrel for Brent crude in 1992 to US$19 a barrel in 1993 before rising again later. Forecast prices are tabulated in Exhibit 3.13. Various scenarios for supply and demand suggest that it might be possible to manage OPEC relationships to the extent that Saudi Arabia will be able to maintain the 8 million b/d minimum at the cost of real prices remaining close to the 1992 level for most of the remainder of the decade.

If full Iraqi exports become available by 1995, this implies that Iraq and Kuwait will together add 4 million b/d to world supplies (additional 3 million b/d from Iraq and 1 million b/d from Kuwait). During the same period, non-OPEC output is expected to decrease by a net 1.32 million b/d. To neutralise the effect of 2.68 million b/d of additional supplies, world demand would need to grow by 2 per cent a year, which is higher than the most optimistic assumptions. We expect world demand to

Exhibit 3.13

Nominal and real (in 1992 terms) prices for Brent crude, 1980 - 2000

	Nominal	*Real*
1980	30.68	54.30
1981	34.00	54.66
1982	33.20	49.63
1983	29.70	42.26
1984	28.10	38.14
1985	27.29	35.52
1986	14.45	18.37
1987	18.34	22.57
1988	15.00	17.77
1989	18.25	20.81
1990	23.40	25.36
1991	20.00	20.71
1992	19.30	19.30
1993[1]	19.00	18.60
1994[1]	20.00	19.00
1995[1]	21.80	19.20
1996[1]	22.50	19.60
1997[1]	23.70	20.00
1998[1]	25.90	20.59
1999[1]	28.20	21.62
2000[1]	30.80	22.75

[1]Forecasts.

Exhibit 3.14
Crude prices, 1904 - 2000

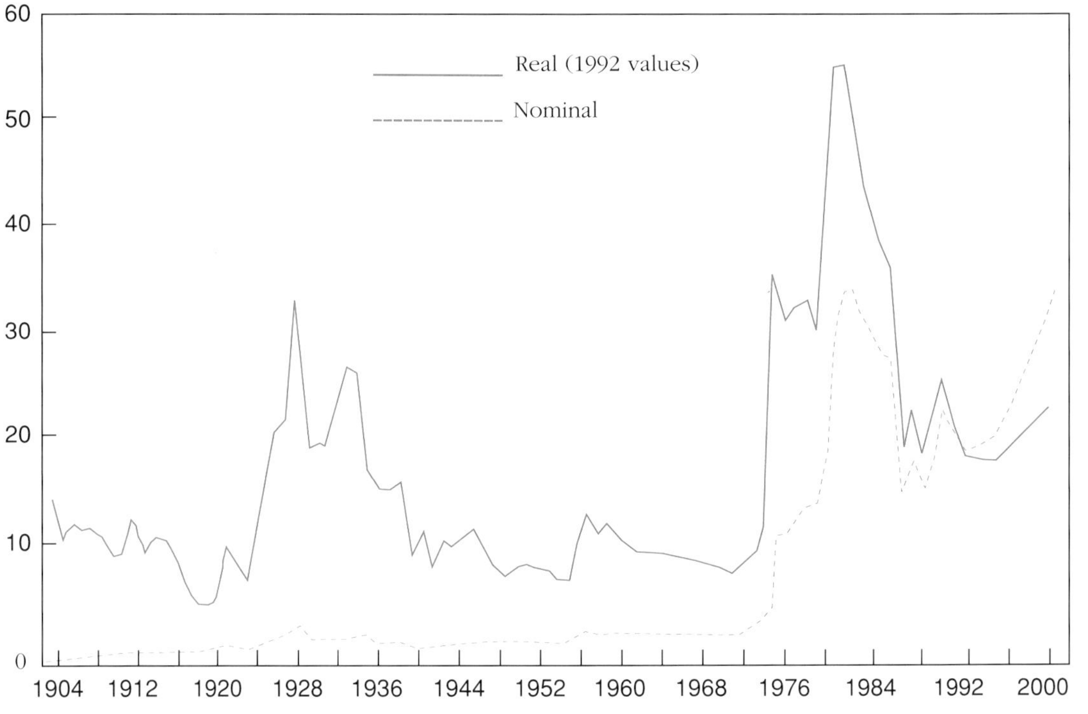

increase by not more than 1.1 per cent a year during this period, especially as additional energy taxes currently being contemplated will dampen future demand. This is likely to keep oil prices under pressure until the mid-1990s. Saudi Arabia will remain the marginal producer with the lowest price tolerance.

World demand growth of 1.4 per cent per annum will add 5 million b/d from 1995 to 2000, however. In the second half of the 1990s growth in demand should be somewhat higher because of higher economic growth but also because developing countries such as China and the eastern European nations will constitute a larger portion of total demand. Supplies outside OPEC (excluding the CIS) will decline in the second half of the 1990s, so that all incremental demand must be supplied from the Gulf countries. The market should therefore tighten during the late 1990s, leaving room for a gradual rise in real oil prices. Exhibit 3.14 shows prices from the start of the century to date and provides forecasts to 2000.

Energy taxes and their impact on the world oil market

The European Commission recently approved a draft directive on energy tax, which would raise taxes on energy consumption in an effort to stabilise carbon dioxide emissions at their 1990 level by the year 2000. However, included in the directive was a provision that approval would be conditional on acceptance of similar measures in the US and Japan.

Exhibit 3.15

Comparative prices and taxes, 1991 (US$ a barrel)

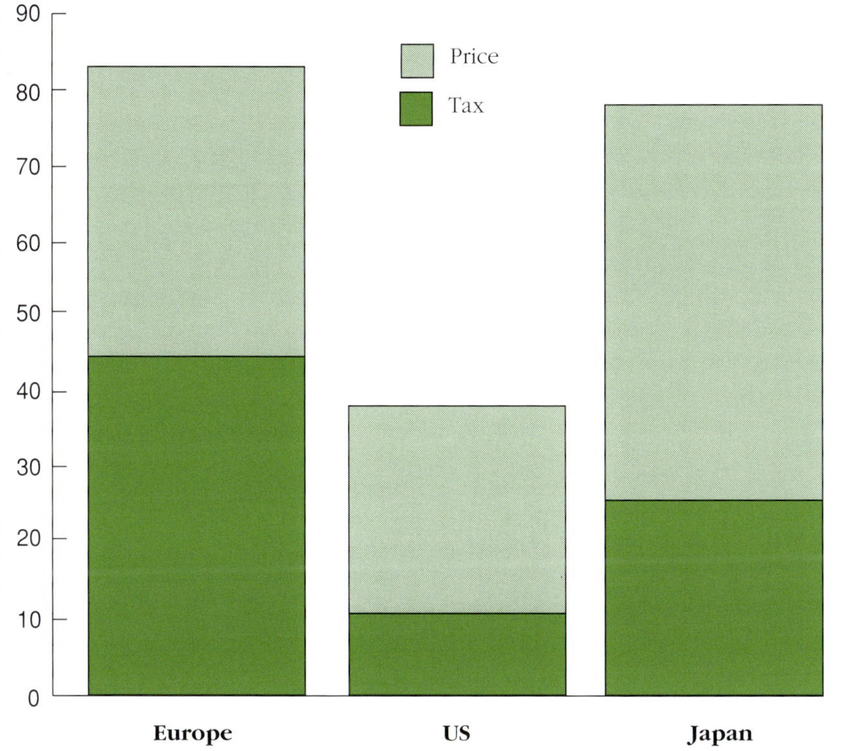

Exhibit 3.16

The evolution of oil prices and taxes in Europe

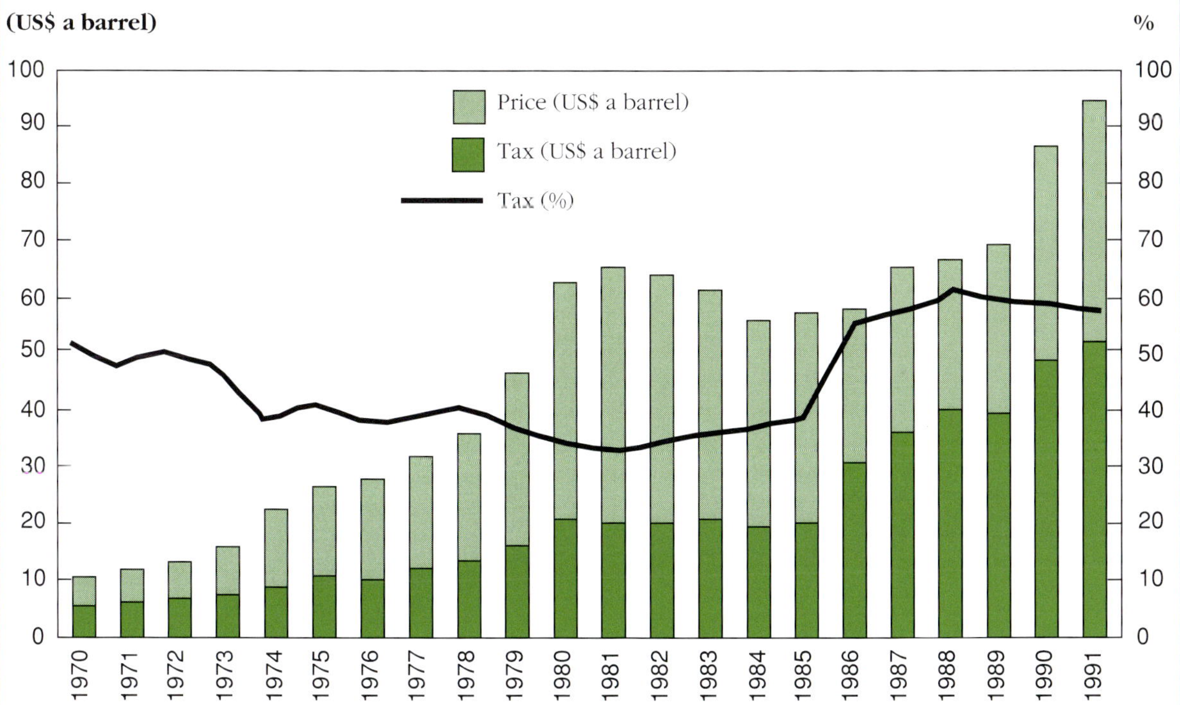

The tax would amount to the equivalent of an additional US$3 per barrel of oil in 1993, rising by US$1 annually to US$10 per barrel by the year 2000. OPEC countries lobbied heavily against the tax, arguing that it represented an unfair burden on world demand for oil. European industry leaders also argued that they would lose international competitiveness if other industrialised countries did not implement similar measures.

There is little doubt that European governments have been the most enthusiastic taxers of oil. Oil has been relatively heavily taxed in Europe since the 1950s, when concern over the future of the indigenous coal industries in the face of competition from cheap oil supplies led some governments to impose taxes on fuel oil to protect coal. Subsequently, Europe's vulnerability to the price shocks of the 1970s persuaded most European governments to increase taxes on oil further in order to stimulate fuel switching. More recently, European moves to reduce acid rain and encourage the use of unleaded petrol have stimulated the growth of a variety of "environmental taxes". The European governments' keenness to tax oil has made oil prices for European consumers among the highest in the industrialised world. In 1991 the weighted average final selling price of a barrel of oil sold to end-users in the 12 EC member states was US$83 a barrel, compared with US$78 a barrel in Japan and only US$38 a barrel in the US. Around 54 per cent of the final selling price of a barrel of oil sold in Europe is made up of taxes imposed by consumer governments, compared with 33 per cent in Japan and 29 per cent in the US (see Exhibit 3.15).

Between 1973 and 1991 the taxes on petrol increased dramatically in Europe (see Exhibit 3.16). During this period the average price of imported oil to Europe rose by 72 per cent from US$11.60 a barrel to US$20 a barrel, while the average tax increased more than eightfold. In 1980 the difference between Arab Light crude and the average EC end-user price of petrol was about US$30 a barrel. By 1991 this gap had widened to US$40 a barrel. Thus, although other factors such as inflation, the removal of lead and other environmental costs have had an effect on refined product prices, taxation has essentially caused the spread between crude oil and average retail petrol prices in the OECD to grow by about US$35 per barrel in a period of 10 years.

While the CIF price of a barrel of crude oil to the EC at the end of 1991 was approximately US$20, the tax on petrol reached approximately US$52 a barrel. Consequently, the estimated petroleum product tax receipts accruing to the EC governments in that year were US$195 billion for a 10.3 million b/d consumption. The revenue received by the oil-exporting countries, conversely, was around US$64 billion. The contrast becomes more vivid if we look at figures for individual countries. In Italy, Denmark, France and Germany, for example, the average 1991 taxes on a barrel of petrol were US$140.90, US$97.30, US$108 and US$101.30 respectively (Exhibit 3.17 gives full details). On the other hand, the average price of imported oil to these countries was US$22 a barrel (including transport cost) and US$30 a barrel of petrol after adding refining costs. It is ironic that the petroleum tax receipts for Italy, with a consumption of some 1.9 million b/d, are estimated at US$50 billion in

Exhibit 3.17

Oil taxes levied in the EC, the US and Japan, 1991

	Petrol			*Heating Oil*			*Heavy fuel oil*		
	Total[1] tax (US$ a barrel)	*Fixed tax (US$ a barrel)*	*VAT tax (%) (a)*	*Total[1] tax (US$ a barrel)*	*Fixed tax (US$ a barrel)*	*VAT tax (%) (a)*	*Total[1] tax (US$ a barrel)*	*Fixed tax (US$ a barrel)*	*VAT tax (%) (a.b)*
EC									
Belgium	92.1	64.4	25.0	5.3	0.0	17.0	0.0	0.0	0.0
Denmark	97.3	71.3	22.0	61.4	43.5	22.0	0.0	0.0	0.0
Germany	101.3	83.6	14.0	12.8	7.3	14.0	2.6	2.6	0.0
Greece	77.0	46.5	36.0	24.5	20.4	8.0	8.9	8.9	0.0
Spain	84.7	70.7	12.0	20.7	14.6	12.0	2.3	2.3	0.0
France	108.0	85.2	18.6	20.9	11.3	18.6	3.4	3.4	0.0
Ireland	100.1	73.8	21.0	16.1	9.1	12.5	1.8	1.8	0.0
Italy	140.9	111.1	19.0	97.6	76.3	19.0	10.3	10.3	0.0
Luxembourg	54.9	44.1	12.0	2.1	0.0	6.0	0.4	0.4	0.0
Netherlands	118.7	92.8	18.5	18.6	10.0	18.5	4.4	4.4	0.0
Portugal	113.0	101.5	8.0	66.1	58.3	8.0	11.0	11.0	0.0
UK	89.1	69.1	17.5	3.5	0.0	17.5	2.3	2.3	0.0
US	16.5	15.7	1.5	1.8	1.8	0.0	0.0	0.0	0.0
Japan	65.2	61.0	3.0	1.6	0.0	3.0	0.9	0.0	3.0

[1]Total tax = fixed tax + VAT

(a) VAT in Europe (lower tax for unleaded petrol. In the US & Japan only unleaded petrol is sold)

- Consumption tax in Japan.
- Average state sales tax in US.

(b) Heavy fuel oil is used mainly by commercial consumers.

Sources: IEA *Energy Prices & Taxes*, 1991 and Center for Global Energy studies, *Global Oil Report*, December 1991.

1991, while the export revenue of the UAE, which produced 1.9 million b/d, were approximately US$12 billion.

Although the EC tax is claimed to be non-discriminatory, since it is imposed on all fossil fuels and on nuclear power, it does discriminate against oil. If the tax is intended to limit carbon dioxide emissions, then coal should be taxed at a higher rate than oil because it is more polluting. The proposed EC tax grades oil and natural gas, which are comparatively cleaner than coal, in a manner which is not consistent with their relative carbon contents. The share of oil in fossil fuel consumption declined in the OECD from 59 per cent in 1973 to 50 per cent in 1990, while the share of coal, which is known to be the highest carbon dioxide emitter, increased from 20 per cent to 25 per cent during the same time. This is largely due to excessive petroleum taxation and generous coal subsidies. In effect, oil taxes are far in excess of its contribution to carbon dioxide emissions. It is disappointing, therefore, to see the latest EC energy tax proposal reinforcing these demand imperfections and price distortions.

Environmental considerations

The oil producers are concerned that the proposed tax, while presented under an environmental pretext, is basically intended to raise government revenues. The economies of OPEC and the developing countries are likely to suffer if the carbon/energy tax is introduced. The higher oil prices in Europe will reduce demand for petrol and bring lower oil revenues for OPEC, with an estimated annual loss of around US$15 billion. Oil producers may be compelled to restrain future increases of their production capacity. Furthermore, the implementation of a carbon tax would lead to higher import costs from Europe, as carbon taxes transmit into the energy prices which play a major role in determining unit production costs. This implies that EC manufacturing exports to OPEC and other developing countries will be more expensive.

Saudi Arabia called on the EC to abandon the proposed tax and stressed that the levying of taxes is ineffective in dealing with issues of global dimensions. Instead, it called for recognition of mutual interests as one of the basic pillars of fruitful cooperation between states. Saudi Arabia has always respected and safeguarded the interests of other countries and was the first to take measures to alleviate the crisis arising from the Iraqi invasion of Kuwait in August 1990. The Kingdom invested up to US$5 billion to boost its production capacity and make up for the missing supplies from Iraq and Kuwait. The Kingdom will continue to play its part in stabilising the oil market because of its concern for growth in the world economy and it wishes others to reciprocate by being equally cooperative.

Saudi Arabia is not indifferent to the environment and wishes to contribute to its protection. Nevertheless, taxation may not be the best policy tool in this respect. Taxes rarely give clear market signals to increase efficiency nor to reduce emissions. The excessive petroleum taxation in the European Community is a case in point. Taxes per barrel of petroleum products increased from approximately US$7 in 1973 to US$56 in 1991, while emissions increased over this period. Petroleum product taxation in the EC was increasing at an annual rate of 5 per cent in the second half of the 1980s while *per capita* emissions were also increasing at an annual rate of 1 per cent. If the concentration on taxes were replaced by more research into cleaner and more environmentally friendly petroleum products, such as reformulated and unleaded petrol, with minimal emission of nitrogen oxides, that would be more in the interests of producers and consumers.

The technology to produce high quality petrol is well established; the international oil companies must now join the oil producers to develop this further. The manufacturing plants require large supplies of LPGs and ample energy resources. The Gulf region is able to supply NGLs and basic petrochemical products in large quantities and to do so more cheaply than most other areas. The capital, the technology and the operating expertise can be made available anywhere. The Gulf region would therefore be the ideal venue for joint venture investments to produce less polluting oil products and petrol additives such as MTBE, TAME or ethanol.

Conclusion

The responsibility for a balanced oil market in the 1990s depends as much on the oil-consuming countries as it does on the major oil-producing countries. OECD governments control the level and structure of oil demand in the same way, albeit with less drama, as OPEC governments control the level of oil supply. Oil taxes, tariffs, subsidies for oil substitutes and dozens of other instruments already exist to influence demand and this renders the future outlook uncertain. Protectionist policies can be effective only in the short term but cannot change the world's geology. Instead of engineering lower oil demand through taxation, and creating inefficiencies in the process, greater cooperation with the Gulf producers would secure reliable sources of clean oil supply at low prices for consumers worldwide.

Although there is clear evidence that higher prices encourage greater energy efficiency and may help to reduce carbon dioxide emissions, it is also important to realise that the sensitivity of demand to rising prices is subject to the law of diminishing returns. The greatest improvements in efficiency can be obtained in countries where prices are lowest, ie the US, Latin America, South East Asia and eastern Europe. Levying a carbon tax on those fuels that are hardly taxed at all, or in those countries that have less onerous tax regimes, would have a much greater impact on global carbon dioxide emissions than would a large tax on fuels that already bear the burden of high prices, as is the case in Europe.

In the same way that consumers would like security of supply and greater certainty that future oil requirements will be met at reasonable prices, producers would like security of demand and certainty that government policies in the OECD region will not stifle growth on the demand side. Simply building up capacity in the Gulf will not by itself balance the oil market; the consuming countries should work as well on removing bottlenecks aimed at dampening future demand for oil. Producers may otherwise rethink their long-term strategy of spending huge sums of capital (needed elsewhere for domestic economic development) to boost production capacities, if they will be forced eventually to mothball the new oil wells because of depressed demand.

The major oil-producing countries may also reconsider their relationships with those trading partners whose discriminatory measures against the basic commodity that they export will greatly affect economic growth prospects and the future welfare of their people. Reciprocal measures may eventually be imposed on industrial imports originating from countries that hinder the free flow of trade. If the new carbon tax on oil is implemented, oil producers could themselves engineer higher oil prices that would have the same effect as the tax, ie reducing oil and energy consumption and stabilising carbon dioxide emissions.

Saudi Arabia and the other major oil-producing countries will continue to acquire downstream ventures in the US, Europe, South East Asia and the developing countries. This will undoubtedly reduce the volume of crude oil that will be available for trading on the open market. By the year 2000 there is the possibility that as much as one-quarter of total OPEC output will be taken out of the crude oil market and sold directly to the end-user through the downstream ventures acquired by the various oil producers. However, as the spot market declines, money is likely to be drawn increasingly to the burgeoning world future markets for the management of risk.

With the trend towards downstream integration continuing, the principal division among oil producers is likely to move from that between OPEC and non-OPEC countries to the distinction between countries with integrated oil industries (and secure outlets for their crude output) and those which lack such facilities. The integrated producers will become more concerned with responding to the market and price competition may shift from the crude oil market to the market for refined products. OPEC may still be able to work with crude production quotas but indirect price control through production ceilings will be a weak mechanism. As the countries with large excess capacity move further towards global downstream integration, they will find their interests diverging from the rest of OPEC and will have more in common with the major oil companies. A larger share of the burden of defending prices will fall on those oil producers (both outside and within OPEC) without downstream assets. Such countries will indirectly become swing producers.

Further downstream integration by OPEC members will change the composition of the global oil market. The industry may well be dominated by fewer, but larger, international oil companies. These companies, some of which will be state owned, will have greater vertical control over the oil market, the outcome of which could be greater stability of prices. A consolidation of the industry and the involvement of oil-producing nations in downstream ventures overseas will probably have important policy implications as well. Oil producers will have a bigger stake in seeing healthy economic conditions in consuming markets. This will help alleviate some of the energy security concerns of these countries by providing them with continued access to crude oil.

4 The industrial challenge

Introduction

Industrialisation in Saudi Arabia has been progressing at a very rapid pace, with the government spearheading the process. A strong industrial base has been built, along with the related infrastructure, to encourage future industrial projects by the private sector. The advancement of the industrial sector, with the aim of reducing the Kingdom's dependence on oil, is now widely perceived as being the most likely route to economic growth in the 1990s.

There are many niches in the domestic market that have not yet been filled and where investments may prove profitable in the years ahead. There exists a growing market for consumer products in the Kingdom, with a total population of around 14 million and a *per capita* purchasing power among the highest in the world. A much larger regional market, where Saudi products have a strong competitive advantage, can also be targeted.

The fifth Five-Year Development Plan (1990 to 1995) aims at growth rates of 7.8 per cent in manufacturing, to be achieved mainly through increased private sector investment. The total investment required for manufacturing (excluding petroleum refining) over the plan period is estimated at SR43.8 billion (US$11.7 billion), of which the private sector is expected to provide SR28.5 billion (US$7.6 billion), with the rest coming from the government and government-owned companies. Industrial development includes the establishment of basic industries, especially petrochemicals, and expansion of light industry, which grew in response to the growth of the domestic market. The development of basic industries has been undertaken mainly by the public sector because of the large amounts of capital required, while light manufacturing has been left to the private sector, which has benefited from government incentives and support.

A wide range of incentives is provided for industrial ventures in the Kingdom. Interest free loans of up to 50 per cent of the cost of the project can be obtained from the Saudi Industrial Development Fund (SIDF) for periods of up to 15 years. Other incentives include tax holidays of 10 years, exemption from tariff duties on imported equipment, raw materials and spare parts, subsidised land leases for factory sites, preferential treatment for domestic companies in the awarding of government contracts and export promotion measures. Some products are also subject to a 20 per cent protective duty in the early stages of production; these include cement, plastic products, steel pipes and tubes, fencing wire, electric poles, iron bars, detergents and soaps.

Industry in Saudi Arabia also benefits from a skilled, non-unionised labour force and reasonably consistent government industrial policies and regulations. The country has ample capital resources, no exchange controls, low utility costs and state of the art infrastructural facilities, including ports, airports, hotels, roads and telecommunications. Following the sweeping price cuts and a range of incentives introduced recently, Saudi Arabia has become one of the cheapest countries in which to operate for local or foreign companies. Domestic prices of petrol, electricity and natural gas are among the lowest in the world and the range of subsidies provided by the government is unmatched. Industry and all other parts of the economy also have the benefit of the Kingdom's openness to the outside world and its receptiveness to modern business ideas. To some extent, there is now industrial service back-up available, including distribution operations, advertising agencies, project finance, maintenance and specialised transport companies.

With all the advances achieved in developing the Kingdom's industrial sectors, there remain few constraints that need to be addressed. These include the lack of sufficient industrial management expertise and technical skills among the national population, unavailability of the necessary information base, bureaucratic constraints complicating the process of obtaining industrial licences, inadequate research on technological advancement, lack of proper marketing for national products, an industrial legal code lacking comprehensiveness and the openness of the domestic markets to imports from all over the world. Another problem is the rates at which joint venture partners are taxed at the end of the tax-free which, at between 35 and 45 per cent, are much higher than the 27 per cent average in the industrialised countries. Furthermore, taxes are levied on total profits generated, rather than distributed profits, and this discourages the reinvestment of earnings in the joint venture. Another constraint has been the limited entrepreneurial vigour of the country's private sector. Saudi businessmen have in general been geared both psychologically and economically towards trade and service activities, where returns are substantial and the payback period is short. This has restricted their involvement in industrial activities which require more risks and long gestation periods for profitability. However, this has been changing recently and today there is a nucleus of Saudi entrepreneurs leading the private sector's industrial activities.

Overview of industrial activities

Saudi industry is comprised of five major sectors: oil refining, managed by Saudi ARAMCO and SAMAREC; large scale petrochemicals and steel industries managed by SABIC; general manufacturing industries run entirely by the private sector; small scale light industries with over 20,000

Exhibit 4.1

Total GDP and manufacturing GDP at current prices, 1983 - 91 (SR billions)

	1983	*1984*	*1985*	*1986*	*1987*	*1988*	*1989*	*1990*	*1991*	*1992*[1]
Total GDP	377.7	351.4	313.9	271.1	275.5	285.1	310.8	376.5	401.3	421.4
GDP in manufacturing	26.9	27.4	24.5	19.7	23.8	24.5	26.2	28.8	31.4	33.4
Manufacturing as a % of total GDP	7.1	7.8	7.8	7.3	8.6	8.6	8.4	7.6	7.8	7.9
Growth in manufacturing GDP (%)	10.7	1.9	-10.6	-19.6	20.8	2.9	6.9	9.9	9.1	6.4

[1]Our estimate.

Sources: Central Department of Statistics, Ministry of Finance and National Economy.

workshops; and new advanced technology projects promoted through military offset schemes such as the Saudi-US Peace Shield Offset Program, the Saudi-UK Al-Yamamah Economic Offset Program linked with the sale of Tornado aircraft to the Kingdom, and the Saudi-French Sawari II Offset Program. Petrochemical industries in the Kingdom at present generate 22 per cent of total manufacturing value added; petroleum refining accounts for 40 per cent; other manufacturing such as chemicals, cement, building materials and engineering products account for the remaining 38 per cent.

Exhibit 4.1 shows the growth in manufacturing GDP since 1983; the effects of the oil glut in the mid-1980s can clearly be seen, with domestic demand falling sharply and reducing output.

Over the period since its inception up to the end of the year 1991/92 the Saudi Industrial Development Fund has sanctioned a total of 1,442 loans for the establishment of 1,160 industrial projects located throughout the Kingdom. Commitments to these projects totalled SR19,802 million (US$5,280 million). Repayments to the Fund have reached SR9,780 million (US$2,608 million) and the recycling of repayments has enabled the Fund to continue its lending activities without acquiring additional funding from the government. During the fiscal year 1991/92, the Fund approved 68 loans with a total value of SR1,749 million (US$466 million) thus representing the second highest annual value industrial loans committed since its inception. The Fund's loan commitments during the year exceeded the previous year's actual commitments of SR953 million (US$254) by 83.5 per cent (see Exhibit 4.2). Its commitments over the last five years exceeded those approved the prior five years by 15 per cent.

Chemical products sector

The chemical products sector occupied the leading position by the size of loan commitments. By the end of 1991/92, the total funds allocated to approved projects in this sector amounted to SR5,171 million (US$1,379 million) or 26.1 per cent of the Fund's total commitments to all industrial projects. During the fiscal year 1991/92 the Fund approved commitments totalling SR1,114 million (US$297 million) for establishing 17 new industrial projects and for expanding four operating plants. The largest

Exhibit 4.2

Approved SIDF loans for new projects by sector, 1991/92

	Number		*Value (SR millions)*	
Sector	*1991/92*	*Cumulative total*	*1991/92*	*Cumulative total*
Consumer products	25	343	368	3,749
Chemical products	21	226	1,144	5,171
Building materials	5	256	34	6,322
Engineering products	16	336	163	4,354
Other products	1	19	40	206
Total	**68**	**1,180**	**1,749**	**19,802**

Source: Saudi Industrial Development Fund annual report, 1991/92.

two loans approved that year were extended to this sector. Among the new loans committed to this sector are two loans each of SR400 million for two new projects in Jubail, one for production of Soda Ash with an annual production capacity of 264,000 tons, and the other for the production of 500,000 tons of ammonia and 600,000 tons of urea per annum. Also two loans were extended to establish two factories in Riyadh, one for SR34.3 million for the production of 24, 830 tons of sodium silicate and sodium aluminate and the other for the production of 12,500 tons of paints annually. Expansion loans included one of SR160 million for a factory in Jubail for production of 438,000 tons of oxygen and 109,500 tons of nitrogen per annum.

Engineering products sector

The engineering products sector occupied the second position in terms of loan size. Since its inception to the end of 1991/92, the Fund approved loans to projects in this sector totalling SR4,354 million (US$1,161 million) or 22 per cent of the Fund's loan commitments to all projects. During the year, the Fund approved 16 loans for the engineering products sector valued at SR163 million or 9.3 per cent of total loan commitments. These loans were extended to 12 new industrial projects and four expansions of existing plants. New loans included two loans for establishing two factories in Riyadh, one valued at SR5.9 million for production of 10,000 household washers and the other of SR11.8 million for production of 257,000 air conditioners (window and split units). Also one loan of SR6.4 million to a factory in Jeddah to produce 980 tons of industrial fasteners (nuts and bolts) and a loan of SR8.6 million to set up a factory in Riyadh to produce 12,000 tons of steel pipes.

Consumer products sector

The sector jumped to third position by the size of loans extended over the period from inception of the Fund up to the end of 1991/92. Cumulative commitments to this sector totalled SR3,749 million (US$1 billion) or 18.9 per cent of the total loans granted till the end of the year. In 1991/92 the Fund approved 25 loans to this sector for a total value of

SR368 million of 21 per cent of the total loan commitments during the year. These loans were extended to 15 new projects and 10 expansions. Among the new loans approved in this sector was one of SR55.2 million for expansion of a carpet factory in Jeddah as well as two other loans totalling SR12.5 million to expand a Jeddah based factory for production of biscuits and another loan of SR10.8 million to expand a factory in Riyadh for the production of ice cream.

Building materials and cement

The total loans extended to projects in the building materials sector amounted to SR6,322 million (US$1,685 million) or 32 per cent of the Fund's overall commitments since its inception. Thus it occupied the fifth position among all other industrial sectors. During the year, the Fund sanctioned five loans to this sector totalling SR34 million which were extended to three new projects and two expansions. Among the loans approved for this sector was a loan for a project in Riyadh for producing 1,620 tons of tiles polishing stones per annum and expansion loans included one for a Dammam-based factory for producing 900,000 tons of suspended ceilings. Loan approvals in the cement sector totalled SR3,459 million by the end of 1991/92 or 17.5 per cent of the Fund's total loans to all industrial sectors. These loans were extended for establishment and expansion of eight cement projects located in various regions of the Kingdom with installed capacities of over 13 million tons per annum which satisfied the local demand for this product.

Industrial joint ventures

The Fund has continued, since its inception, to encourage the establishment of joint venture projects to enable foreign partners, particularly well-established international companies to transfer modern technology of the Kingdom. During 1991/92 the Fund approved 11 loans to joint venture projects: four in the chemical products sector; three in the engineering products sector; two in the consumer products sector; and one in each of building materials and other industries sectors. The total amount of loans granted to these projects amounted to SR166 million (US$44.2 million). The total equity of these projects was about SR105 million (US$28 million) of which SR39 million (US$10.4 million) or 37 per cent represents foreign shareholdings. Analysis of the data on joint venture projects approved by the Fund since its inception shows that 372 joint venture projects have been approved to date representing 32 per cent of the number of Fund's financed industrial projects. The amount of loans granted to these projects totalled SR7,378 million (US$1,967 million) representing 37.3 per cent of the value of commitments to industrial projects by the end of 1991/92. Furthermore, foreign participation has represented about 36.3 per cent of the total equity in these projects. The engineering and chemical products sectors have continued to lead other manufacturing sectors in terms of loan commitments to approved joint venture projects. The US has remained the leading partner, accounting for about 24 per cent of total equity in these projects.

Exhibit 4.3

The number of companies and their capital in Saudi Arabia (SR millions)

	1991		*1990*		*1989*		*1988*		*1987*	
	Capital	*Number*	*Capital*	*Number*	*Capital*	*Number*	*Capital*	*Number*	*Capital*	*Number*
Saudi	73,270.6	5,789	70567.4	5,780	68,065.4	5,678.0	64,983.2	5,551.0	64,474.6	5,293
Non-Saudi	91.3	21	84.6	24	65.8	18.0	50.3	14.0	50.3	14
Joint ventures	16,090.2	1,222	16,185.3	1,303	16,129.2	1,323.0	15,735.7	1,326.0	15,513.1	1,297
Total	**89,452.1**	**7,032**	**86,837.3**	**7,107**	**84,260.4**	**7019**	**80,769.2**	**6,891**	**80,038.0**	**6,604**

Source: Saudi Arabia *Statistical Yearbook*, Central Department of Statistics, 1991.

Exhibit 4.4

Factories in operation in the Kingdom

Year	*Total manpower of operating factories*	*Total capital of operating factories (SR millions)*	*Number of operating factories*
1979	89,129	34,202	1,206
1984	134,547	93,189	1,929
1985	137,372	94,003	1,983
1986	138,784	94,353	2,017
1987	140,620	94,805	2,061
1988	142,934	95,449	2,132
1989	144,923	96,085	2,193
1990	147,584	96,797	2,251
1991	151,098	97,682	2,316

Source: Saudi Arabia *Achievements of the Developments Plans (1970-1991)*, facts and figures, Ministry of Planning 1992.

Of the total 7,000 companies registered in the Kingdom by the end of 1991 with a capital of SR89.5 billion (US$23.9 billion), there were more than 2,316 factories of which around 100 are major industrial businesses. The Saudi companies were 5,789 with a capital of SR73.3 billion (US$19.5 billion), while there were only 21 non-Saudi companies and 1,222 joint ventures with a capital of SR16.1 billion (US$4.3 billion) (see Exhibit 4.3). Apart from SABIC the giant petrochemical company, the largest enterprises involve cement, building supplies, paper, cables, steel pipes and food processing. Annual sales of Saudi industrial products were worth more than SR44.9 billion (US$12 billion) in 1991, satisfying a major part of domestic needs with a rising export portion as well. The Kingdom has become the Arab world's leading industrial state. Over 15 per cent of Arab manufacturing in value terms is produced in Saudi Arabia. Total manpower of operations factories in the Kingdom rose from 89,179 in 1979 to 151,098 in 1991 (see Exhibit 4.4).

The number of licences issued for industrial projects increased from 145 in 1987 to 250 in 1990 and 349 in 1991. The authorised capital of industries established during this period rose from SR452 million (US$120 million) in 1987 to SR15.6 billion (US$4.2 billion) in 1990. The

Exhibit 4.5

Licences issued and authorised capital of industries established, 1987 - 90

	1987		***1988***		***1989***		***1990***		***1991***	
	Number of licences	*Authorised capital*	*Number of licences*	*Authorised capital*	*Number of licences*	*Authorised capital*	*Number of licences*	*Authorised capital*	*Number of licences*	*Authorised capital*
Food and beverages	36	42	28	125.4	42	287.1	36	181	66	1,676
Textiles & clothing	4	5	5	39.2	11	8.8	[1]15	[1]99.9	[1]47	[1]477
Leather products	5	–	3	–	4	12.0	–	–	–	–
Wood products	3	28	6	33.8	11	27.7	8	82.9	–	–
Paper products	1	11	10	42.8	4	34.8	8	11.2	–	–
Chemicals, rubber & plastics	35	194	42	143.0	54	147.9	88	6,107.6	97	10,000
Ceramics & glassware	2	–	2	10.6	5	7.4	[2]19	[2]44	–	–
Construction materials	10	78	9	52.3	17	13.3	–	–	–	–
Metal, machinery & equipment	33	80	38	250.1	53	64.6	74	256.7	78	1,324
Other manufacturing & storage	16	14	9	61.5	4	32.2	2	29.6	–	–
Total	**145**	**452**	**152**	**758.7**	**205**	**635.8**	**250**	**6,812.7**	**349**	**15,600**

[1]Includes leather products.
[2]Includes construction materials.

Source: Saudi Arabia Ministry of Industry and Electricity, 1991.

major industries established are chemicals, representing 28 per cent of the total number of licences issued in 1991 and around 64 per cent of authorised capital. Basic metal industries came next, with 22 per cent of total number of licences and 8.4 per cent of authorised capital. Food and beverage industries accounted for 18.9 per cent of total licences issued and the balance, less than 18 per cent went to small scale market oriented industries such as textiles, wood and paper products among others (see Exhibit 4.5).

The total sales/turnover of Saudi companies was close to SR17 billion (US$4.5 billion) in 1992 (see Exhibit 4.6). This figure does not include Saudi Aramco, the oil giant that is responsible for the production of most of the Kingdom's crude oil. The break down by sector shows the industrial companies accounting for 35 per cent of total sales/turnover in 1992, while the diversified companies – many of them involved in industrial activities – generated 20 per cent of the total (see Exhibit 4.7). The total sales of the top ten industrial companies (excluding Aramco) reached SR62 billion (US16.5 billion) in 1992, with Saudi Arabian Marketing and Refining Company (SAMAREC) at the top accounting for around 56 per cent of the total followed by Petromin Mobile Yanbu Refinery (PEMREF) with around 21.5 per cent, SABIC 14.4 per cent and Saudi Cable 2.2 per cent (see Exhibit 4.8). Among diversified companies, Dallah Al Baraka came at the top with total sales of SR9.54 billion (US$2.54 billion), followed respectively by Al Rushaid Group, Al Fadl Group, Olayan Saudi Company and AA Turki Group (see Exhibit 4.9).

Exhibit 4.6

Total turnover of the top 100 companies, 1985/86 - 1991/92 (SR millions)

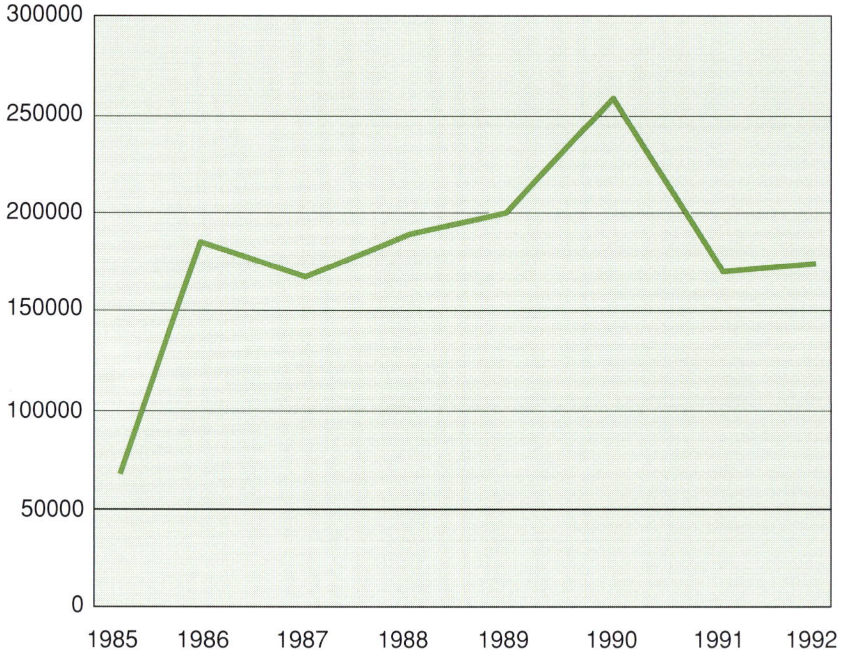

Exhibit 4.7

Top ten industrial companies

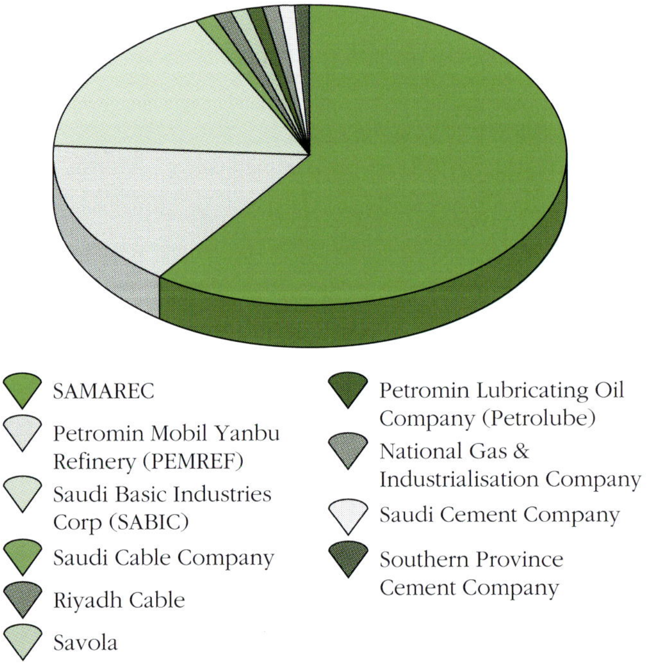

Total sales/turnover in 1992 of SR62 billion (US$16.5 billion)

Exhibit 4.8

Sector breakdown

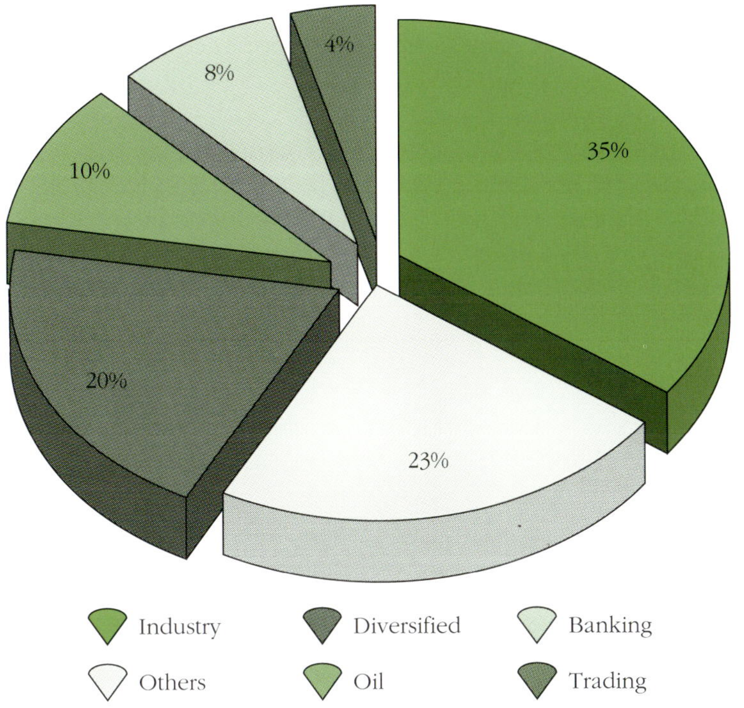

Exhibit 4.9

Top 10 diversified groups (SR millions)

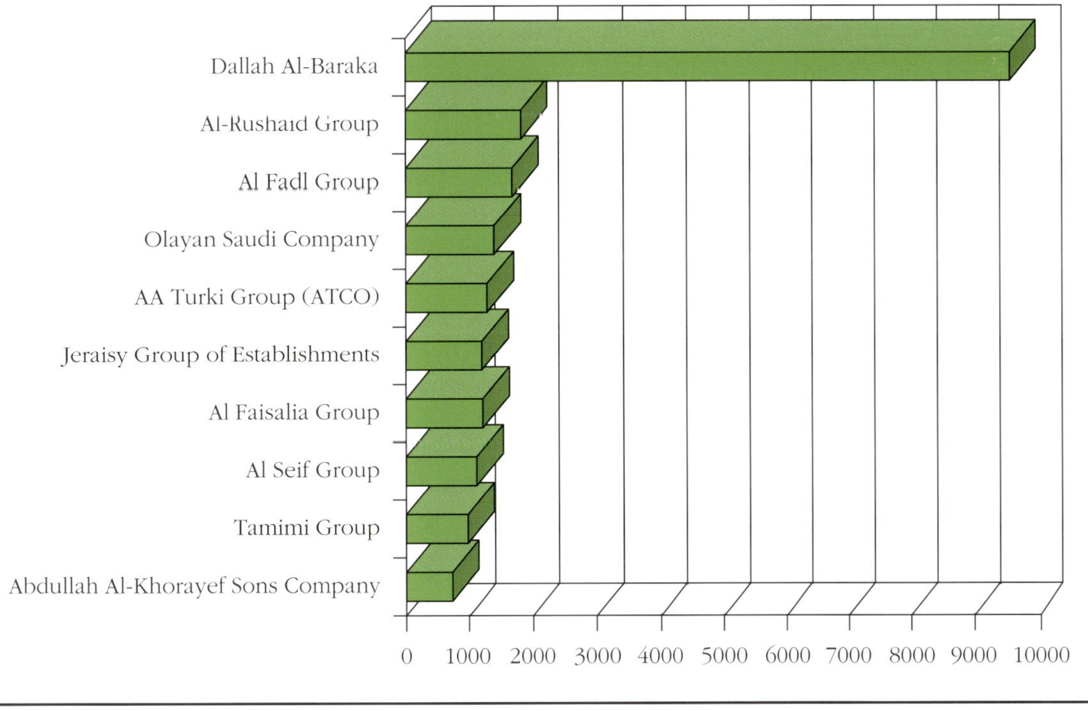

The constituents of the Kingdom's industrial sector

The manufacturing sector is expected to lead economic growth during the 1990s. Industrialisation is given prime importance in the development strategy of this decade and the private sector is being called upon to take the lead. The country is still considered too dependent upon its hydrocarbon resources and economic diversification will be pursued more forcefully to reduce the impact of fluctuations in world oil prices on the Saudi economy. The most important industries in the Kingdom are related to petrochemicals but other manufacturing industries have experienced considerable growth over the past few years.

Petrochemicals

In order to exploit more fully the country's abundant hydrocarbon resources and broaden the production and export base, the government, through SABIC, has made substantial investments in the development of the primary petrochemical industry. These investments have been guided by a two-phase strategy. In the first phase (1976 to 1987) a number of large, capital-intensive and export-orientated petrochemical projects were completed in the two industrial cities of Jubail and Yanbu'. These plants focused on the production of bulk products such as ethylene, polyethylene and methanol and of downstream products, including derivatives of ethylene. In addition, SABIC's activities include the production of fertilisers (urea, sulphuric acid and melamine), metals (steel rods and bars) and intermediate petrochemical products (vinyl chloride monomer, polyvinyl chloride and MTBE); it is also involved in supporting industries such as nitrogen. Most of these projects are joint ventures between foreign partners and SABIC, with a significant part of the financing provided by the Public Investment Fund (PIF). SABIC is ranked by *Chemical and Engineering News* as the 32nd largest chemical producer in the world.

Total production of petrochemical products and fertilisers reached around 13 million tons in 1991, up from 2.5 million tons in 1984. About 95 per cent of the Kingdom's output is exported to more than 70 countries. These exports have been subject to restraint in a number of major markets. In the European Community, to which SABIC ships around 25 per cent of its output, petrochemical imports from all sources are subject to quantitative restrictions. Japan also regulates such imports through quantitative measures. In addition, urea exports from Saudi Arabia to the EC are subject to anti-dumping duties and preferential treatment to Saudi Arabian petrochemicals under the EC's Generalised System of Preferences (GSP) scheme was eliminated with effect from 1990.

The investment strategy for the second phase (to 1995) calls for the maintenance of Saudi Arabia's present share in the world market for petrochemicals (about 6 per cent). The aim is to increase total capacity by 50 per cent from 13 million metric tons a year in 1991 to 19.5 million metric tons a year in 1995 (see Exhibit 4.10 for details). The new investment requirement is estimated at US$8 billion, which will be financed partly by

Exhibit 4.10

SABIC production and expansion plans (thousands of metric tons per year)

Product	*Existing capacity*	*Planned increase in capacity*	*Planned capacity in 1995*
Ethane-based industries			
Ethylene	1,970	500	2,470
Ethylene glycol	800	400	1,200
Ethylene dichloride	560	–	560
Styrene	360	54	414
Crude industrial ethanol	300	–	300
Vinyl chloride monomer	300	–	300
Propylene	–	300	300
Butadiene	–	100	100
Benzene (BTX)	–	70	70
Polyethylene	1,100	370	1,470
PVC	200	100	300
Polystyrene	100	38	138
Polypropylene	–	200	200
Melamine	20	–	20
Caustic soda	450	–	450
Methane-based industries			
Methanol	1,410	630	2,040
MTBE	500	1,400	1,900
Ammonia	1,100	500	1,600
Urea (gran & prill)	1,430	600	2,030
Other products			
Nitrogen	219	270	489
Oxygen	438	438	876
Steel	1,750	500	2,250
Total	**13,007**	**6,470**	**19,477**

Source: SABIC, 1991.

retained profits and soft loans from SIDF and foreign export credit agencies; borrowing from domestic commercial banks is expected to make up 30 to 40 per cent of the total, with part of this figure obtained through syndications involving foreign banks. SABIC plans to invest about US$6 billion in new plants by 1995, while the smaller, but dynamic, private sector will invest about US$2 billion over the same period.

Investment in the petrochemical sector is being directed towards expanding the capacity of existing product lines and establishing new ones, such as propylene and benzene, which will utilise existing raw materials. A list of selected SABIC expansion projects is given in Exhibit 4.11 The strategy of SABIC has been to develop close links with those companies considered to be leaders of technology in the global petrochemical industry. The key criterion is to build the most modern and advanced plants available to allow economies of scale and the ability to cope with market trends. The aim is to encourage new uses and applications for products. All projects are based on detailed feasibility and market studies.

Exhibit 4.11

SABIC expansion projects

Company	*Current production (metric tons per year)*	*Expansion project (metric tons per year)*	*Cost*	*Completion date*	*Contract signed*	*Contractor*
Petrokemya (Arabian Petrochemical Company)	Ethylene (650,000) Polystyrene (100,000) Butadiene (50,000)	Ethylene cracker (500,000) Butadiene (100,000) Benzene (70,000)	US$ 1 billion	1994	1990	Mitsui Engineering and Shipbuilding (Japan)
Ibn Sina (National Methanol Company)	Methanol (770,000)	MTBE (500,000)	US$300 million	1993	1991	Fluor Daniel (USA)
Yanpet (Saudi Yanbu Petrochemical Company)	Ethylene (720,000) Polyethylene (500,000) Ethylene Glycol (340,000)	Polyethylene (50,000) Ethylene glycol (80,000)	US$100 million			
Al-Razi (Saudi Methanol Company)	Methanol (640,000)	Methanol (660,000)	US$150 million	1993	1990	Mitsubishi Heavy Industry (Japan)
Sadaf (Saudi Petrochemical Company)	Ethylene (760,000) Ethanol (300,000) Styrene (360,000) Ethylene dichloride (560,000) Caustic soda (450,000)	Ethylene dichloride (280,000) Caustic soda (225,000)				
Sharq (Eastern Petrochemical Company)	Ethelene glyede (660,000)	Polyethylene (280,000)	US$400 million	1994	1991	Mitsubishi Heavy Industry (Japan) & Shinwha (S.Korea)

Exhibit 4.11 *cont.*

SABIC expansion projects

Company	*Current production (metric tons per year)*	*Expansion project (metric tons per year)*	*Cost*	*Completion date*	*Contract signed*	*Contractor*
Ibn Zahr						
(Saudi European	MTBE (500,000)	MTBE (700,000)	US$200 million	1991	1995	Snamprogetti (Italy)
Petrochemical Company)		Polypropylene (200,000)		1991	1993	John Brown (UK)
Gas						
(National Industrial Gases Company)	Gas oxygen (438,000)	Nitrogen (220,000)	US$55 million	1991	1993	Linde (Germany)
	Liquid oxygen (13,000)	Gas oxygen (435,000)				
	Nitrogen (219,000)					
Safco						
(Saudi Arabian Fertiliser Company)	Urea (230,000)	Ammonia (600,000)	US$306 million	1990	1993	Chiyoda (Japan)
	Sulphuric acid (100,000)	Urea (500,000)				
Hadeed						
(Saudi Iron & Steel Company)	Metal product (1,700,000)	Flat steel (100,000)	US$1.5 billion			
Ibn Hayyan						
(National Plastic Company)	Polyvinyl chloride (200,000)	Polyvinyl chloride (100,000)				

Projected growth in world demand has to be satisfied and the Kingdom is the leading candidate to accomplish this. Any criticism of building new plants at a time of oversupply should be directed at companies which are expanding without having SABIC's local raw material advantage. Saudi Arabia has an added advantage even over other OPEC countries which enjoy similar access to raw materials in that it has the infrastructure in place and has experience in operating and marketing, which cannot be developed quickly. By pressing ahead with expansion schemes when the market is hitting a trough, SABIC will be well placed to catch the next major upswing in demand for petrochemicals.

To maintain its competitive edge, SABIC is boosting its research and development capabilities to provide more technical support to its customers worldwide. SABIC's research and development centre in Riyadh will help to speed up research into new technologies and will develop new commercial applications for them. In doing so, the new complex will contribute to the enhancement of SABIC's position as an international exporter. The complex has a computerised technical information centre and five research laboratories. Activities concentrate on upgrading production by enhancing existing technology and testing new chemical product formulations.

The role of the private sector in Saudi Arabia's petrochemical

Exhibit 4.12

Major private sector projects in petrochemicals

Company	*Project*	*Start/ complete*	*Cost (US$ millions)*
Saudi Venture Capital Group	Joint venture with Total (Compagnie Française des Pétroles) for a plant to produce 250,000 metric tons a year of paraxylene and 100,000 metric tons a year of benzene.	1992/97	300
Arabian Industrial Development Company (NAMA)	A three-unit complex at Jubail to produce five downstream petrochemicals, with joint venture partners from abroad.	1993/95	150
Saudi Chemical Investment (Chemvest)	Joint venture with Mobil of Delaware for a plant in Yanbu' to produce 880,000 metric tons a year of MTBE.	1992/95	840
	A joint venture with Amoco of the US to produce 400,000 metric tons a year of paraxylene.	1993/96	150
Xenel Industries through The National Company for Petrochemical Industries (Teldene)	Joint venture with International Chemical Industries & Trading Company (ICIT) for a plant in Jubail to produce 250,000 metric tons a year of Soda ash.	1992/94	242
	A joint venture with Himont of the US for a plant in Yanbu' to produce 300,000 metric tons a year of propylene.	1992/94	400
Al-Hamrani Group	A joint venture with the finnish company Neste Oy for a plant in Jubail to produce 10,000 metric tons a year polyester resins.	1991/93	100

industry has grown considerably in recent years and is expected to expand further through the 1990s. The private sector is planning to invest about US$2 billion in downstream petrochemical plants, utilising as raw material the products of the basic petrochemical industries; major private sector projects are listed in Exhibit 4.12. Private sector participation is expected to increase in years to come, helped by SABIC's decision to assist nascent projects with the benefits of its experience and technical knowledge. SABIC has taken 10 per cent stakes in two new private sector

Exhibit 4.13

Profiles of selected industrial investment opportunities in plastics and petrochemical related industries in Saudi Arabia[1]

Project type/products	*Estimated investment cost (US$ millions)*	*Proposed capacity*	*Return on investment*
Large/medium sized projects		**Tons/year**	%
Styrene - butadiene rubber (SBR)	130.7	60,000	10.7
Phenolic resins - novolaks & resoles	26.7	24,000	10.9
Acrylonitrile polymer (SAN)	92.4	50,000	22.5
Acrylonitrile polymer (ABS)	93.2	50,000	24.6
Polyamide 6 chips	61.0	50,000	56.4
Polyamide 6 fibres	162.0	20,000	14.0
Phenol/acetone	181.0	120,000	25.6
Cumene	59.0	171,000	11.0
Purified terephthalic acid (PTA)	324.0	240,000	11.0
Carbon black	31.0	30,000	21.0
Small end user projects		**Units**	%
Rotational moulding			
Information counters	2.0	87,377	19.4
Buffets	2.3	9,954	22.6
Outdoor toilets	2.0	2,400	22.3
Pick-up box covers (canopies)	2.0	4,830	26.4
Fertiliser hoppers	1.5	875	19.2
Agricultural trailer boxes	1.9	761	16.4
Large landscaping containers	1.5	1,500	18.1
Injection/blow moulding			
Garden chairs	2.16	240,000	25.6
Garden tables	2.24	60,000	23.4
Insulated containers for cold water	6.71	260,000	25.4
Plastic packages for pharmaceutical products	2.94	–	21.4
Plastic suitcases	1.33	70,000	37.0
Extrusion moulding			
Plastic poles	3.47	869,500	19.4
Plastic fences	3.47	1,000,000	20.6
Miscellaneous		**Tons/year**	
Fishing nets	2.07	158	22.5
Artificial leather	4.16	2,000,000 m^2	27.3
LLDPE stretch wrap film	2.32	1,440	15.3

[1]Detailed studies on most of these projects are available with SABIC, the Saudi Consulting House and Gulf Organisation for Industrial Consulting (GOIC).

Source: Saudi German Development and Investment Company, 1992.

industrial investment companies, the Arabian Industrial Development Company (NAMA) and the Saudi Industrial Development Company (SIDC). It has also undertaken preliminary economic feasibility studies for 27 ventures in the petrochemicals and plastics related industries within the framework of a programme it is adopting to acquaint the private sector with the opportunities available in the industrial field. A list of the industrial ventures that SABIC recommends for implementation is given in Exhibit 4.13.

Other manufacturing

After the petrochemical sector, metals, machinery and equipment ranks first in terms of the number of licences issued between 1987 and 1990 (198) and in terms of authorised capital (SR651.4 million), followed by food and beverages and then construction materials. Most private manufacturing activity in Saudi Arabia in the early 1980s was concentrated in the construction materials sector (cement, insulation materials, pipes, bricks and wood products). However, owing to the decline in construction activity after 1983, there has been a shift toward enterprises engaged in food processing, engineering, chemicals, light consumer products and metal fabrication, with particular emphasis on high value added projects.

A significant part of the further industrial development undertaken by the private sector is expected to be in technology-intensive industries under defence-related offset programmes, particularly the Peace Shield programme with US companies and the Al-Yamamah programme with UK companies. There is also a similar offset programme being established with France. These programmes call for the reinvestment of up to 35 per cent of the technical content value of major defence contracts in high technology industries in the country. Total investment in the economic offset programmes is expected to generate more than US$4 billion in new industrial projects by the end of this decade. Saudi Arabia contributes 50 per cent to each of the three programmes mentioned above. Upon completion, they could generate about 75,000 new jobs and create national substitutes for foreign industries.

Many industrial development initiatives are not exclusively of government origin. The National Industrialisation Company (NIC), a private sector initiative with government support, was established in 1984 and has since invested in 45 companies ranging from aircraft repair companies to glass manufacturers and canning companies. NIC provides start-up capital, invests in existing industries and creates industrial service and support projects in the private sector. The company has 10 major projects totalling SR2 billion (US$533 million) planned for the next four years (see Exhibit 4.14). The largest is a scheme to set up a newsprint factory at a cost of SR950 million (US$253 million) that will supply not only all of Saudi Arabia's needs but also export throughout the Middle East.

NIC's lead in developing private sector manufacturing industry was followed by the Saudi Venture Capital Group in 1986 and the Saudi Advanced Industries Corporation. More recently the Saudi Industrial Development Company (SIDC), capitalised at SR400 million (US$107 million), was formed with the aim of investing in a broader range of

Exhibit 4.14

National Industrialisation Company (NIC) projects

Company	*Project*	*Start/complete*	*Cost (SR millions)*
Athath	Furniture manufacturing	1991/93	43
Al-Rawad	Plastic sheets	1992/94	21
Rassas	Lead smelting	1992/95	80
	Car batteries	1992/94	53
Warak	Newsprint	1992/94	950
Asha'a	X-ray film	1991/92	23
Maadaniah	Foundry	1992/94	130
	Electric insulators	1992/94	65
	Military uniforms	1993/95	108
Zoujaj	Float glass	1992/94	565
Total			**2,038**

industries, including second and third generation petrochemical plants, import substitution industries and small offset projects. The Arabian Industrial Development Company (NAMA) was set up in 1991 with 300 investors and a total capital of SR250 million (US$67 million). Its aim is to generate more investment by bringing in local and foreign joint venture partners. The Saudi Industrial Export Company was formed in 1989 to provide export marketing and distribution services for all Saudi companies.

The master plan for the Kingdom's two biggest industrial cities of Jubail and Yanbu' calls for an expansion of almost 100 per cent over the next five years, about the same growth rate as that of the last five years. Much of the new expansion is expected to come from smaller companies investing in the secondary petrochemicals market. Jubail (on the East coast) and Yanbu' (on the West coast) were established in 1975. They are home to about 15 primary petrochemical industrial ventures that use Saudi feedstock to make products for domestic use and for export, along with dozens of secondary industries and nearly 100 support businesses. The success of the two industrial cities has caught Saudi officials by surprise. The Royal Commission for Jubail and Yanbu', which manages planning and infrastructure and reviews joint venture proposals for the two cities, had not anticipated such a fast rate of expansion, particularly by the larger companies such as SABIC. In addition, many smaller companies have been formed to invest in manufacturing in the secondary petrochemicals market and the trend is expected to continue. This may be the best way to get the Saudi private sector profitably involved in energy.

Prospects for new industries

In studies carried out in the last few years by the Organisation for Industrial Consulting (GOIC), the Gulf Investment Corporation, SIDF, SABIC and NIC among others, several industries with good potential have been identified. The most important are discussed below.

Downstream industries in the petroleum and petrochemical sectors.
These include manufacturers involved in second and third generation

petrochemical projects, plastics intermediates, solvent fertilisers, tyres, rubber products, paints, nylon and polyester fibres, detergents, animal feeds and other miscellaneous products. These industries can draw on relatively cheap basic products as well as cheap intermediate and finished products, including those which can be processed on an export basis. They also enjoy the major comparative advantage of the Middle East region, namely abundant and low cost energy sources, such as natural gas and hydrocarbon fuels in general. The petrochemical industry is likely to continue to be the most important sector during this decade in terms of investment allocation, revenue generation and diversification.

Industries based on mineral resources

Industries based on those resources which exist in economic quantities in Saudi Arabia (eg iron ore, potash, copper, bauxite, phosphate, gold and limestone) are both capital- and energy-intensive; both these resources are relatively abundant in the Kingdom. Saudi Arabia is preparing to exploit bauxite in the Zubaira region, which has deposits of over 200 million metric tons. Developing such mineral-based primary industries normally creates external economies and opportunities for forward integration that render investments in secondary product industries more profitable.

Processed foodstuffs

The production of such foods as breakfast cereals, biscuits, dairy products, macaroni, chocolates, jam, sweets, date products, baby food and canned products, as well as investment in fast food outlets, will continue to gain ground in the short term. The 300 food processing plants and outlets in the Kingdom are reported to have an annual output of 8 million tons and sales worth SR5 billion (US$1.3 billion) a year. A report by the Eastern Province Chamber of Commerce & Industry points out that there are many more opportunities for import substitution in this sector and urges companies to capitalise on agriculture's increasing output as the basic raw material for food processing.

Import substitution industries in the consumer products field

This sector includes general, light, consumer-related industries for which a sizeable market already exists, eg soaps, detergents, furniture, cosmetics, garments, jewellery and paper products. The easiest way to seek opportunities here is to look at the leading brands in the market and then see if these can be produced locally, preferably in joint venture deals with the exporter itself. If established brands start being manufactured locally, they will immediately enjoy a secure market. The manufacture of these products also creates demand for a whole range of other related products and materials.

Synthetic and assembling industries

Several of these industries already have large markets for their products in the Gulf area in particular and in the Arab region in general. Examples include the manufacturing and assembling of certain types of consumer durables, vehicles and industrial equipment serving the oil industry, agriculture, light industries, desalination plants, metal construction, electric inter-connection projects and the medical products industry. A report by GOIC estimates that demand for cars in the GCC will rise to 257,000 a year by 1995 and 285,000 a year by the turn of the century. Local production of spare parts and components, preferably in joint ventures with current exporters, could prove profitable.

Industries that serve the national and regional defence and security sectors
Requirements in these two sectors are large and constant. Dozens of industrial projects can be identified that will serve this sector and hence minimise dependence on other countries.

Industries that serve the oil sector
Oil is the largest industry in the country and its needs and requirements are numerous throughout the different stages of production (exploration, extraction, transport and refining). Since the 1950s the oil industry has been contributing to the development of a large associated business sector and many industrial projects have emerged to serve it.

High technology and engineering industries
The development of such industries would make it possible for Saudi Arabia to attain a degree of technological independence and would help in the transfer and assimilation of technology. Possible products include electrical switchgear, pumps, valves, computer and telecommunications components and the development of Arabic computer systems.

Financing of industrial projects

The Saudi industrial sector may need close to US$5 billion in project finance over the next few years. This is over and above the US$1.3 billion that has already been committed (US$500 million for Ibn Zahr, US$500 million for Hadeed and US$300 million for Ibn Sina, among other, smaller projects). Commercial banks will be asked to provide at least half of this amount, with the remainder coming from shareholders and, to a lesser extent, from the PIF or the SIDF. In the first stage of Saudi industrialisation, when projects originally got off the ground, commercial bank borrowing represented only about 10 per cent of capital investment. Another 30 per cent was contributed by equity shareholdings (including foreign joint venture partners), while the balance came in the form of concessionary loans from the PIF and SIDF. Government equity and subsidised PIF loans may no longer be forthcoming. Since most of the companies have been operating successfully for several years, it is deemed that the time has come for them to stand on their own feet and justify their borrowing requirements to Saudi banks. It is worth noting in this context that SIDF loans will depend in the future less on fresh infusions of government cash and more on the resources made available from repayments of earlier loans now falling due. Henceforth, even concessionary finance will have to be self-supporting.

There is ample wealth in the hands of the private sector, with overseas investment estimated at US$100 billion and the propensity to save being quite high. In future investors may be called upon to raise their own equity participation in projects to, say, 50 per cent instead of the 25 per cent that currently prevails. This will reduce dependence on concessionary loans from the state and borrowing from commercial banks, freeing the resources of these institutions so that they can extend credit to a larger number of projects than would otherwise have been possible. Equity support will also force owners to have a greater personal commitment to their projects and will bring the lowest cost of funding and the largest offers of finance.

Commercial bank involvement

Saudi industrialists have consistently called on the commercial banks to help finance the private sector's industrial projects. However, despite improved balance sheets, commercial banks remain reluctant, with credit extended to industry continuing to play a minor role in overall commercial bank lending activities. Loans to industry actually declined both in value and as a percentage of total commercial bank credit from 1987 to 1989, before rising again in the last two years (see Exhibit 4.15).

The dilemma for the commercial banks has focused around the incompatibility of industry's borrowing needs, which are essentially medium to long term, with the predominantly short-term nature of their deposit base. Saudi capital markets are still at the early stages of development, which makes it difficult for banks to issue long-term debt instruments. The Kingdom still lacks equitable standards of protection for bank creditors and few banks will consider setting up credit relationships with a client without at least a three-year track record. Large industries with joint venture projects face fewer problems in obtaining commercial finance than do small and medium industries, owing to the direct participation of the government in the equity capital of such projects. Aside from these considerations, most commercial banks simply do not have the in-house capability of assessing the viability of industrial projects.

Until recently project financing in Saudi Arabia was synonymous with straightforward project lending by financial institutions. The lender assessed the project loan on the basis of the financial strength and credit

Exhibit 4.15

Commercial bank loans to industry in Saudi Arabia (SR millions)

	1986	*1987*	*1988*	*1989*	*1990*	*1991*	*June 1992*
Industry & manufacturing	5,452	4,749	4,126	4,083	5,138	6,324	7,262
Total	88,503	63,570	70,977	74,279	67,119	84,855	106,919
% of total	6.2	7.5	5.8	5.5	7.7	7.4	6.7

Source: SAMA *Quarterly Bulletin*, 3rd quarter, 1992.

standing of the sponsor to determine the borrower's ability to pay. During the boom years the name of the borrower was in many cases sufficient to satisfy lenders. In view of the retrenchment of traditional commercial banks' lending, however, project financing is gradually evolving from straightforward lending to encompass more advanced concepts of financial engineering.

The sophisticated commercial banks in the Kingdom are increasingly resorting to complex project finance when considering the borrowing requirements of industrial projects. The main characteristic of project finance is non-recourse to the sponsor. Here, project lenders look primarily at the cash flows and earnings of the project as sources of funds from which a loan will be repaid and to the assets of the project as collateral for the loan. In other words, the lenders examine the ability of the project to pay for itself, rather than looking to the credit standing of the borrower. For the borrower, the separation of the project's credit risk from the rest of his business has obvious advantages, since his other assets will not necessarily be called upon to support the project.

Project financing in its true form holds considerable promise for the development of industrial projects in the Kingdom. The resource-based nature of the country's projects lends itself readily to the assessment of the risk involved. Petrochemical, refining and aluminium projects, for example, with marketing guaranteed by foreign partners, represent a reliable source of funds from which loans can be repaid. Project financing as a clearly defined credit package is also crucial in encouraging the cautious domestic banks and the local and regional development institutions to use their resources for industrial development.

To encourage greater flows of financing from the Kingdom's commercial banks, a joint financing mechanism needs to be developed that will pool the resources of the country's industrial development funds with those of the commercial banks. While development institutions could extend financing to industrial projects at the longer end of the maturity profile, commercial banks would step in at the shorter end to provide working capital, bonding requirements and import finance facilities. Commercial banks could also participate in export finance schemes for creditworthy exporters. Banks in the Kingdom may be enticed to take a longer-term exposure to a specific industrial project if a joint or parallel financing scheme can be worked out with the development institutions. For example, commercial and development loans may be linked through a cross-default clause, whereby a payment default on the commercial loan will constitute a default on the concessionary loan and will trigger suspension of disbursement to the borrower from the development institution.

Industry growth projection

Growth in industry can come from four main sources: internal growth due to population and income increases; import substitution; export development; and high-technology industries under the Economic Offset Programme. Domestic demand for Saudi-made goods estimated at SR40 billion in 1991 is projected to increase by 4 per cent annually as a result of population growth and income increases. Compounded over 9 years, domestic demand could rise by 42 per cent to SR56.9 billion in the year 2000, an increase of SR16.9 billion. A conservative estimate is that 22 per cent or about SR24 billion of the SR108.8 billion in 1991 imports can instead be made locally. By the year 2000 this import substitution potential will grow by 50 per cent to SR36 billion.

Non-chemical exports, which in 1991 amounted to only SR5.8 billion, could easily double by the year 2000 to SR11.6 billion if export promotion policies are adopted. By the turn of the century, chemical exports are projected to increase to SR16 billion from SR9 billion in 1991 while other new export-oriented industries are projected to produce products worth SR2.4 billion. This gives an estimate for total exports in the year 2000 of around SR30 billion almost double the 1991 figure. Additional growth can come from the high-technology manufacturing and maintenance companies being developed under the various economic offset programmes, with a preliminary projection for the year 2000 of SR2 billion (see Exhibit 4.16).

The conclusion that one can derive here is that both import substitution and export development offer important opportunities for industrial growth. As Exhibit 4.17 shows, there is still a sizeable percentage of domestic demand currently being met by imports, whether in food processing, chemical industries, textiles, building materials or electrical equipment. Increasingly more of the products that are imported can be produced domestically, benefiting from the support and protection provided by the government. Most imports are subject to tariffs at the rate of 12 per cent with a 30 per cent duty on tobacco. However, in order to promote import-substituting industrialisation, a limited number of manufactured imports are subject to protective tariffs of 20 per cent (detergents and soap, plastic products, marble and cement tiles, macaroni, confectionery, furniture, cement, iron bars, among others). On the other hand, imports of certain inputs and essential foodstuffs (sugar, rice, tea, meat, barley etc.) are allowed free of tariffs. Other incentives include exemption from import taxes on material and equipment required for local production, exemption from taxes on profits for the foreign partner in an industrial joint venture, ready made industrial sites low energy costs,

Exhibit 4.16

Saudi industry: estimated turnover in the year 2000

	SR billions
1991 turnover	40.0
Increase in the year 2000 due to:	
Growth in domestic demand	16.9
Import substitution	36.0
Growth of non-chemical exports	5.8
Growth of chemical exports	7.0
New exports	2.4
Offset projects	2.0
Total industrial turnover in the year 2000	**110.1**

Exhibit 4.17

Domestic demand for Saudi made products

Industrial category	*Industrial sub-sectors*	*% of domestic market met by Saudi made products*
Food industries	Vegetable oil	60
	Biscuits	30
	Spaghetti	35
	Canned vegetables	35
Chemical industries	Adhesive products	45
	Perfumes & cosmetics	15
	Plastics	30
Textiles & apparel	Ready-made clothes	7
	Textiles	8
	Towels	15
	Shoes	6
Building materials	Glass	10
	Aluminium products	15
Electrical equipment	Batteries	15
	Refrigeration	20

Source: Local production: consumption and exports (Arabic), Riyadh Chamber of Commerce and Industry, 1990.

abundance of inexpensive feedstocks, capital loans and grants, freedom of capital movement and repatriation of profits, preferential purchasing of local products by the government.

While import substitution is an important goal, more emphasis will be put in the future on export promotion. Saudi Arabia is strategically located for export oriented industries to the surrounding Arab states, Turkey, the Indian Sub-continent, East Africa, Southeast Asia, China and Central Asian states of the previous Soviet Union. Most of these countries are in their early stages of development and thus a small growth involves huge new markets, particularly for basic commodities. There is a market of 350 million people in the Middle East and Muslim Africa alone to which Saudi Arabia through the various national and regional organisations and their programmes have direct favourable access. The Kingdom has also signed bilateral trade agreements with several of these countries that greatly enhance its preferential export markets.

Investors in export oriented industries can benefit from the available schemes providing credit for exports at the Arab and Islamic levels. On the Arab level, use can be made of financial guarantees against commercial and non-commercial risks from the Kuwait-based Inter-Arab Investment Guarantee Corporation. Export credit is also extended by the Arab Trade Finance Programme of the Arab Monetary Fund whose aim is to help support trade flows between the Arab countries. On the level of trade exchanges between Islamic countries, the investor can enjoy the benefits of the Longer Term Trade Financing Scheme of the Islamic Development Bank which specialises in financing the export of non-traditional commodities between Islamic countries. Besides, the Saudi commercial banks also offer trade finance and other related services and the Saudi Industrial Exports Corporation is doing very well in marketing Saudi products abroad and in undertaking market research, providing information and advising Saudi exporters.

Conclusion

It has become evident that, for industrial strategy in the Kingdom to succeed, it should take into consideration the need to develop manpower, services, financial and capital markets, engineering, maintenance, consultancy and research and development facilities. Only those projects that do not require long-term subsidies and protection to become commercially viable should be considered. A comprehensive strategic outlook for industrial development at both the national and regional levels needs to be drawn up and implemented. Priority should be given to new projects which are complementary (through either backward or forward integration) with existing industries.

A sliding scale protection tariff formula directly proportional to the ratio of value added of an industry to total value needs to be implemented, with infant industries benefiting from higher tariff rates for a specific period of time only. Industries applying for protection should adhere to certain levels of specification and certain standards and should be able to compete on price and quality in the local markets. Too much protection would reduce competition and lead to high prices for industrial products, harming consumers and dampening future export potential.

The lack of proper marketing is considered one of the serious problems affecting industry in the Kingdom. Industrialists here concentrate most of their efforts on production problems and pay less attention to marketing. Little freedom is given to marketing directors to take the initiative and provide input on consumer preferences to production managers. Promotional activities for local products are slack and are not targeted to specific buyers. Those who invested in industry imagined that, if a market for a certain quantity of an imported product existed and they were able to manufacture that quantity of the same product locally, they would be able to capture that market. This argument has been proved wrong by the several industrial failures in the 1980s. Conversely, it is noticeable that many of the industries that have been successful have grown out of good marketing operations; the entrepreneur has established a certain brand image and a strong selling base, then integrated backwards into manufacturing.

Just as in other developing countries, an indigenous tradition of research is lacking. Research is considered to be more of an academic exercise than a vital ancillary to industry and technology transfer. Only a small fraction of the Kingdom's GDP has been spent on research and development, compared with 2 per cent in the US and 3 per cent in Japan and several other industrialised countries. If research is not encouraged and a change in the general attitude towards employment in the productive sectors of the economy brought about, manufacturing activities may end up perpetually dependent upon foreign labour and technical expertise. Research programmes in universities, centres such as the King Abdulaziz City for Science and Technology and big industrial companies such as SABIC have started to address this issue but more needs to be done to develop indigenous research capabilities.

These are still the early stages of Saudi industrialisation. The Kingdom is trying to compress into a couple of decades development that has taken industrial countries a century or more to achieve. There is a need to develop indigenous manpower and managerial skills and to promote attitudes that are helpful to industrial development. During the boom years of the 1970s and early 1980s the sudden easy access to wealth created a "get rich" society in which the relationship between productivity and reward was largely diluted. Much has changed since then and new attitudes towards industrialisation in the Kingdom have been developed. The more young people pursue vocational training studies and careers in science and engineering, the better the prospects are for industrial development to become a self-perpetuating economic activity.

5 The changing character of the construction sector

Introduction

The outlook for the Kingdom's construction sector is quite positive, with ample business opportunities arising from a string of new industrial projects, huge expansion of oil production capacity, a new generation of petrochemical plants and refineries and several defence, and other public sector, projects. The retrenchment period that lasted throughout most of the 1980s came to an end in 1990. A strong upturn started in the first half of that year but was overshadowed by the Gulf crisis and many construction plans were either cancelled or postponed until after the end of the crisis. Activities have revived strongly since then, with sizeable construction contracts emanating from both the public and the private sectors.

Construction activity in Saudi Arabia started to pick up in earnest in the second half of 1991 and has surged ahead in 1992. New shopping complexes, commercial centres and recreation areas are being built and planned. Private villas and palaces have proliferated and more than 300 housing compounds have been started in the rush to provide accommodation for the increasing number of expatriates involved in defence, industry and private projects. Some 500 industrial facilities are planned in the Kingdom over the next few years and the expansion plans of ARAMCO, SABIC and SAMAREC are now underway. All of this augurs well for the Kingdom's building and construction companies, some of which are also beginning to look outside the Kingdom for continued growth.

Responding to the increased business, prices of building materials have risen, providing an important boost to a sector that accounts for around one-fifth of all factories in the Kingdom. The local cement industry has also improved its performance in 1991 and 1992. Production at the eight cement factories in Saudi Arabia is expected to reach almost its full capacity of around 13 million tons in 1992, compared to total production of 10 to 11 million tons in previous years, of which up to 2 million tons was for export. Exhibit 5.1 gives a breakdown of total capacity in the Kingdom. As the cement industry has recovered, share prices of cement companies have rallied, with values going up by more then 60 per cent in the first half of 1992. Sales and profitability at all factories has also risen considerably in 1992, a trend expected to hold as construction activity continues to grow and demand in the export market increases.

Exhibit 5.1

Production capacity of Saudi Arabian cement companies at 31 December 1991

Company	*Production started*	*Plant location*	*Number of kilns*	*Production capacity*
Arabian Cement Company	1959	Jeddah[1]		
	1985	Rabegh	4	1,200,000
Saudi Cement Company	1961	Hofuf	5	1,300,000
Yamama Cement Company	1966	Riyadh	6	2,580,000
Qassim Cement Company	1980	Qassim	2	1,260,000
Yanbu Cement Company	1981	Yanbu'	4	1,200,000
Southern Province Company	1981	Abha	2	1,650,000
Saudi-Bahraini Company	1981	'Ain Dar	4	1,800,000
Saudi-Kuwaiti Company	1985	Kursania	2	2,100,000
Total				**13,090,000**

[1]This plant was closed in 1985 after construction of a new plant in Rabegh.

Construction prospects in the Kingdom are attracting international interest at a level not seen since the early 1980s. Several international companies who were driven out of the market in the late 1980s, when the pool of public sector contracts was shrinking and competition was intense, are again actively pursuing new contracts in the Kingdom. The new opportunities are arising at a time when prospects for major construction work in the US, Europe and, to a lesser extent, Japan have been greatly reduced because of the domestic downturn in these areas. Those international contractors with a longstanding relationship with Saudi Arabia are expected to benefit from the steady revival of design and construction activities. They will not get preferential treatment in contract awards but their presence in the Kingdom will allow them to be more competitive. Management and equipment are in place and the firms have smaller start-up costs, making it easier for them to put in low bids for projects.

The heavy financial cost incurred by the government because of the Gulf crisis and the rising deficits over the past few years could lead to a decline in certain public sector projects, especially civil development schemes, while contracts for operations and maintenance and priority projects in oil, refining and the petrochemical sectors are increasing. Contractors remain apprehensive about the availability of finance for the planned projects and are uncertain whether the expected increase in defence construction and the industrial expansion will offset the slowdown in civil and infrastructural projects. However, several public sector companies are tapping the long-term lending market to fund current expansion plans. This is indicative of a trend towards financing construction projects by borrowing. To acquire a competitive edge, contractors bidding for large public sector projects may find it advantageous also to provide financing schemes in their offers.

The spate of new projects in various sectors is made more attractive by an improvement in payment procedures, which were a source of grievance for many contractors in the 1980s. Official payments have improved markedly since early 1990, when the government put an end to the practice of using payment delays to balance the books and manage cash disbursements. Payments are a good deal better than in the past and, while there can still be delays in final disbursement because of differences in accounting, these are neither as common, nor as serious, as in the past.

The changing character of the Saudi construction sector

The history of the construction industry in Saudi Arabia is marked by a succession of groups of contractors from different parts of the world acquiring a dominant position. During the oil boom period from the mid-1960s to the early 1980s construction activities were led by European and American contractors, who built the foundations of the country's infrastructure and oil facilities. In the 1980s the lead position was taken by contractors from South Korea, the Netherlands, the Indian sub-continent, Turkey and Southeast Asia, who proved to be more competitive on price during a period of declining Saudi financial surpluses. The 1980s also saw considerable growth in the number, size and capability of local contractors. They benefited from measures introduced by the government specifically to ensure that they received an adequate share of construction contracts.

Following the end of the Iran-Iraq war in 1988, and with the move towards specialised industrial and defence-related projects, American and European contractors were in demand once again. In 1990 and 1991 American companies ranked top of international firms involved in Saudi Arabia's construction sector, capturing an estimated 25 per cent of total contracts awarded. Work initiated by ARAMCO to increase Saudi Arabia's oil production capacity, the expansion of the Ras Tanura refinery, the increase in defence contracts and those related to the Peace Shield programme helped to boost the share of US companies. Italian contractors came next with an estimated 12.4 per cent of new projects, capturing sizeable civil and industrial contracts. UK contractors ranked third with a 6.5 per cent market share, boosted by the Al-Yamamah programme. Japanese and French companies followed, with estimated market shares of 6.1 per cent and 5.0 per cent respectively. Full details are given in Exhibit 5.2.

South Korean contractors have seen their share of contracts drop since the mid-1980s. The country does not have an export-orientated defence industry, while the large civil engineering and building construction projects where they enjoy a comparative advantage have been declining. The same is also true for contractors from the Indian sub-continent. Turkish firms entered the Kingdom's consulting and contracting market relatively late in the boom years but managed to make headway initially, largely at the expense of the South Koreans. Turkish contractors accounted for the largest part of contracts awarded to firms grouped under "Others" in Exhibit 5.2.

The construction market in Saudi Arabia is still considered sizeable by international standards. The value of contracts awarded in 1990 and 1991 is estimated at around US$5.6 billion, 60 per cent higher than in 1988

Exhibit 5.2

Individual countries' shares in construction contracts, 1974 - 91 (%)

	US	*UK*	*France*	*Germany*	*Italy*	*Japan*	*South Korea*	*Saudi companies*	*Others*[1]	*Total (US$ billions)*
1974-1979	17.6	7.2	10.8	10.9	8.5	9.5	5.1	5.3	25.8	17.3
1980-1982	9.1	4.9	8.9	7.1	6.7	9.5	10.9	13.0	29.9	24.6
1983-1985	15.1	7.9	10.6	2.9	5.9	8.2	11.6	13.0	24.8	14.3
1986-1987	13.5	5.5	4.6	5.5	7.2	5.9	4.8	16.0	36.7	2.8
1988-1989	18.0	7.0	7.5	6.5	6.8	4.3	3.1	20.2	26.6	3.5
1990-1991[2]	25.0	6.5	5.0	3.4	12.4	6.1	3.0	22.2	16.4	5.6

[1]Includes contractors from the rest of Europe, Canada, Turkey, China, Southeast Asia, the Arab countries and the Indian sub-continent.

[2]Estimate based on the *Top 250 International Contractors* published by *Engineering News-Record*, New York.

Source: Figures are derived from specific projects reported by *Saudi Economic Survey*, *MEED* and other domestic and International sources.

and 1989 but well below the peak of US$24.6 billion reached in 1980 to 1982. The low point of US$2.8 billion was in 1986 and 1987 but the trend has been upwards ever since. The Kingdom's share of the total GCC construction market is believed to have reached 70 per cent in 1990, following Iraq's invasion of Kuwait, compared with 58 per cent in 1989.

New priorities are evident in the recent upturn of construction activities in the Kingdom, with emphasis shifting from the high growth sectors of the 1970s and early 1980s (roads, airports, electricity, schools, hospitals, telecommunications, transport, public facilities and civil works in general) to defence, industrial infrastructure, operation and maintenance and expansion of petrochemical plants, refineries and oil production facilities. In 1990 and 1991 approximately 32 per cent of all new contracts were for oil-related projects, including expansion of production capacity, refineries and petrochemical plants; this was roughly double the amount of general building. The change of emphasis is opening more opportunities for local contractors, who enjoy a near monopoly on the lower technology end of the market, while the specialised fields remain the domain of international contractors.

We are witnessing a change in the sector's financial requirements, with the move from booming cash markets a decade ago to tighter credit conditions. Even though projects are now generally smaller than the infrastructural contracts of the 1970s, many of them require some form of financing. Two competitors for a massive telecommunications expansion scheme in Saudi Arabia have included financing proposals in their bids for the US$3 billion contract. This is indicative of a new trend, with the government and public sector companies borrowing, many of them for the first time, to finance large construction projects.

The Middle East construction market

The Middle East, and particularly Saudi Arabia, is emerging as an increasingly active market for international contractors. According to the annual *Top 250 International Contractors* report published by the New York-based *Engineering News Record* (ENR), the leading international contractors saw a 17 per cent increase in Middle East contracts in 1991, bringing the total to US$23.3 billion. Besides the six GCC States, the Middle East region includes Iran, Iraq, Turkey, Egypt and the North African countries. The Middle East followed both Europe and Asia in terms of the total value of contracts, with Europe accounting for US$30.45 billion in total contracts and Asia US$27.07 billion. However, the Middle East posted the second largest increase over 1990, following Europe which registered a 20 per cent increase. Asia came third at 10.6 per cent. Among the GCC countries, Saudi Arabia boasted the highest number (59) of international contractors working in the country in 1991, followed by the UAE with 44 contractors, Kuwait with 25, Bahrain with 19, Qatar with 17 and Oman with 14.

US firms clearly dominated the contracting market in the Middle East in 1991, with 59 companies winning 55 per cent of all contracts. That amounted to US$16.02 billion worth of business. This share was higher than the US share of the world market, which was only 46 per cent. European firms were second, with a total of 95 companies winning 31.3 per cent of contracts, worth a total of US$9.16 billion. Among the European firms, Italian companies had the biggest share, with 27 firms winning 11 per cent of the contracts, worth a total of US$3.22 billion. UK firms followed, with 13 companies winning 9.3 per cent of the contracts, worth a total of US$2.73 billion. Three Dutch firms won 2.7 per cent of the market (worth US$804 million); 10 French companies won 1.6 per cent (US$465 million); and 13 German firms won 0.6 per cent (US$189 million).

Japanese firms accounted for only a small proportion of the Middle East market in 1991, with 28 companies taking 2.7 per cent of contracts, worth a total of US$805 million. In contrast, four South Korean companies won 5.2 per cent for a total value of US$1.54 billion. One Lebanese firm alone took 3.4 per cent (US$983 million); one Bulgarian company captured 3 per cent (US$870 million); and 18 Canadian firms accounted for 0.8 per cent (US$229 million). Overall, 225 firms won contracts in the region in 1991. Turkish contractors, quite active in the Middle East during the 1980s, were hit particularly hard by the Gulf crisis, as large projects in Iraq had to be abandoned; no new Middle East business was reported.

The top 10 international contractors operating in the Middle East in 1991 were the Clinton, New Jersey-based Foster Wheeler Corporation, the San Francisco-based Bechtel Group Inc, the Irvine, California-based Fluor Daniel Inc, the London-based John Brown/Davy, The M W Kellogg Co, based in Houston, CRSS Inc, also based in Houston, the Seoul-based Daewoo Corporation, the Athens-based Consolidated Contractors International Co SAL, the Milan-based Snamprogetti Spa and the Bloomfield, New Jersey-based ABB Lummus Crest Inc. These contractors together billed a total of US$19.6 billion in the region in 1991.

The Middle East design market

According to ENR, the leading 200 international design firms billed US$1.31 billion for design services in the Middle East in 1991. This was the third largest amount for any region of the world (global billings for design firms totalled US$10.1 billion), with Europe and Asia taking first and second positions. The Middle East design market was heavily dominated by US firms, with 78 American companies accounting for 57 per cent of the region's market, billing a total of US$741.1 million.

European design firms together held 29.5 per cent of the market, with 85 companies billing US$384.9 million. A partial breakdown of the European firms active in the region revealed the following: 20 British companies held 9.4 per cent of the market, worth US$122.4 million; 10 Dutch firms accounted for 6.3 per cent, equal to US$81.7 million; 14 German companies held 3.6 per cent, translating into US$47.6 million; five French firms accounted for 3.4 per cent, worth US$43.9 million; eight Italian companies held 0.9 per cent, equal to US$11.4 million; and 1 Yugoslavian firm accounted for 0.2 per cent, translating into US$2.8 million. Canadian design firms held 3.1 per cent of the region's market, amounting to US$41 million, divided between 10 companies. Japanese firms accounted for another 1 per cent of the market, equal to US$13.6 million, shared by 14 companies. All other firms, numbering 13, accounted for the remaining 9.6 per cent, worth some US$125.8 million. Within this last category was one Lebanese firm (Dar Al-Handasah), which alone accounted for 7.7 per cent of the region's 1991 billings, or US$101 million.

While the market was growing in 1991, competition for business became noticeably more fierce. Clients were moving towards consortia of suppliers, contractors and design firms working together. There was also a trend towards more local participation in projects. The volume of work was growing, with much of it involving restoration of major projects built during the 1970s. In addition, Gulf countries were less easily enticed by the lowest bids, as was sometimes the case previously, and more conscious of quality concerns.

The top 10 firms working in the Middle East, according to ENR, were San Francisco-based Bechtel Group Inc, Houston-based CRSS Inc, Beirut-based Dar Al-Handasah Consultants, Bloomfield, New Jersey-based ABB Lummus Crest Inc, Pasadena, California-based Parsons/Main, Houston-based Brown & Root Inc, London-based John Brown/Davy, Montreal-based SNC-Lavalin International, Paris-based TECHNIP and The Badger Co Inc of Cambridge, Massachusetts. These firms together accounted for US$802.1 million of the total market. Saudi Arabia led the region in terms of the number of design firms working in the country in 1991, with 84 companies participating.

The position of Saudi contractors

Saudi contractors were able to raise their share of the new contract market to around 22 per cent in 1991 from 13 per cent in the early 1980s. This uptrend is natural, as many local contractors built up considerable technical and financial experience during the boom years. Several local contractors are now able to undertake work which a few years ago could be done only by large, foreign firms. With their low overhead costs, local firms are able to remain competitive on price, while foreign contractors need to plough back their profits into future work. Saudi contractors are likely to retain their comparative advantage within the GCC itself, as state boundaries are disregarded when partnerships are formed between national companies from the different member countries. Such partnerships are now treated as local firms when bidding for contracts within the GCC.

Until now the activities of Saudi contractors have centred on housing projects, offices, shopping complexes, operation and maintenance, public utilities, roads and government buildings. Many have acted as sub-contractors for international contractors and some have entered joint venture agreements with them. Construction for private sector clients is supported by concessionary finance from state-backed credit institutions and this is providing steady business for local contractors.

The authorities have taken certain measures in the last few years aimed at assisting the local construction industry. Many large government contracts which previously tended to be awarded to foreign firms have been divided into smaller contracts which can be handled by local contractors. Of more importance, however, is the requirement introduced in 1983 that 30 per cent of all government projects awarded to foreign contractors must be sub-contracted to domestic companies. Moreover, since 1982 wholly-owned foreign companies are allowed to work only on hospitals, airports and factory projects. All other construction ventures must be undertaken by companies having at least 25 per cent local equity participation. In addition, all government contracts of a value below US$50 million for roads, bridges and small or medium-sized buildings are typically awarded to domestic companies.

Major contract opportunities in the Kingdom

As mentioned before, major construction opportunities today lie in oil production and in the refining and petrochemical industries, natural gas, industrial projects, power and water schemes and defence-related projects. Maintenance of public services and infrastructure will also provide lucrative contracts for many years to come. With about 40 per cent of the cost of constructing a building, plant or oil refinery being spent on power generation, water supply, drainage installations, cooling and air conditioning, there will obviously be great potential in maintenance. In the past few years budget allocations for operations and maintenance of projects have ranged between SR18 billion and SR25 billion (US$4.8 billion and US$6.6 billion). A large part of the country's major infrastructure is around 20 years old and therefore requires major maintenance work. The hot and humid weather that the Kingdom experiences for six to eight months a year reduces the average life expectancy of concrete structures and buildings from 80 years in Europe and the US to around 30 years. However, increased efficiency and the streamlining of operations will create a higher degree of competitiveness in this market.

Expansion of oil production

Saudi ARAMCO's accelerated plans to raise the company's maximum sustainable oil production capacity to 10 million b/d by 1995 will involve an overall capital cost of US$16 billion and plans for the development of light crude oil finds in the Central Region are projected to cost US$500 million (see Chapter 3).

Even though the main programme management contracts have already been awarded, there will be a series of large construction awards as the scheme gathers pace. Each field's development will be divided into a set of major contracts. The first phase of developing Hawiya will involve three gas oil separation plants (GOSPs), a seawater injection plant, a pumping system and several pipeline packages. The total cost of the development is estimated at US$900 million. Other imminent contracts involve building a GOSP and infrastructure at Al-Hawiya field, GOSPs at Qatif and Khursaniyah and wet crude handling facilities for Zuluf. They will be let as either procure-build contracts, under which Saudi ARAMCO buys equipment itself, or as turnkey contracts.

Plans for the petrochemical industry

SABIC has an ambitious expansion programme for existing plants that is expected to increase production capacity from its 1990 level of 13 million metric tons to almost 20 million tons by 1995 at a total cost of around US$6 billion. The programmes are expected to increase production of existing products and to add new ones such as benzene and polypropylene. SABIC's affiliate, Ibn Zahr, has signed a contract to build a polypropylene plant in Jubail over the coming two years; it will have an annual capacity of 200,000 tons and will use feedstock from the new ethylene cracker (500,000 metric tons per year) to be produced by the Arabian Petrochemical Company (Petrokemya) as part of that company's two-year expansion programme. Ibn Zahr has also signed an agreement to build a plant to produce 700,000 metric tons a year of MTBE.

The Eastern Petrochemical Company (Sharq) has signed a US$420 million contract with Chiyoda of Japan to almost double its ethylene glycol capacity to 660,000 tons by 1994. The National Industrial Gases Company (Gas) awarded a US$55 million contract to raise nitrogen production from 219,000 tons to 490,000 tons and oxygen from 438,000 to 876,000 tons by 1993. The National Chemical Fertiliser Company (Ibn Al-Baytar) has already launched a US$250 million project to produce 1.31 million tons of fertilisers, phosphates and urea to service farmers. Saudi Iron and Steel Company, which produces 1.4 million metric tons a year of steel reinforcing bars, rods and wires will nearly double its capacity by 1993. The company is also looking at a US$1.5 billion scheme to construct a new complex for the production of flat products. Safco, the Saudi Arabian Fertiliser Company, has signed a turnkey contract worth SR1.15 billion (US$306 million) with Chiyoda of Japan to build a new complex in Jubail to produce ammonia and granular urea. The Al-Jubail Fertiliser Company (Samad) is building a new plant at its Jubail site. Estimated to cost US$400 million, the new 2-ethyl hexanol plant will have an annual capacity of 150,000 metric tons. Davy Process Technology has started design work on the plant, which is due to come onstream in mid-1994. Further discussion of SABIC's plans can be found in Chapter 4.

The refining sector

SAMAREC has unveiled the broad lines of a US$5 billion, 10-year plan to modernise and upgrade its refineries in the light of growing demand. The plan aims to improve the profitability of Saudi refineries by maximising output of high value products, particularly unleaded petrol, for domestic and export markets. When the plan is completed in the year 2000 it is projected that SAMAREC will have an exportable surplus of some 350,000 b/d of unleaded petrol. The plan is scheduled for implementation in three phases. The first phase envisages the development of SAMAREC's domestically-orientated refineries at Yanbu' (capacity 170,000 b/d), Riyadh (120,000 b/d) and Jeddah (95,000 b/d), with new units to produce high octane, unleaded petrol for local market requirements. In addition, the Yanbu' plant will undergo extensive upgrading to raise capacity to 240,000 b/d. Foster Wheeler of the US is to provide front-end engineering management and be responsible for the overall supervision of Phase 1.

The second phase will involve the modernisation and upgrading of the refineries at Ras Tanura (original capacity 530,000 b/d, now reduced to 300,000 b/d as a result of the loss of a distillation unit through fire damage in late 1990) and Rabigh on the Red Sea coast (capacity 325,000 b/d). Brown and Root of Houston was awarded a 10-year contract for the Ras Tanura refinery in October 1991. When the project is completed, by the year 2000, Ras Tanura will be the world's largest and most sophisticated refinery. The third phase (1995 to 2000) will entail the modernisation and upgrading of the joint venture export refineries at Jubail (Petromin/Shell) and Yanbu' (Petromin/Mobil), with the installation of new units for the production of high-quality unleaded petrol and distillates, as well as additional upgrading work on the Ras Tanura plant. The design capacities of the Jubail and Yanbu' refineries are 250,000 b/d each but both plants have recently been operating at 300,000 b/d.

Several contracts are being initiated by the Saudi private sector as well. For example, an MTBE plant with a capacity of 800,000 metric tons a year is to be established by Mobil and Chemvest, a local private firm. It will be located at Yanbu', with all output going to Mobil, although each partner will have a 50 per cent stake. The NIC and the Saudi Venture Capital Group (SVCG), both private companies, are looking at an extensive programme of industrial projects. Following their lead are two newer industrial investment firms, the SIDC, created in 1989, and the Arabian Industrial Development Company (AIDC), being promoted by the Eastern Province Chamber of Commerce & Industry. It is estimated that private industrial projects in the 1990s could entail fixed capital investment of several billion riyals.

Defence projects

Defence-related construction promises to expand dramatically over the next few years. Saudi Arabia has indicated that it requires several new airbases and, at the very least, that it will expand existing facilities. A steady stream of military contracts is expected over the next five to 10 years, with an estimated total expenditure of around US$13 billion. Several contracts have already been awarded for the huge Al-Kharji airbase project. Two new military cities have been proposed at Jizan in the southwest and near Medina in the Central Western Region. The Al-Yamamah defence pact with the UK includes a military complex at Sulayyil. A proposal to build underground storage for arms and ammunition is also being considered. The Saudi Ministry of Defence and Aviation is also building a network of strategic storage facilities for oil products, including six underground depots near military bases, in a programme said to cost over US$6 billion. Swedish firms in the local joint venture, ABV Rock Group, have been contracted for related work, while the group itself will act as programme manager. The ambitious plans to expand defence infrastructure will undoubtedly attract interest from international contractors specialising in this field.

Civil construction programmes

Power

Saudi Arabia's rapid emergence as an industrial nation has led to a pressing need for more power generation. Future plans to upgrade and extend electricity supplies throughout the Kingdom are forecast to cost between SR2.6 billion and SR3 billion a year. In January 1992 ABB Asea Brown Boveri was awarded a SR1.17 billion (US$312 million) contract to build the Kingdom's first combined cycle plant at Rabigh on the Red Sea coast. Another contract, worth US$300 million, to expand Rabigh power station was given to Mitsubishi Heavy Industries. A giant new power station will be built in Asir Province in the south. The plant will initially have a capacity of 1,000MW but there are plans to increase this to 2,500MW later. Three other power projects involving the addition of 400MW of generating capacity in the Central Region and Southern Region are also in the pipeline, each estimated to cost US$50 million.

Water

The Kingdom's dependence upon desalinated water creates a constant flow of project opportunities. In July 1992, the Saline Water Conversion Corporation (SWCC) awarded the US$228 million Medina/Yanbu' contract, which involves installing two reverse osmosis (RO) plants, to Mitsubishi Heavy Industries. The US$138 million Jubail expansion contract, involving an RO plant with a capacity of 20 million gallons a day, was awarded to Germany's Preussag. Two other projects which SWCC is contemplating are the expansion of the Al Khobar plant (expected cost US$750 million) and a new desalination plant to serve Jeddah (expected cost US$900 million). Fichtner of Germany signed a contract for design and engineering for the water desalination project, called Jeddah 5. The project will entail building a new plant adjacent to the Mecca/Taif desalination unit 120 kilometres south of Jeddah and water from the plant will be transported by pipeline. In Abha a large dam is being built at a cost of SR330 million (US$88 million) to control flood waters and to store water for irrigation. There are also opportunities for small scale suppliers. For example Metito International of the US has recently won more than 20 contracts to supply and install water plants in various parts of the Kingdom.

Transport projects

The basic highway system has been established in the Kingdom, and second and third-grade networks are being developed. In the main urban areas, major new highway programmes are expected in the 1990s. For example, a new study has been commissioned into the possibility of building a new urban motorway system to relieve congestion in western Riyadh.

The fifth Five-Year Development Plan includes a number of vital projects for the civil aviation sector, aimed at upgrading services. The most important of these are the expansion of the King Abdulaziz International Airport in Jeddah to enhance its handling capacity and the establishment of an intermediate college for aviation. The plan also provides for the development of an industrial estate at King Khaled International Airport in Riyadh and the setting up of a number of plants specialising in high technology products under the economic offset programmes. The King Fahd International Airport in the Eastern Province is in the finishing stages of first phase construction and will be ready for operation in 1993. This will be the Kingdom's third international airport and is being built at a cost of SR7.6 billion (US$2.026 billion). It is expected to serve about 4 to 6 million passengers a year on opening, rising to 14 million by the year 2000 and 16 million by 2005.

Private sector industries

A newsprint paper factory (Al Warak) estimated to cost SR950 million (US$253 million) is under construction, promoted by the NIC. A private sector soda ash plant is to be set up in Jubail at an estimated cost of SR900 million (US$240 million) with the technical assistance of the Dutch firm Akzo Chemicals. The plant will be fully operational by the end of 1995 and will have an annual output of 264,000 metric tons. It is expected to be the largest in the Middle East when commissioned. The client is the Jeddah-based International Chemical Industries & Trading Company (ICIT). Steel cans manufacturer Al-Jomaih Company has announced plans to boost its capacity by expanding its product range. The expansion will reportedly give it the largest such operation in the region and the project is likely to cost SR100 million (US$26.6 million). Bechtel has been selected to act as project manager for the Arabian American Chemical Company (Aramchem) MTBE plant, the Kingdom's largest-ever private scheme in Yanbu'. This scheme has been promoted by Saudi Chemical Investments (Chemvest). The company is also promoting a US$500 million private-sector paraxylene plant to be built in Jubail. Other potential industrial projects include a 150,000 tone a year copper smelter.

Public projects

University attendance has more than doubled over the past 10 years and is forecast to continue growing at about 15 per cent a year. In anticipation of this increase, a number of colleges and university campuses are now being planned. King Saud University plans to build a new campus in

Abha, estimated to cost SR1.5 billion (US$400 million). The campus will cater for 2,500 male and 1,600 female students and the project includes a medical college. Almabani General Contractors was recently awarded a SR200 million (US$53.3 million) contract for the expansion of the Qassim campus of King Saud University. The contract is to build a college for agriculture and veterinary medicine studies and will be completed in three years. Contracts still to be tendered in this project include construction of accommodation for 1,200 male students, administrative buildings, a central library, festival halls and other facilities. The General Organisation for Technical Education and Vocational Training has been allocated a budget of SR1.18 billion (US$314 million) for 1992/3 to set up several new technical, agriculture and other institutes. The largest hospital scheme in the Kingdom for half a decade, a 500-bed facility to be constructed for the National Guard in al-Hasa in Eastern Province, has been announced, and bids for the US$1,000 million scheme are due early 1993. The Binladen Organisation of Jeddah was awarded a SR800 million (US$228.5 million) contract to build a general hospital in Taif for the Health Ministry.

Urban development

The Riyadh Construction Company (RCC) is to be floated on the Saudi stock market in 1993. Its objective is to raise finance for new projects for the city of Riyadh and in part, to displace public agencies as the dominant force in planning the city. The last great public scheme in Riyadh – the Qasr al-Hukm (Justice Palace) development, which cost more than SR 900 million (US$240 million) – was completed in 1992. The scheme was the fruit of the Arriyadh Development Authority (ADA), a government agency created to coordinate the development of Riyadh. The RCC is to develop some of the outstanding parts of the Justice Palace scheme. Similar companies have or are being established in Makkah, Medina, Taif, Al-Baha, Abha and Tabuk. With the population of Saudi cities growing at the rate of more than 5 per cent a year, the demand for office buildings, housing and basic infrastructure is set to expand steadily for the foreseeable future. In Jubail industrial city, where the population is projected to double to 40,000 people by the year 2000, a rush housing programme has been announced to deal with an emerging housing shortage. Rising property values are reported across the Kingdom, providing an incentive for private property developers. A new range of opportunities is being created by attempts to develop tourism within the Kingdom. Hilton International has been appointed to manage two new hotels to be built in Jeddah and Medina for business visitors and pilgrims.

Financing Saudi construction activities

Exhibit 5.3 shows the changes in GDP in the construction sector since 1983. As can be seen, although its long decline in absolute terms was halted in 1989, it continues to fall as a percentage of total GDP. With the drop in public sector expenditure on construction, commercial banks were invariably called upon to provide the required financing. The

Exhibit 5.3

Total GDP and construction GDP at current prices, 1983 - 91 (SR billions)

	1983	*1984*	*1985*	*1986*	*1987*	*1988*	*1989*	*1990*	*1991*[1]
Total GDP	377.7	351.4	313.9	271.1	275.5	285.1	310.8	376.5	423.2
GDP in construction sector	52.9	44.9	38.7	34.0	33.3	32.0	32.5	34.1	37.0
Construction as a percentage of total GDP	14.0	12.8	11.0	12.5	12.1	11.2	10.5	9.1	8.7
Growth in Construction GDP (%)	-3.6	-15.1	-13.8	-12.1	-2.1	-3.9	1.6	4.9	8.5

[1]Estimates.

Sources: Central Department of Statistics, Ministry of Finance and National Economy.

rescheduling of existing loans to several contractors and the capitalisation of interest owed contributed to a large commercial bank exposure to the sector, more than was the case with other sectors in the period from 1985 to 1989. Commercial banks in general have been shying away from increasing their credit exposure to local contractors, especially the weak and poorly capitalised ones.

Total bank lending outstanding to the construction sector has generally been on a declining trend in the last few years and the percentage share of construction in total outstanding credit facilities extended by commercial banks in the Kingdom has also dropped. Total outstandings fell from SR13.2 billion (US$3.5 billion) in 1984 to a low of SR10.7 billion (US$2.86 billion) in 1989 and rose slightly in 1991 to an estimated SR10.8 billion (US$2.88 billion). The percentage of total bank lending accounted for by the sector dropped to 13.3 per cent in June 1991 from a high of 23 per cent in 1985.

Almost US$37 billion worth of construction projects may be contracted over the next five years. Saudi ARAMCO requires about US$16 billion, SABIC's expansion programme is expected to cost US$6 billion, while SAMAREC needs US$5 billion. Power and water projects, together with various other industrial projects, will add another US$10 billion worth of new contracts during the next five years. Nearly a third of the US$37 billion requirement is expected to be borrowed from commercial banks and around 20 per cent may be funded by or through foreign contractors, with the rest to be provided from government budgets and the internal resources of the public sector companies.

The traditional view of Saudi Arabia as a cash-rich construction market needs to be revised. The country is becoming more of a credit than a cash market. Although future oil revenues are expected to rise gently, public sector finances have been burdened by the cost of the Gulf War and commitments to huge future outlays on defence. Contractors anxious to capture a slice of the business available should be ready to provide financing proposals in their bids for major contracts. The increasing need to offer finance, engineering and project management in a single package will put pressure on the traditional consultant and contractor, unless stronger links with the financial community are forged. This is not just a matter of good relationships but also an ability actually to work together, possibly in joint ventures. Contractors and bankers who have developed skills in project financing may have a competitive edge in today's markets.

Exhibit 5.4

Major borrowings by public sector companies, 1989 - 92

	Date	*Amount (US$ millions)*
External borrowing		
Saudi ARAMCO	March 1992	2,000
Vela	March 1992	900
Internal borrowing in dollars		
Vela	January 1992	300
Ibn Zahr	April 1992	500
Ibn Sina	August 1992	275
Sharq	August 1992	350
Internal borrowing in local currency		
Hadeed	May 1991	133.3[1]
Sceco West	July1991	320.0[2]

[1]SR500.
[2]SR1,200.

Three of Saudi Arabia's leading public companies have tapped the long-term lending market to fund current projects. ARAMCO drew on the international markets for a US$2 billion loan to help finance its capacity expansion plans. Vela, Saudi ARAMCO's shipping subsidiary, raised a US$300 million loan from the domestic Saudi market in January 1992, followed by another US$900 million loan from the international market to finance the acquisition of a large crude oil tanker fleet. Hadeed, the iron and steel producing affiliate of SABIC, borrowed SR500 million (US$133 million) from the domestic market to help pay for its expansion scheme. The Saudi Consolidated Electrical Company for the Western Province (Sceco West) took a SR1.2 billion (US$320 million) loan to support the cost of a new power plant in Rabigh. In April 1992 Ibn Zahr signed a US$500 million loan to finance expansion with a syndicate of Saudi and Gulf banks. This was followed in August by Ibn Sina and Sharq, who signed loans of US$275 million and US$350 million respectively with a group of Saudi and Gulf banks. Exhibit 5.4 tabulates these loans.

Private Saudi companies are following the same pattern, borrowing commercially for construction or expansion of industrial plants to supplement concessionary long-term credit provided by the PIF and the SIDF. This represents a marked change in the established pattern of financing. In the early 1980s the bulk of financing came from the PIF. Now that most of the companies have been operating successfully for some time, they are required to borrow on commercial terms. This is obviously the overall strategy the government wants to see followed in the future. Expansion plans must be commercially justified and financed from the firms' own resources, either directly from cash flows or by borrowing against reasonable projections of future income.

Conclusion

Construction activities in Saudi Arabia are picking up momentum in an atmosphere of confidence reminiscent of that of the first half of the 1980s. Many companies that stayed through the Saudi recession have been reassessing their situations, cutting overhead expenses and repositioning themselves strategically for the upturn in construction activities. Long-term plans for expansion of existing plants or building of new ones are now appearing, with the bulk of contracts to be awarded between 1993 and 1995.

The Kingdom is becoming more of a credit than a cash market, with public sector companies going into the markets for finance. This trend is expected to continue and international contractors anxious to capture forthcoming contract awards should be ready to include financing proposals in their bids for major projects. Those who are able to provide finance, technical capabilities and management skills in a single package will greatly enhance their competitiveness. In this respect, it would be advantageous for contractors to establish close relationships with banks in the Kingdom who have a good understanding of the risks involved and are able to provide sophisticated project finance schemes for their clients.

Competition in the 1990s for a growing Saudi construction market will be intense, with narrow profit margins. State budgets are tightly controlled and customers in both the private and the public sectors are more conscious of costs. Many projects are put to tender more than once to ensure that the lowest bid is closer to the amount budgeted for the project and more local contractors are bidding for projects that were the sole domain of international contractors just a few years ago. Local companies source their labour from low cost Asian countries and government policies are already in place to promote local contractors. In such a competitive environment the advantage of being on the spot increases. A foreign construction company with a formal, legal joint venture presence can develop its business and promote its interests better than competitors who lack a domestic base. Those on the spot will have easier access to the whole GCC market and will be better able to benefit from incentives available within the GCC.

6 Agriculture: constraints and opportunities

Introduction

Saudi Arabia has been among the world's fastest growing food producers, with GDP in the agricultural sector growing at an average annual rate of 8.1 per cent between 1980 and 1985 and 13.4 per cent between 1985 and 1990. Agricultural production increased by around 7 per cent in 1991 and the same growth rate is forecast for 1992 and 1993. The agricultural sector employs around 10 per cent of the workforce and, including fishing, its share of total GDP rose from 2.5 per cent in 1983 to 7.4 per cent in 1989, before edging down to 6.7 per cent in 1991. The average consumption of agricultural products by a Saudi family is put at around SR938 (US$250) a month, among the highest in the world, and an increasing amount is being met from domestic production. Land under cultivation totalled 1.831 million hectares in 1991, almost twice the area cultivated in 1986. The value of agricultural commodities produced in Saudi Arabia was estimated at nearly SR19.5 billion (US$5.2 billion) in 1991, compared to agricultural and feedstock imports of SR11.1 billion (US$2.96 billion).

The Kingdom's agricultural production continues to surge, with the value of farm and livestock products exported in 1991 reaching SR1,419 billion (US$378 billion), of which around SR398 million (US$106 million) was accounted for by extra wheat production and SR325 million (US$86.6 million) by exports of vegetables and fruit. In the last 10 years wheat has been the engine of growth in Saudi agricultural production, with total production rising from 154,000 tons in 1973 to a record 3.9 million tons in 1991. Large wheat farmers have been able to improve the efficiency of their operations to achieve yields of over five tons per hectare, among the world's highest. Today the Kingdom is the world's sixth largest wheat exporter and among the largest producers of dates. It has also attained self-sufficiency in various agricultural crops, eggs, fish and dairy products.

The growth of agricultural output has been mostly due to the price support policy and other incentives provided by the government, as well as to the adoption of modern farming techniques. Despite the extreme climatic conditions and limited water resources, agriculture was given a priority because of social, political and economic factors. The Kingdom's perceived vulnerability and overdependence on imported food was a key consideration. By promoting agricultural development, the government aims to diversify the economy further away from hydrocarbons, to achieve self-sufficiency and food security in many more agricultural crops, to improve the welfare of the rural population and to limit migration to urban areas. Through extensive state subsidies and price support programmes, agriculture has served as an effective way to spread wealth and prosperity to the rural population. It has also contributed to the development of the agricultural areas of central and southwestern Saudi Arabia.

Under the Fifth Five-Year Development Plan (1990 to 1995), agriculture's share of GDP is expected to grow to 9 per cent by 1995, achieving an average annual growth rate of 7 per cent in value-added. Wheat production is targeted to decline at the expense of barley and other crops. Local production of red meat, white meat, vegetables, fruit and fish is projected to increase by between 4 per cent and 8 per cent a year. Close to SR14.4 billion (US$3.84 billion) is allocated to the agricultural sector for the period, of which SR6.9 billion (US$1.84 billion) will be for loan support through the Saudi Agricultural Bank.

The plan identifies several policies that the government would like to implement, including the cultivation of land in areas with potentially renewable water resources; areas with critical groundwater depletion rates will be identified and regulations introduced on appropriate water pumping rates and the number of hectares to be cultivated. The growing of new crops will be encouraged where feasible and the government will continue to undertake research on problems specific to Saudi agriculture. The plan also calls for the regular review of agricultural support prices to promote optimum cropping patterns and the prudent diversification of agricultural production.

The major constraint to the future development of the agricultural sector is the availability of water resources and the scarcity of arable land. Less than 1 per cent of the area of the Kingdom has the potential to be exploited for agricultural crops. There are limited water resources and, with the exception of the southwestern region, the potential for renewable surface water supply is minimal, with non-renewable underground aquifers providing approximately 80 per cent of the water requirements of agriculture. Demand has increased rapidly in recent years and, since 1988, agriculture has accounted for almost 90 per cent of total water requirements (14 billion cubic metres), with wheat production alone accounting for one-third of that figure. The government realises that this depletion rate of underground water supplies may not be sustainable in the long term and policies are being implemented to address the imbalance between supply and demand.

Government support for agriculture

The strong performance of the agricultural sector in the past few years is mostly attributable to generous government subsidies and price support policies, as well as to the land reform programmes. To encourage private investment in agriculture, the authorities have allocated substantial funds to improve infrastructure, including irrigation, storage and drainage and secondary roads linking production areas with marketing centres. The land distribution and reclamation programme, which started in 1968, aims at allocating land, mostly in smaller plots, to increase the area under cultivation and encourage crop and livestock production. The beneficiaries are required to develop a minimum of 25 per cent of the land within two to five years. Upon compliance, the full ownership is transferred to the beneficiary. Over 1.4 million hectares were distributed through this scheme during the 1980s. In addition, the government has sought to expand the arable area by stepping up land reclamation.

The government has also committed substantial resources to subsidising agricultural imports and machinery and to maintaining procurement prices above world market prices for producers of certain agricultural crops. Direct agricultural subsidies from the government grew at an annual average rate of about 9 per cent between 1984 and 1987 to SR6.9 billion (US$1.84 billion), before declining sharply to an average of SR4 billion (US$1.07 billion) in 1988 and 1989, as the provision of subsidies was curbed by budgetary constraints. However, in the last two years they have risen again, reaching SR7.95 billion (US$2.12 billion) in 1991.

In addition to the various subsidies provided by the government (as detailed in Exhibit 6.1), the agricultural sector also benefits from several indirect subsidies, including free water for irrigation, subsidised fuel and electricity, duty free imports of raw materials and machinery and a tax holiday of up to 10 years for foreign partners in agricultural joint ventures. There is a 12 per cent duty on most imported agricultural crops and

Exhibit 6.1

Saudi Arabian agricultural subsidies

Product	*Subsidy*
Irrigation engines & pumps	50% of official price fixed by Ministry of Agriculture and Water
Tractors & other earthmoving equipment used in agriculture	45% of official price
Animal feed	SR 100/ton
Poultry farm equipment	30% of total cost
Dairy farms equipment	30% of total cost
Airfreight transportation for imported cows	Full cost of air transport (50 cows or more per shipment)
Palm trees (newly planted)	SR50/tree (minimum 30 trees)
Potato seeds	First five tons free, each additional ton up to five tons sold at SR1,000
Improved seed for wheat, barley, sorghum	Distributed by Ministry of Agriculture & Water, mostly free
Fishing boats & nets	A grant of up to SR10,000 per person engaged in fishery business

Exhibit 6.2

Loans extended by the Agricultural Bank, 1979/80 - 1991/92 (SR thousands)

	Short-term loans		*Medium-term loans*		*Total loans*	
Years	*Number*	*Amount*	*Number*	*Amount*	*Number*	*Amount*
1979/80	3,557	22,734	16,225	1,105,951	19,782	1,128,686
1980/81	9,310	39,226	35,818	2,491,640	45,128	2,530,866
1981/82	5,556	29,456	31,890	2,903,445	37,446	2,932,902
1982/83	3,454	25,270	35,432	4,140,757	38,886	4,166,027
1983/84	1,759	18,510	22,085	3,477,252	23,844	3,495,763
1984/85	1,024	17,315	13,722	2,304,484	14,746	2,321,800
1985/86	305	3,901	8,904	1,547,323	9,209	1,551,225
1986/87	475	4,178	6,588	1,015,010	7,063	1,019,188
1987/88	253	2,548	4,539	838,728	4,792	841,276
1988/89	143	1,471	3,607	753,055	3,750	754,526
1989/90	178	1,782	3,964	852,521	4,142	854,303
1990/91	131	2,163	3,992	1,014,482	4,123	1,016,646
1991/92	118	1,534	3,615	755,307	3,733	756,842

Source: Saudi Arabian Agricultural Bank, Annual Report 1410/1411 H.

livestock, with a 20 per cent duty on imports of poultry allowing a significant poultry industry to develop.

The agricultural support programme is administered by the Ministry of Agriculture and Water, the Saudi Arabian Agricultural Bank and the Grain Silos and Flour Mills Organisation (GSFMO). The Ministry of Agriculture and Water is responsible for land reclamation, crop selection, seed development, improved animal husbandry and ultimately the use and development of water resources. The Agricultural Bank provides interest free loans to farmers, mainly for purchase of farm machinery and drilling of wells. With the completion of major investments in the early 1980s, net disbursements by the bank have been declining (see Exhibit 6.2).

Exhibit 6.3

Agricultural subsidies disbursed through the Agricultural Bank, 1979/80 - 1990/91 (SR thousands)

Years	*Engines & pumps*	*Agricultural machinery*	*Animal feed*	*Poultry raising equipment*	*Dairy farm equipment*	*Transport of imported cows*	*Fishing boats*	*Total*
1979/80	163,799	115,171	125,725	8,335	373	11,142	11,050	435,598
1980/81	297,122	179,116	126,752	3,462	437	8,521	70	615,483
1981/82	348,965	261,904	327,808	12,476	5,757	22,353	–	979,266
1982/83	472,250	370,558	432,377	15,265	1,903	29,205	–	1,321,560
1983/84	361,043	298,203	334,004	12,308	536	16,439	–	1,022,535
1984/85	355,886	285,652	710,124	14,787	674	10,762	–	1,377,888
1985/86	241,836	199,664	534,386	3,272	137	14,535	–	993,833
1986/87	217,317	167,147	–	8,881	–	11,178	–	404,525
1987/88	148,395	108,105	179	3,324	122	4,516	–	264,644
1988/89	152,995	96,053	13,823	2,713	–	2,657	–	268,242
1989/90	1,153,535	98,741	200	1,466	1,489	4,282	–	259,552
1990/91	84,023	63,471	290	1,041	212	–	–	149,037

Source: Saudi Arabian Agriculture Bank, Annual Report 1410/1411 H.

Total subsidies granted reached SR149 million (US$39.7 million) in 1990/91, down from SR259.5 million (US$69.2 million) the year before and way below the figure of SR1,321.5 million (US$352.4 million) in 1982/83. Exhibit 6.3 lists the areas for which subsidies were granted.

Total loans extended by the bank since its inception in 1964/65 reached SR25,728 million (US$6,861 million) in 1991. Short-term loans constituted less than 1 per cent of the amount extended, while SR25,447 million (US$6,785 million) was disbursed in medium-term loans. Loans concentrated on the provision of water (comprising drilling and casing of wells, irrigation equipment, engines, pumps and piping), agricultural projects of different types (production of wheat, dairy products, greenhouse vegetables, etc) and agricultural machinery, including accessories. These three loan categories constituted about 95.5 per cent of total loans extended in 1990/91. Loans associated with the provision of water alone accounted for 44 per cent of the total or SR443 million (US$118 million). Exhibit 6.4 gives a full breakdown of the categories in which loans were advanced. Small farmers and owners of medium-sized farms were the main beneficiaries, as more than 87.6 per cent by number of loans extended in 1990/91 were for less than SR400,000 (US$106,666).

Financing is also available from the bank for agricultural joint ventures. Loans extended are interest free for up to 80 per cent of the first SR2 million (US$533,000) in project costs and 60 per cent beyond that, to a maximum of SR20 million (US$5.33 million). Agricultural loans normally extend for 10 years, with a grace period of from one to two years. Financing and credit support for export-orientated investment or trade

Exhibit 6.4

Agricultural loans by category, 1990/91 (SR thousands)

Category	*Number*	*Amount of loans*	*% of total*
Engines	2,620	58,460	5.75
Pumps	2,760	67,117	6.60
Sink pumps	91	1,062	0.10
Booster pumps	34	139	0.01
Agricultural machinery	9,763	153,928	15.14
Piping	132,000	9,020	0.88
Generators	39	464	0.04
Electric generator	1	29	–
Electric dynamo	37	274	0.02
Irrigation equipment	1,065	113,325	11.14
Well drilling	1,776	194,077	19.09
Offshoot for wind breaks	20,000	128	0.01
Mountain terraces	–	598	0.05
Silos	20	1,781	0.17
Plastic sheds	2,046	16,452	1.61
Fishing boats & gear	244	21,527	2.11
Bee-hives & bee-keeping equipment	1,878	882	0.08
Fertilisers	–	1,664	0.16
Seeds	–	444	0.04
Ploughing	–	54	–
Agricultural projects	263	375,211	36.90
Total		**1,016,646**	**100**

Source: Saudi Arabian Agricultural Bank, Annual Report 1410/1411 H.

finance may in some cases be available from the Islamic Development Bank, the Inter-Arab Investment Guarantee Corporation or the Arab Monetary Fund.

The GSFMO implements official procurement policy by purchasing locally produced wheat and barley at guaranteed prices for domestic sales and for export. The GSFMO uses its retained earnings to supplement output subsidies disbursed through the budget. The government paid a total of SR7,945 million (US$2,119 million) for the 1991 wheat crop of 3.9 million tons. This amounted to a payment of US$543 a ton for Saudi wheat, compared with world prices of around US$110 a ton. Domestic needs are around 1 million tons and the surplus is either stored or exported. GSFMO has been expanding its storage capacity, which currently stands at 2.58 million tons.

Important changes in procurement prices have been introduced over the last few years to contain wheat production and rationalise the product mix. The procurement price for wheat has been reduced gradually from SR3,500 (US$1,000) a ton in the early 1980s to SR1,500 (US$400) a ton in 1988 for the seven large agricultural companies (which account for about 20 per cent of total wheat output) and to SR2,000 (US$533) a ton for other producers. The price for large farmers was dropped again to SR1,500 (US$400) a ton in 1989. The major agricultural companies were also asked to transfer 30 per cent of land under wheat cultivation to the production of barley and a ceiling of 200,000 tons has been set for purchase of wheat from these companies at the official price.

In order to rationalise the product mix further, the subsidy for barley was reduced by two-thirds in 1987 to SR100 a ton, with a maximum selling price of SR200 a ton for imported barley. This subsidy was eliminated in 1988 and a domestic procurement price for barley of SR1,000 (US$277) a ton was introduced. In order to avoid any potentially adverse price effects from this measure, the GSFMO was accorded a monopoly for the import of barley. In addition to wheat and barley, the government also provides fixed subsidies for certain other crops including rice (SR0.3/kg), corn and sorghum (SR0.25/kg), dates (SR0.25/kg) and imports of concentrated feeds other than barley.

Agricultural products

Output of several agricultural crops has increased significantly over the past 10 years, with the value of crops and livestock reaching US$5.2 billion in 1991, much higher than the 1985 level of US$3.2 billion. Wheat has been the principal growth sector, followed by livestock. Exhibit 6.5 gives details of growth in production since 1985.

Preliminary estimates indicate that wheat production may have declined slightly in 1992, after reaching an all-time high of 3.9 million tons in 1991, representing an increase of 8.3 per cent on the previous year. The area planted with wheat has remained high, exceeding 700,000 hectares and the crop has grown substantially every year since the government introduced the price support scheme. Growth was fastest when the purchase price was highest: the crop virtually doubled in both 1982 and

Exhibit 6.5

Value of agricultural production, 1985 - 91 (US$ millions)

	1985	*1986*	*1987*	*1988*	*1989*	*1990*	*1991*
Crops	1.799	2.043	2.216	2.560	2.654	2.912	3.156
Livestock	1.424	1.503	1.647	1.784	1.838	1.973	2.079
Total	3.223	3.546	3.863	4.344	4.492	4.885	5.235
Increase on previous year (%)	27.2	10	8.9	12.5	3.4	8.8	7.1
Wheat share (%)	35.3	38.2	36.5	39.2	38.1	39.3	40.7

Source: Saudi Arabia Quarterly Report, January 1992.

1983 when the price was US$1,000 a ton. After the price was dropped to SR2,000 (US$533) a ton, growth dropped to 54 per cent in 1985 and 6.6 per cent in 1986. The price for large farmers fell again in 1989, although there was no change for small farmers, who account for 84 per cent of the crop, and output that year remained virtually static at 3.2 million tons.

The rise in wheat production was despite an official policy of encouraging farmers to switch to other crops, particularly barley. New regulations were introduced in mid-1991 to establish tighter government control over the sector and to limit the area planted with wheat. Nevertheless, farmers increased the application of nitrogen and phosphate fertilisers to boost yields of existing wheat fields. The area planted with barley rose from 7,000 hectares in 1985 to 491,000 hectares in 1991 and production increased from 10,000 tons to 500,000 tons but the Kingdom continues to import large amounts of the crop. The barley procurement price of SR1,000 (US$267) a ton is less than the SR1,500 (US$400) received by the seven major wheat growers and well below the SR2,000 (US$533) a ton received by the smaller farmers. Furthermore, the average barley yield continued to lag behind that of wheat. The fundamental economics of wheat and barley need to be changed to induce a wider shift from the production of wheat into barley, as the two are grown during the same period of the year.

Total production of fruit and vegetables rose from 706,000 tons in 1970 to more than 3 million tons in 1991, satisfying more than 50 per cent of the domestic market for vegetables and 20 per cent for fruit. According to the Saudi Ministry of Agriculture and Water, the Kingdom produced close to 2.54 million tons of vegetables in 1991, up from 1.56 million in 1984. Watermelon production is estimated at about 600,000 tons annually and prices are relatively low. The 45 per cent subsidy for purchases of trucks for farm use has added to the incentives for melon cultivation. Tomato production has ranged between 370,000 and 400,000 tons annually. The new tomato paste processing plant should provide a catalyst for gains in future tomato production. Vegetables which can be produced quickly should do well on land where wheat is harvested from May to July. Some farms near Hail have succeeded in growing peanuts as a crop to follow wheat and experiments with vegetables and fodder crops are still going on. Concern about the demand for farm labour to pick vegetables has apparently caused some farmers to favour fodder crops, which can be grown and harvested mechanically.

Saudi Arabia is among the world's four leading date producers, with total production in 1991 amounting to 545,000 tons, while total fruit production, including dates, reached 800,000 tons, up from 607,000 in 1984. The US$14 subsidy for each date palm planted has succeeded in expanding production and boosting exports. Commercial fruit production has also been developed, particularly in the region near Tabuk, but remains short of local demand. The Kingdom's apple production reached close to 32,000 tons in 1991, compared with imports of around 200,000 tons, while production of oranges is put at 63,000 tons, compared with imports of 205,000 tons. Production of grapes has expanded rapidly and now exceeds 110,000 tons annually. Production of the best varieties of fruit by commercial orchards has increased in the Asir highlands, all the way from Tabuk down to Taif, and some of this produce is currently being exported. The potential for more fruit exports remains high.

Saudi Arabia is the world's largest importer of live sheep, around 6 million in 1991, accounting for most of red meat consumption. Mutton is the preferred meat and a number of projects to breed sheep have developed. Local mutton production rose gradually in the 1980s from 66,000 tons in 1984 to 134,000 in 1991. Similarly, local beef production has grown steadily to around 32,000 tons, partly as a by-product of the burgeoning dairy industry. Domestic production of poultry surged in the 1980s, reaching 290,000 tons in 1991, the highest in the Arab world.

Egg production was around 170,000 tons in 1991, of which about 10 per cent was exported. The dairy sector is also well developed in the Kingdom, with a number of large plants supplying fresh milk and yoghurt. Milk production has risen substantially from 384,000 tons in 1984 to 550,000 in 1991. The Kingdom's consumption of fresh and frozen fish was put at 95,000 tons in 1991, of which 50,000 tons were accounted for by local catches. Fish farming is being encouraged and the national fishing company, Saudi Fisheries, that was set up in 1980, has played a key role in the revival of this sector. Exhibit 6.6 gives full details of Saudi Arabian agricultural production in recent years.

Imports and exports of agricultural products

The Kingdom's agricultural imports, including livestock, totalled SR11,120 million (US$2,965 million) in 1991, up from SR10,292 million (US$2,744 million) in 1989. Exhibit 6.7 shows both imports and exports between 1989 and 1991. Imports of live animals and meat products accounted for 33 per cent of the total. Even with the 12 per cent duty on red meat, imports remained generally less expensive and domestic demand for imported products continued to rise, reaching 163,000 tons in 1991. The 20 per cent import duty on poultry helped support domestic production and led to a sharp fall in imports to around 180,000 tons in 1991, mostly from France and Brazil. Imports of dairy products continued to rise, reaching 240,000 tons in 1991, with a total value of SR1,916 million (US$511 million), while fish imports, mostly from South East Asia and the other GCC countries, reached SR286 million (US$76.3 million).

Exhibit 6.6

Saudi Arabian agricultural production, 1984 - 91 (thousands of tons)

	1988-90 average price (US$ a ton)	*1984*	*1985*	*1986*	*1987*	*1988*	*1989*	*1990*	*1991*
Grain									
Wheat	553	1,398	2,135	2,544	2,647	3,192	3,208	3,600	3,900
Corn	193	5	5	9	15	20	35	36	35
Barley	267	7	3	13	136	186	315	400	500
Sorghum	208	35	43	31	126	128	130	140	145
Vegetables									
Potatoes	300	13	12	22	26	31	32	38	42
Onions	291	20	17	16	15	14	17	18	19
Watermelons	188	625	621	534	555	573	575	580	595
Other melons	430	176	169	181	212	230	238	242	245
Pumpkins	145	44	45	47	54	57	58	60	62
Egg plant	150	31	37	39	44	46	43	45	46
Tomatoes	204	328	331	370	334	356	385	393	430
Cucumbers	185	26	49	54	66	74	84	85	87
Carrots	240	19	20	18	24	25	27	30	31
Squash	250	28	42	46	55	67	70	74	90
Other vegetables	380	251	270	320	338	372	415	427	446
Fruit									
Oranges	400	27	42	47	51	54	56	62	63
Grapes	481	79	80	72	109	96	99	99	110
Peaches	780	7	9	11	10	13	14	15	16
Apples	685	8	11	14	19	24	28	30	32
Apricots	650	13	15	16	17	19	20	21	22
Pears	595	9	9	10	11	14	16	17	18
Pomegranates	212	10	13	11	14	15	17	18	18
Dates	333	454	456	460	502	505	528	542	545
Livestock & animal products									
Beef & veal	1,730	25	26	27	28	28	29	30	32
Mutton & lamb	2,937	66	92	99	109	112	115	122	134
Goat meat	1,789	12	12	13	17	19	22	23	25
Poultry	2,608	141	186	196	236	248	249	270	290
Milk	835	384	403	428	487	508	534	546	550
Eggs	1,985	104	134	138	114	152	154	165	170

Source: Ministry of Agriculture and Water, Riyadh, 1992 and US Department of Agriculture, Washington DC, 1991.

Imports of cereals have been declining recently, dropping to SR1,527 million (US$407 million) in 1991 from SR2,633 million (US$702 million) in 1989. The Kingdom is a net exporter of wheat, even though it imports 150,000 tons of wheat seeds a year. Grain imports are dominated by barley (around 4 million tons a year), rice, corn, soybean and other cereal products. Fruit and vegetables, both fresh and canned, constitute the largest import item, reaching SR2,271 million (US$606 million) in 1991. Even though domestic production has been rising, a large proportion of total consumption of fruit, onions, potatoes and cucumbers is accounted for by imported goods. Imports help keep prices reasonable for consumers and fill seasonal shortages. The import duty of 12 per cent serves as a small protection for domestic producers, who also

Exhibit 6.7

Agricultural imports and exports, 1989 - 91 (SR millions)

	Imports			*Exports*		
	1991	*1990*	*1989*	*1991*	*1990*	*1989*
Live animals	1,700	1,509	1,558	153	62	61
Meat products	1,954	1,526	1,202	98	16	24
Dairy products & eggs	1,916	1,752	1,551	278	143	122
Fish	286	204	242	15	20	40
Cereals	1,527	1,698	2,633	398	660	940
Fruits & vegetables	2,271	2,072	2,073	325	158	184
Sugar	300	338	327	48	55	22
Coffee, tea & spices	1,010	860	586	25	14	20
Feed grains	155	114	120	79	48	51
Total	**11,120**	**10,073**	**10,292**	**1,419**	**1,176**	**1,464**

Sources: Ministry of Finance & National Economy, Central Statistical Office, Foreign Trade Statistics, 1991.

benefit from subsidies for fertiliser and credit and machinery. The Kingdom has became the leading Middle Eastern importer of feed grains, providing the potential for expanding output of meat and milk.

In the last few years the European Community (EC) has provided around 25 per cent of the Kingdom's agricultural imports. This includes more than 2 million tons of barley and large quantities of dairy products and canned foods, estimated at a value of around US$1,700 million in 1991. The US provides 10 per cent of total agricultural imports, dominated by bulk items (barley, corn and rice) and high value items (including fresh fruit, fruit juice, nuts and canned foods). There has been an expansion in US exports of soybean oil, frozen poultry and some fruits. Other major suppliers are Turkey, Australia, New Zealand, Thailand, France and Brazil. Saudi imports from eastern Europe and China fell in the late 1980s because of competition from the EC and the US. Some smaller suppliers have gained, while others have dropped out. Chile, for example, has greatly expanded exports of grapes, apples, pears and some other horticultural products. Turkey has increased deliveries of sheep and pulses, while India recently crowded out Pakistan in exports of basmati rice to the Kingdom.

Wheat, eggs, dairy products, fruit and vegetables constitute the bulk of Saudi agricultural exports. Surplus crops amounting for SR1,419 million (US$378 million) were exported in 1991, up 20 per cent on the year before. Wheat exports reached SR398 million (US$106 million), fruit and vegetables brought in SR325 million (US$87 million), while the value of dairy products and eggs exported reached SR278 million (US$74 million). The domestic market for wheat is no more than 1 million tons and this has forced the government to launch an export programme in the mid-1980s to dispose of surplus production. According to the London-based International Wheat Council, Saudi Arabia exported around 2.1 million tons of wheat for the year ending June 1992, up from 1.58 million in 1986 but below the record 2.43 million in 1988. The Kingdom donates sizeable amounts of its wheat output every year to developing countries, with the rest exported to western Europe, mainly Portugal, (202,600 tons), other Arab countries (200,000 tons), the Far East, mainly Indonesia and Malaysia, (545,900 tons) and Africa (717,000 tons).

Constraints and opportunities

The transformation of the Saudi agricultural sector from traditional farming to largescale commercial farming has entailed significant economic cost, particularly through the subsidies provided to farmers (direct payment, price support and others) and through depletion of non-renewable water resources. Achieving balanced growth and deriving the social and political advantages associated with agricultural development are, however, more important to the government than the cost of supporting farmers.

The Kingdom is not the only country to have a price support programme for farmers, nor is it the most expensive programme. The EC, the US, Japan, Switzerland and Sweden among others provide ample subsidies to their respective agricultural sectors. The amount of support provided as a percentage of value of agricultural production is highest in Switzerland (80 per cent), followed by Japan (60 per cent), Sweden (59 per cent), the EC (49 per cent) and the US (30 per cent). Subsidies disbursed to Saudi farmers in 1991 were around SR7.95 billion (US$2.12 billion). Including the SR756 million of loans extended by the Agricultural Bank and other subsidies of SR149 million, total support for the agricultural sector was SR8.855 billion (US$2.361 billion). This constituted 45 per cent of the farmgate value of agricultural commodities produced in the Kingdom and compares favourably with the corresponding levels in the industrialised countries (shown in Exhibit 6.8).

A more sensitive subject is agriculture's drain on the country's limited water resources. A definite assessment of these resources does not yet exist and the impact of the current depletion rate cannot therefore be precisely evaluated. Ignorance often breeds misconceived worries, which is why the authorities need to complete their assessments as soon as possible and provide an up-to-date evaluation of these resources. The government's concern about water use has been voiced in the chapter on

Exhibit 6.8

Worldwide subsidies to agriculture, 1991

	Amount (US$ billions)	*As % of agricultural production*
Switzerland	5.2	80
Japan	31.5	66
Sweden	2.7	59
EC	85.6	49
US	28.1	30
Saudi Arabia	2.3	44

Source: OECD figures as reported by the *Economist*, 28 November 1992 and our estimates for Saudi Arabia.

agricultural production in the current five-year plan. It states that:

> with the exception of the southwestern region, the Kingdom has an arid climate and very low rainfall. Thus, the potential for renewable surface water is very limited. With the rapid expansion in farm holdings, largescale agricultural projects have relied primarily on water supplies from non-renewable underground aquifers, which provide over 80 per cent of the agricultural sector's water requirements. The demand for underground aquifers' water supplies has increased enormously over the past 10 years. Further largescale spatial expansion of agriculture would lead to a critical imbalance between water demand and sustainable water supply, which might negatively affect the role of agriculture in the long term.

A major objective in the water sector during the period of the current plan is to reduce the rate of water consumption in the Kingdom. According to the plan, "This can be achieved through conservation measures, higher efficiency in the use of water and by switching agriculture away from highly water-intensive crops, especially in areas that depend almost exclusively on non-renewable water resources". Total water use in the Kingdom will be reduced by 8 per cent from 16.2 billion cubic metres a year in 1990 to 14.9 billion cubic metres in 1995, compared with a total increase of 89 per cent during the period of the fourth plan.

Saudi Arabia has three main types of water resource: non-renewable groundwater, renewable ground and surface water and desalinated water. Its average rainfall is low and irregular; while the average is over 300mm a year in the mountains of the Hejaz and Asir, it can be as low as 30 to 90mm a year in the northeastern and central areas. The Rubh al-Khali (empty quarter) in the southeast can be without water for up to 10 years. The western coastal plain and particularly the southern part, the Tihama, receives 60 per cent of the country's total rainfall. Rainfall there has been caught in a series of dams, such as those at Jizan, Najran and Abha, which reduce the run-off eastward into the desert and westward down the coastal plain to the sea. The renewable water resources are composed of renewable ground and surface water fed from rainfall, with an average annual supply of around 1.85 billion cubic metres, accounting for about 11 per cent of total annual water consumption.

Desalinated water provides the bulk of the country's drinking water in major cities but constitutes only about 2.5 per cent of the Kingdom's annual water consumption. With 22 plants producing 2 million cubic metres daily, the Kingdom has become the largest producer of desalinated water in the world, accounting for around 30 per cent of world output. The Saline Water Conversion Company (SWCC) runs the majority of the desalination plants and more are being built to boost the supply of potable water. Desalinated water cannot sustain agricultural production because it is too costly to produce. The cost varies between SR2 and SR10 a cubic metre, depending on the plant.

Treated wastewater is still a very underdeveloped aspect of water supply and consumption, accounting for not more than 1 per cent of annual consumption. The most important source of water in the Kingdom is the non-renewable fossil aquifers, which account for about 87.5 per cent of water consumption. However, the supply is finite and the increasingly rapid depletion of this source is causing considerable concern. It is reported that the extraction level from these aquifers has dropped by 100 metres in the past 10 years.

The opportunities in the Saudi agricultural sector remain sizeable. The goal of achieving balanced agricultural growth and promoting import substitution for certain crops has not yet been attained. Gains from increased production of selected crops will allow overall agricultural production to grow, will generate imports for the thriving agro-industries and will contribute to the diversification of the Kingdom's economy. The new commodities chosen for expansion are likely to be tested for their adaptability to Saudi growing conditions, as well as their comparative advantage and profitability for farmers. World market prices and prospects for future trade will have an impact on the extent to which farmers are encouraged to grow a particular crop.

Diversification of agricultural production is expected to receive a higher priority in the years ahead. Wheat overproduction will be reduced and other crops currently imported will be encouraged. Conditions exist to allow Saudi Arabia to become a significant producer of vegetables which can be grown and harvested in several months (eg cucumbers, green beans and squash). Some varieties of sweetcorn, potatoes, peanuts and pumpkins mature quickly and could possibly be planted in May and harvested in July on land used to grow wheat during the winter.

There is also an increasing awareness of the need to reduce wastage of crops by improving storage, transport and preservation facilities. The increasingly sophisticated domestic consumers and the requirement of the export markets demand better quality and are prepared to pay higher prices for it. Marketing companies are being set up to purchase, grade, pack and distribute produce from local farmers. Additional facilities to preserve excess production and to upgrade packaging and distribution for the domestic and world markets will be needed. Future reductions in subsidies will require greater efficiency in agricultural production and this will undoubtedly create opportunities for project management expertise, machinery and equipment (including maintenance) and better seeds, fertilisers and pesticides.

There will also be opportunities in food processing, a sector that the authorities are keen to develop, with a targeted growth rate of 10 per cent annually. In 1990 the Food Products Company was established as a joint stock firm with the specific aim of using Saudi agricultural output. Eleven projects have been selected for investment, including animal feed, date processing, pasta, frozen vegetables, potato chips, meat processing, baby food and cornflakes. Savola is planning to establish a sugar factory, while the National Industrialisation Company and other industrial ventures also have plans for a number of food-processing projects.

The trend in world trade and the requirements of the General

Agreement on Tariffs and Trade necessitate a gradual reduction of agricultural subsidies, especially for wheat, with more resources allocated to barley and hardy crops that require less water. The achievements so far in the agricultural sector and the linkages established with the burgeoning food-processing industry suggest that growth in this sector is bound to continue, even though the composition of crops produced might change in the next few years.

7 Financial and capital markets

Introduction: the process of financial development

Financial development and economic growth are closely linked. In the early stages of economic development financial markets tend to be either non-existent or fragmented. A large part of national savings is invested in physical assets (durable consumer goods, real estate and precious metals), which contribute little to economic growth, and the balance is simply left in cash or in domestic and foreign currency bank accounts. The lack of diversified financial instruments forces savers to invest excessively in their own business activities. The structure of private sector capital is built upon the foundation of family firms, with the owners unwilling to relinquish control over their companies by going public.

Underdeveloped financial markets have various economic limitations. Commercial banks tend to be predominantly confined to deposit and loan activities and the mentality associated with such services. Regulations do not encourage the rise of specialised financial institutions. Companies often choose the traditional methods of raising funds, depending too much on internal sources of capital and borrowing from commercial banks and specialised credit institutions. The supply of equity and debt instruments tends to be limited, while the demand for these instruments is restrained by the absence of viable secondary markets. Securities, if unmarketable, lose their attraction as liquid instruments and savers become reluctant to purchase them. Besides, financial underdevelopment suppresses entrepreneurial activities, accentuates speculation, increases inflationary pressures on physical assets and encourages capital outflow as better opportunities are sought abroad.

The process of increasing the productive capacity of a country to generate economic growth requires the full mobilisation and efficient utilisation of available domestic resources. Financial development stands at the very centre of this process. Financial markets, which act as a filter of information on available resources, provide savers with the chance to diversify their assets and enhance their yield, while borrowers will be able to draw on a larger pool of resources. Financial development involves not only the creation of new financial instruments and financial intermediaries and institutions but also the regulatory and legal framework within which such development can take place. The process can be hampered by financial repression from policies such as interest rate ceilings, high levels of monetary growth, controls on the movement of capital or rigid exchange rate policies.

"Financialisation" is a complex process involving changing public perceptions, a higher level of financial sophistication and the availability of a wide range of financial services and monetary assets. During the early stages, government and public corporations start issuing their own debt and equity instruments. These institutions command the trust and confidence of the public at large and can expect a good response to their public issues. Even if countries do not need to borrow domestically, a government bond scheme helps to create a benchmark for corporate bonds. The advantages of issuing debt instruments are not limited to generating additional revenue for the government; equally importantly, such instruments serve as a tool for better implementation of effective monetary policy (discounting bills, open market operations and so on) and simultaneously provide new domestic investment channels for the private sector.

With time, as debt and equity instruments become more widely accepted, commercial banks, insurance companies and industrial and commercial institutions can start floating their own issues. This creates a range of financial products differentiated by credit risk and quality. Eventually, secondary markets will be established to ensure liquidity and to promote confidence in the financial system. Development of capital markets is being actively pursued in Saudi Arabia. The government has been issuing public debt instruments to finance its budgets, to manage domestic liquidity more effectively and to create new investment media for the private sector. As government bonds and Treasury bills gain depth and acceptability, they will open the way for other debt instruments to be introduced.

The Saudi stock market has regained the vigour it exhibited before the Gulf crisis, attracting new share flotations and a range of domestic investment. The surge in market activity has been the result mainly of a general feeling of confidence and optimism in the Kingdom arising from the recent upturn in economic activity and the improvement in the region's geopolitical atmosphere. The return of money sent abroad during the Gulf crisis has boosted the already substantial domestic liquidity and has also contributed to the stock market boom. The excess liquidity available in the domestic banking sector that is normally deposited with banks abroad was estimated at US$25 billion at the end of 1991. Money kept outside the banking system, believed to be around SR30 billion (US$8 billion), is also finding its way into the stock market. Another important factor has been the drop in Saudi riyal interest rates (in line with the corresponding decline in US dollar interest rates), which has increased the appeal of Saudi shares and government development bonds to investors. Three-month riyal deposit rates dropped to 3 per cent in the fourth quarter of 1992, compared to 9.9 per cent in the first quarter of 1989.

The Saudi riyal market

Exchange rate policy

Saudi Arabia follows a managed exchange rate policy, with stability against the dollar as its most important element. Given the current system of floating exchange rates for the world's major currencies, economies without a diversified production base and which are well integrated into the world economy are more vulnerable to external disturbances and have found it advantageous to peg their currencies to a major international currency or to a basket of currencies. Since prices of Saudi Arabia's exports are mostly denominated in dollars (oil, petrochemicals, wheat; etc), while a good portion of the Kingdom's overseas investment is believed to have be in dollar-based assets, it is logical for the monetary authority to emphasise stability of the riyal against the US dollar.

In the 1950s and 1960s the newly created Saudi currency was linked to the gold standard, while its value was mostly expressed in sterling. After sterling was devalued in 1967 and the dollar price of gold was raised in 1971 and 1973 the daily value of the currency started to be expressed in dollars, though still technically linked to gold. IMF regulations required exchange rates to be held within 2.25 per cent on either side of the dollar gold parity. As the dollar value continued to fall in the international markets during the first half of the 1970s, the Kingdom was attracted to the IMF's Special Drawing Right (SDR) as a substitute for gold. The SDR is a basket of currencies with the US dollar accounting for 40 per cent, the Deutschmark for 21 per cent, the Japanese yen for 17 per cent and the French franc and pound sterling for 11 per cent each. In 1975 the riyal became officially pegged to the SDR at the rate of SR4.2825. The chosen SDR benchmark was the pre-1973 SDR, which was very close to the dollar in value. In practice, riyal exchange rates were allowed to fluctuate within margins of 7.25 per cent of the fixed relationship with the SDR.

Until 1980 the riyal appreciated against the US dollar, as the latter weakened against major currencies. Since then, however, a number of considerations have influenced determination of the exchange rate and have led to an effective pegging of the Saudi riyal to the dollar, the intervention currency, with limited flexibility. During the period from 1981 to 1984, when the dollar appreciated against other major currencies, the pursuit of this policy led to an appreciation of the riyal against the SDR by about 17 per cent, in effect breaching the declared margins around the SDR parity. On the other hand, when the dollar lost ground in the exchange markets, the riyal in turn depreciated against the SDR. By September 1992 the riyal had lost 25 per cent of its SDR value (see Exhibit 7.1 for details).

During the first half of the 1980s the riyal was devalued several times against the dollar but only by small amounts. The largest devaluation, at 2.6 per cent, was on 1 June 1986 when the riyal was revalued from SR3.645 to SR3.745 to the dollar. This followed a 1.1 per cent devaluation in June 1985 and several other, smaller devaluations in the preceding years. There

Exhibit 7.1

Saudi riyal exchange rates, 1981 - 92

	Riyal/ US dollar	*US dollar/ SDR*	*Riyal/ SDR*	*Divergence from parity (%)*
1981				
Feburary 11	3.335	1.23834	4.12986	-3.57
March 3	3.345	1.21578	4.06678	-5.04
April 22	3.355	1.20341	4.03744	-5.72
May 14	3.365	1.17968	3.96962	-7.31
May 18	3.375	1.17475	3.96478	-7.42
May 25	3.385	1.17164	3.96600	-7.39
June 7	3.395	1.14400	3.88388	-9.31
June 22	3.405	1.15402	3.92944	-8.25
August 8	3.415	1.11360	3.80294	-11.20
December 31	3.415	1.16396	3.97492	-7.18
1982				
April 5	3.425	1.11561	3.82096	-10.78
June 30	3.435	1.08860	3.73934	-12.68
December 31	3.435	1.10311	3.78918	-11.52
1983				
March 30	3.445	1.07574	3.70592	-13.46
August 7	3.465	1.04679	3.62713	-15.30
August 14	3.475	1.04154	3.61935	-15.49
December 25	3.495	1.04087	3.63784	-15.05
December 31	3.495	1.04695	3.65909	-14.56
1984				
January 8	3.505	1.03610	3.63153	-15.20
March 18	3.515	1.06257	3.73493	-12.79
June 6	3.505	1.04959	3.67881	-14.10
August 12	3.525	1.01857	3.59046	-16.16
September 10	3.535	1.00576	3.55536	-16.98
September 18	3.555	0.99586	3.54028	-17.33
December 27	3.575	0.98425	3.51869	-17.84
December 31	3.575	0.98021	3.50425	-18.17
1985				
February 27	3.595	0.94618	3.40152	-20.57
March 7	3.605	0.95040	3.42619	-20.00
June 10	3.645	0.99562	3.62900	-15.26
December 31	3.645	1.09842	4.00374	-6.51
1986				
June 1	3.745	1.14314	4.28106	-0.03
December 31	3.745	1.22319	4.58085	6.97
1987				
December 31	3.745	1.41866	5.31288	24.06
1988				
December 31	3.745	1.34570	5.03965	17.68
1989				
December 31	3.745	1.31416	4.92153	14.92
1990				
December 31	3.745	1.42270	5.3279	24.40
1991				
Q1	3.745	1.34630	5.0420	17.70
Q2	3.745	1.31450	4.9229	14.9
Q3	3.745	1.36800	5.1232	19.6
Q4	3.745	1.43040	5.3570	25.0
1992				
Q1	3.745	1.37170	5.1372	19.9
Q2	3.745	1.43120	5.3597	25.1
Q3	3.745	1.45260	5.5158	28.7

Source: Saudi Arabian Monetary Agency, *Quarterly Bulletins* and IMF *International Financial Statistics*.

has been only one instance in the past (6 June 1984) when the riyal exchange rate was revalued upwards, moving against the direction generally expected in the market presumably to introduce an element of uncertainty and to discourage speculation in the currency. The move was reversed on 12 August in the same year and the downward trend continued.

Devaluation during that period was perceived as a controlled adjustment to a current account deficit created by the decline in the Kingdom's oil revenues. It raised the riyal value of oil exports denominated in dollars and gave a boost to the Kingdom's emerging non-oil industries, both in the domestic market (import substitution) and internationally (export promotion). It also raised prices of imports, discouraged consumption and helped reduce deficits in the balance of services and transfers.

For the last seven years the value of the riyal has been maintained at SR3.745 to the dollar. To maintain such a fixed exchange rate parity, Saudi riyal deposit rates have generally remained quite close, usually less than 0.5 per cent above or below, comparable dollar deposits (see Exhibit 7.2). The excess liquidity in the market that used to end up in the offshore markets of Bahrain and London has gradually come under control. SAMA'S ability effectively to manage liquidity in the riyal market has improved considerably in the last few years, with the introduction of such instruments as Banking Security Deposit Accounts (BSDAs) and Government Development Bonds. SAMA started issuing short-term Treasury bills in November 1991 to replace the BSDAs.

Few speculative positions (short riyal/long dollar) have been recorded in the last few years, as evidenced by the shrinking gap between riyal and dollar interest rates. When speculation reached its peak in 1986 before the 1 June devaluation, three-month riyal deposit rates jumped more than 5 per cent above comparable Eurodollar rates, with overnight rates at one point reaching 20 per cent. Such speculative fever has subsided recently, with the gap between riyal and dollar rates dropping to less than 0.1 per cent in 1991/92.

It is highly unlikely that the Saudi riyal will be devalued again at any time soon. There are new considerations shaping the Kingdom's exchange rate policy. The main goal is to minimise exchange rate risks for the Saudi private sector to facilitate long-term planning and to encourage repatriation of capital from abroad. The strategy of pegging the Saudi riyal to the dollar also aims at maintaining stability between the GCC currencies. Since most of the Kingdom's exports are oil-related and are priced in dollars, a stable exchange rate against the dollar makes it easier for the authorities to forecast government revenues in local currencies.

Another aim of the fixed dollar parity is to contain transmission of inflation from abroad. During periods when the dollar is firming on the exchange market, for example, the fixed SR/US$ parity leads to the appreciation of the riyal against the currencies of the Kingdom's major trading partners in Europe and Japan. In 1991 the US was the largest exporter to the Kingdom, accounting for 16.7 per cent of total Saudi imports, followed by Japan with 15.3 per cent, the UK with 11.3 per cent, Germany with 7.4 per cent and Switzerland with 6.6 per cent; the other European countries accounted for most of the rest.

Even during periods when the dollar has depreciated, the real

Exhibit 7.2

Saudi Riyal deposit rates and Eurodollar rates compared, 1984 - 92 (% per annum, quarterly averages)

	Three-month SR deposit rates	*Three-month Eurodollar deposit rates*	*Differentials (SR minus US$)*
1984			
Q1	9.62	10.75	-1.13
Q2	11.75	12.19	-0.44
Q3	11.50	11.44	0.06
Q4	8.87	8.62	0.25
1985			
Q1	9.25	9.06	0.19
Q2	7.87	7.75	0.12
Q3	8.87	8.12	0.75
Q4	7.87	7.97	-0.10
1986			
Q1	9.12	7.34	1.78
Q2	8.75	6.81	1.94
Q3	7.12	6.06	1.06
Q4	8.00	6.31	1.69
1987			
Q1	6.44	6.56	-0.12
Q2	6.69	7.12	-0.43
Q3	7.69	8.31	-0.62
Q4	5.37	7.25	-1.88
1988			
Q1	6.63	6.81	-0.18
Q2	7.59	7.60	-0.01
Q3	8.57	8.26	0.31
Q4	9.43	9.10	0.33
1989			
Q1	9.70	9.67	0.03
Q2	9.56	9.61	-0.05
Q3	8.66	8.77	-0.11
Q4	8.22	8.46	-0.24
1990			
Q1	7.94	8.26	-0.32
Q2	8.06	8.32	-0.26
Q3	8.16	8.03	0.13
Q4	7.90	7.89	0.01
1991			
Q1	6.85	6.68	0.17
Q2	5.99	5.99	0.00
Q3	5.61	5.67	-0.06
Q4	4.86	4.84	0.03
1992			
Q1	4.04	4.04	0.00
Q2	3.90	3.89	0.01
Q3	3.24	3.30	-0.06

Source: Saudi Arabia Monetary Agency, *Quarterly Bulletins*, various issues.

effective exchange rate of the Saudi riyal has not dropped proportionately. The real effective exchange rate of the Saudi riyal represents the ratio of an index (with 1985 = 100 as a base) of its weighted average exchange rate against the currencies of the Kingdom's major trading partners. A real effective exchange rate index is broadly defined as a nominal effective exchange rate adjusted for relative movements in Saudi Arabia's domestic inflation (measured by the consumer price index) and the inflation rates of its major trading partners. An increase in the index represents appreciation of the riyal and a decline in the index a depreciation of the riyal. The IMF's *International Financial Statistics* give yearly and monthly values of both the nominal and the real effective exchange rates. The Kingdom has generally recorded low domestic rates of inflation because of low utility prices and the subsidies that the government maintains on various goods and services. As a matter of fact, because domestic inflation in Saudi Arabia has generally been lower than that prevailing in the Kingdom's major trading partners, the currency's real effective exchange rate showed only a slight depreciation in 1991/92, even though the dollar lost around 8 per cent of its value *vis-a-vis* the SDR during this period. The policy of a fixed parity need not, therefore, hamper the competitiveness of the Kingdom's trading sectors.

New financial instruments

More sophistication is gradually being introduced to the Kingdom's exchange markets. Today there exists an efficient forward market, with competitive prices quoted for up to one year. Quotations are available from one to five years from a limited number of banks, mainly on a one-sided price basis. A major impediment to the development of hedging operations in the Kingdom was resolved with the establishment of two benchmarks, SIBOR (Saudi Interbank Offered Rate) and a Saudi prime rate.

Quotes for riyal forward rate agreements (FRAs) are also available from a few banks but no formal market making has yet been initiated. The focus has been on the shorter-dated maturities, with a preference for six-month contracts catering to commercial interests. To date, only limited activity has been undertaken (predominantly wholesale) and it must be stressed that, given this embryonic state, the market is subject to inconsistent liquidity. The absence of futures and options contracts on an exchange-traded basis is a limiting factor.

Riyal interest rate swap activity is extremely limited. This is attributable to the lack of natural receivers in the market. The recent advent of riyal-based fixed rate, medium-term funding operations greatly enhances the potential for future activity. Riyal interest rate caps have received the most favourable response of all the off-balance sheet instruments. Again, relatively few banks are active in this market but commercial demand has been quite widespread. As yet, only short-dated caps have been offered (predominantly for one year), with a commercial preference for one-month fixings, at strikes only modestly above prevailing rate levels.

Markets for government bonds and Treasury bills

The government bond market

The most important financial development in the late 1980s was the issuance of public debt instruments by the Saudi government. The introduction of government bonds and Treasury bills will undoubtedly have a significant impact on the Kingdom's financial markets. Government bonds create a benchmark for corporate bonds and the development of debt markets will give a boost to the region's fledgling stock markets. Chapter 2 contains a discussion of the development of the government bond market in Saudi Arabia. Total development bond outstandings at the end of 1992 are put at around SR140 billion (US$37.3 billion), up from SR71 billion (US$18.9 billion) at the end of 1989. It is estimated that up to two-thirds of the bonds issued have been taken by government institutions, effectively giving the government a liability of SR93 billion (US$24.8 billion) to repay itself. The outstanding public debt held by the private sector does not, therefore, exceed SR47 billion (US$12.5 billion).

Since the inception of the government bond programme, SAMA has been offering a total of SR1.5 billion of two- to five- year bonds every two weeks. The minimum denomination offered through the primary market is SR1 million to the banks, dropping to a minimum of SR50,000 for individual buyers. Primary distribution is undertaken on a subscription basis, ie SAMA posts the yield (*via* the "earnings" mechanism) at which bonds will be sold in the primary market and at which eligible investors can subscribe for an allocation. Exhibit 7.3 illustrates a description of dealing conventions for a sample issue. The aggregate amount of government bonds open to subscription is announced by telex to the banks on Saturday morning (a business day in Saudi Arabia). The earnings for each tranche are posted but with no indication of how many bonds in each tranche are actually available. The banks and the autonomous government bodies have until noon the following Monday to respond to the subscription notice, simply indicating how many bonds of each

Exhibit 7.3

Saudi government bonds, dealing conventions, technical characteristics and pricing mechanism

- **Wholesale dealing size:** SR5 million.
- **Standard bid/offer spread:** 20 basis points.
- **Transaction costs:** none, net quotes.
- **Tax:** (a) there is no witholding tax;
  (b) the bonds are exempt from *Zakat* (religious tax) if held for at least one year or until maturity.
- **Settlement:** seven days (a two-day settlement can be negotiated).
- **Trading hours:** 9 am to 1 pm (except Fridays and official holidays).
- **Listing requirements:** none.
- **Pricing mechanism:** bonds are officially quoted, not in yield terms, but with value statements defined in terms of earnings.

Example

Government bond	Series 5.06
Maturity	5.8.93
Price	106.90/10
Earnings	SR48,000

The earnings are equivalent to the semi-annual coupon in the conventional sense. In this case, SR48,000 x 2=SR96,000 or, restated, a coupon of 9.6% against the initial subscrition principal of SR1 million. The bond equivalent yield in the example is 5.34%. The series number translates to: the sixth issue of the five-year tranche.

tranche are desired. SAMA notifies each subscribing institution during that Monday afternoon of its allocated subscription. In the event of oversubscription, a simple, *pro rata* allocation is made.

Payment for and settlement of the allocated bonds is made the following Monday (seven calendar days later). No physical securities are issued. SAMA, as fiscal agent, employs a book entry mechanism to register ownership of the bonds in the case of banks and autonomous government bodies; other retails buyers are deemed to be beneficial owners of the bonds but the registration remains in the bank's name. Redemption and earnings payments are passed back through the banking system. The institutional infrastructure to accommodate the repository and transfer mechanisms necessary to support a physical securities market is still lacking. Besides, the book entry method keeps SAMA informed about the distribution of the bonds.

Steps were taken recently to improve the liquidity of the government bond market. In August 1988 a repurchase facility was established, permitting banks to discount up to 25 per cent of their holding to SAMA at 28-day maturities. The monetary authority sets the repo rate daily. This facility became more flexible later, with repo maturities permitted to range from 28 days to overnight. During the Gulf crisis banks were allowed to discount up to 50 per cent of their holdings to SAMA. However, offers to discount bonds must be justified by the banks' liquidity needs and should not be made to take advantage of market conditions. The restriction is intended in order that SAMA does not end up acquiring a large, permanent stock of discounted bonds, ie monetising the budget deficit. Borrowing by the government from SAMA is prohibited by law for the same reason.

In early 1989 SAMA approved plans for six Saudi banks (National Commercial Bank, Saudi American Bank, Saudi British Bank, Riyadh Bank, Al Bank Al Saudi Al Fransi and United Saudi Commercial Bank) to act as market makers for the bonds, thus establishing an effective secondary market. The SR50,000 (US$13,300) minimum purchase limit for individual investors was also introduced. By the end of 1992 there were still no figures available for the volume of business on the secondary market. However, it was estimated at around SR300 million (US$80 million) to SR500 million (US$133.3 million) a week. SAMA supports the role of the market makers by providing a liquidity backstop through the repo arrangements described above.

An interesting development took place in June 1990 when residents of GCC countries were permitted to acquire bonds in the secondary market. Commercial banks in the Kingdom were told that they could sell the two- to five-year development bonds to several new categories of investor, including banks operating in the Bahrain-based offshore market, overseas branches of Saudi firms and any institution incorporated, or simply resident, in the any of the six members of the GCC. Finally, SAMA has encouraged banks to offer mutual funds to the public, either exclusively in government bonds or in a mixture of bonds and other securities. This development has enabled investors with much smaller balances to acquire bonds. Banks may also offer repurchase opportunities to their own customers.

From a risk management perspective, the existing limitations of the secondary market are further compounded by a lack of indigenous hedging instruments. Exchange-traded futures and options do not exist and the derivatives market is still very much in the embryonic stage. The domestic banks offer riyal-denominated interest rate caps and FRA products that provide an element of protection for future cash flows but there is nothing currently on offer designed to eliminate principal risk. The close linkage between returns on Saudi government bonds and those on US Treasuries does allow the synthetic implementation of riyal hedging programmes by tapping into the tremendous liquidity available in the US market. The currency risk embedded in this crossborder play should be noted, even though it is generally considered to be minimal given the longstanding parity between the riyal and the dollar.

The Treasury bill market

Saudi Arabia started to issue Treasury bills in November 1991 to tap domestic liquidity and to smooth out short-term cash flow problems. The bills, which are offered in maturities ranging from one to 12 months, also give domestic banks a viable short-term instrument to help them manage their excess liquidity. The bills replaced the SR1.5 billion weekly issues by SAMA of BSDAs that were employed as a liquidity adjustment mechanism. The four-week, 13-week and 26-week bills are issued on a weekly basis (Monday for Wednesday settlement), while the 52-week bills are issued once a month (last Tuesday of the month for Thursday settlement). Again no physical securities are issued and the amount raised varies from one week to another. A detailed comparison between Treasury bills and government bonds is given in Exhibit 7.4. The monthly bonds provide the bulk of government financing requirements, while the bills are intended mainly as a cash management instrument to smooth cash flows and provide short-term bridge financing.

SAMA later introduced a repurchase facility for Saudi Treasury bills, through which banks may raise additional liquidity when needed by selling back up to 75 per cent of their holdings at a specified rate, with an agreement to repurchase them later. In May 1992 a reverse repurchase facility was introduced, aimed at further improving management of day to day liquidity in the interbank market. Banks with excess overnight liquidity may buy Treasury bills under an agreement to resell them to SAMA. The amount available for reverse repos is determined at SAMA's discretion. The reverse repo facility is reserved for residual liquidity of the banks and not as a substitute for outright purchasing of Treasury bills. SAMA sets the daily rate for the repo and reverse repo facilities (a spread of 50 basis points between the two has been holding) and has given itself the option of executing no reverse repos on any single day. This has kept the overnight riyal interest rate from fluctuating outside a narrow 0.5 per cent band and has helped to link deposit rates more closely to corresponding dollar rates (SAMA is unlikely to pay more for riyal liabilities than it is earning on dollar deposits overseas). The purpose of the repurchase and reverse repurchase facilities is to help stem the flow of excess liquidity out of the banking system towards overnight dollar

Exhibit 7.4

Comparison between government bonds and Treasury bills

	Government bonds	*Treasury bills*
Maturities & frequency of issue	Maturities of two, three, four and five years issued every two weeks.	Maturities of four, 13 and 26 weeks issued every week, maturities of 52 weeks issued once a month.
Amount	SR1.5 billion for all issues every two weeks.	Not specified by maturity; total range is between SR1 billion and SR2 billion.
Denomination	Multiples of SR1 million to banks and SR50,000 from banks to customers.	Multiples of SR1 million for banks and SR50,000 to customers.
Secondary market	Exists.	Will exist, banks only to buy primary bills.
Pricing	20 bp to 50 bp above comparable US bonds.	Very close to SR interbank rates but at discretion of SAMA.
Repo facility	25% of banks' total holdings. No reverse repo.	75% of banks' total holdings. Reverse repo available.
Authorised purchasers	Saudi banks and their branches overseas, government institutions, resident investors, GCC resident institutions, mutual funds available to the public.	Saudi banks, government institutions, resident investors, classified non-residents.

deposits and to channel it instead to domestic outlets.

Banks are licensed to trade the Treasury bills in the secondary market and to sell them on to customers who may find it advantageous to reduce their bank deposits in favour of more liquid instruments with a better yield. Banks may sell the bills to customers in denominations of SR50,000 at rates slightly better than corresponding bank deposits. There are no reserves required on Treasury bill holdings, whereas banks must keep 7 per cent of demand deposits and 2 per cent of time deposits as non-interest bearing, required reserves with SAMA.

There is no private bond market to speak of in Saudi Arabia. A domestic Saudi riyal bond market existed until 1978, when SAMA imposed a moratorium on Saudi riyal issues. In the mid-1980s a few dollar-denominated floating rate notes were arranged for local borrowers in the Kingdom by Saudi banks and the Offshore Banking Units in Bahrain. A few Saudi banks are exploring the possibility of issuing certificates of deposit (CDs). If a market for CDs develops, it will greatly assist the broadening of the financial markets in the Kingdom.

The Saudi stock market

Stock market listings in Saudi Arabia have increased substantially during

Exhibit 7.5

Public companies and their capital

Sector	*Number of companies*	*Paid-up capital (SR billions)*	*Percentage of total market capitalisation*
Banks	11	4.20	7.9
Agriculture	8	1.44	2.7
Industry (including cement)	28	17.59	33.0
Electricity	10	23.46	44.1
Services	21	6.50	12.3
Total	**78**	**53.19**	**100.0**

Sources: Saudi Council of Chambers of Commerce and Industry, 1991.

the last decade from 37 joint stock companies with a combined paid-up capital of SR21.2 billion (US$5.7 billion) in 1980 to 78 companies by the end of 1992. The combined capital of listed companies totalled SR53.2 billion (US$14.2 billion) in 1990 and rose to SR65 billion (US$17.3 billion) in 1992, following the increases in capital of such firms as Riyadh Bank, United Saudi Commercial Bank, Savola, Mubarrad, Saudi Industrial Development Company, Al-Baha Investment and Development Company, the Saudi Pharmaceutical Industries & Medical Appliances, Bank Al Jazira, Saudi Cairo Bank, Al Saudi Al Faransi Bank and Saudi British Bank, among others. Electricity companies accounted for the biggest share of that capital in 1990 at 44.1 per cent, followed by industrial firms (including cement companies) at 33 per cent, services at 12.3 per cent, banks at 7.9 per cent and agricultural companies at 2.7 per cent (see Exhibit 7.5 for details).

Share trading

Of the listed joint stock companies only 60 are publicly tradeable, eight agricultural companies, 13 services companies, 19 industrial companies, nine utility companies and 11 financial companies. Only shares of Saudi companies may be traded in the Kingdom. Shares may normally be acquired only by Saudi citizens, except in special circumstances, such as the 1984 SABIC issue when specified portions were made available to GCC citizens.

A decree issued by SAMA in 1985 ruled that all trading in stocks had to be done through banks using a cumbersome system of telex and telephone calls. Also in 1985 the Saudi Shares Registration Company (SSRC) was formed and capitalised at SR11 million, with equal shares held by all banks in the Kingdom. The company acts as an integrated central registry for all shares traded in the market.

More recently SAMA has instituted reforms aimed at boosting trade but its main move, the opening of a central trading hall in May 1987, was abruptly cancelled. A new screen trading system, the Electronic Securities Information System (ESIS), was introduced in 1990 to run parallel to the old system. ESIS is a strictly computerised dealing scheme which will allow greater liquidity in the market.

The mechanism of a share transaction is as follows. Anyone wishing to buy or sell shares in the market approaches a branch of a bank and completes an application form indicating amount and preferred price; buyers have to pay in advance. Banks then try to match buyers and sellers, first within their own branch network and then with the central coordinating unit of other banks through a clearing office at SAMA. Forward dealing and the acceptance of post-dated cheques are both prohibited and banks are responsible for the settlement of shares. Banks may charge a maximum of 1 per cent of the value of the shares traded, split between the buyer and the seller. Officially, brokers are not allowed to be active participants in the Saudi market and banks are forbidden to act as market makers.

Market performance

The depth of the market, ie the value of shares traded as a percentage of total market value of shares outstanding, has generally been low by international standards, averaging less than 5 per cent for many years before rising to around 10 per cent in 1992. The reasons for the thinness of trading and the shallowness of the market are varied. For one thing, as can be seen in Exhibit 7.6, not more than 38 per cent of the shares of joint stock companies are held by individuals and are available for trading. The rest are held mostly by the government, public sector institutions and foreign entities (holding mainly bank shares); and most of these shares are not traded. Another reason is the concentration of ownership of shares in a few hands, with the large Saudi trading families having up to 20 per cent of those shares held by the Saudi private sector. By controlling large blocks of shares, these families obtain board representation and influence on the management of companies. They are, therefore, less likely to sell their holdings; on the contrary, they tend to pick up additional shares of companies in which they are interested whenever possible. This is why the number of shareholders of any Saudi company declines sharply soon after the stock becomes available in the secondary market.

The movement of share prices in the Kingdom has generally reflected economic conditions in the country. Share prices fell in 1983 to 1986, following the drop in the government's oil revenues and the

Exhibit 7.6

Estimated ownership of Saudi joint stock companies, 1988 (%)

Sector	*Government and public sector institutions*	*Banks and pension funds*	*Foreigners*	*Saudi Individuals*	*Others*
Banking	0.1	3.4	39.4	57.1	0.0
Industry	15.0	7.5	5.8	70.5	1.2
Services	71.3	3.6	–	25.1	0.0
Agriculture	6.3	6.7	–	86.7	0.3
Total market	**54.1**	**4.5**	**2.9**	**38.2**	**0.3**

Source: Al Dukheil, Abdulaziz *The Development of the Saudi Stock Market* in *Gulf Financial Markets*, 1988.

Exhibit 7.7

The CCFI share index and changes in GDP, 1983 - 92

Year	*Overall index*	*Change in index (%)*	*Change in nominal GDP (%)*
1983	95.07	[1]-4.7	-17.8
1984	79.56	-17.36	-6.0
1985	60.05	-23.56	-10.8
1986	54.99	-8.43	-13.6
1987	63.59	15.69	1.6
1988	76.12	19.71	1.8
1989	94.21	23.77	9.8
1990	84.68	-10.12	21.6
1991	142.52	68.32	12.4
1992	[2]195.27	[2]37.01	[3]10.0

[1]Second half of the year.
[2]To the end of June.
[3]Estimated annualised growth for the first half of 1992.

Sources: Consulting Center for Finance and Investment, Riyadh and IMF Statistics.

considerable decline in economic activity recorded during that period. Saudi Arabia's nominal GDP was down by 17.8 per cent in 1983, 6 per cent in 1984, 10.8 per cent in 1985 and 13.6 per cent in 1986. In 1987 a steady increase in share prices began, accompanying a general upturn in economic activity. The Consulting Center for Finance and Investment (CCFI) index rose by around 59 per cent from 1987 to 1989, offsetting the 54 per cent loss of the preceding four years. Exhibit 7.7 shows the correlation between GDP and the CCFI share price index.

Prices and trading slumped during the Gulf crisis but were quick to recover after the end of the War. The official stock market index initiated by the Ministry of Finance in 1989 dropped by 10 per cent in 1990, hitting a low of 95.6 at the end of that year's third quarter before rising slightly during the rest of the year. By March 1991 the index was at 114.13, buoyed by the outcome of the War and by a noticeable uptrend in economic activity. It continued to rise steadily throughout 1991 and the first quarter of 1992, as profits of companies showed considerable improvements on the year before. The index ended 1991 at 187.77, a rise of 92 per cent on the year before and was up an additional 19 per cent in the first half of 1992 at 223.97. The index trend was lower in the third and fourth quarters. It ended the week of December 2 at 170.53, down 9.2 per cent from the beginning of the year. The index recorded a loss of 23.9 per cent from its level at the end of the second quarter and 27.1 per cent below the peak it attained on 15 April 1992 of 233.82. Exhibit 7.8 shows changes in the official stock market index.

While the increase in the overall market index in 1991 and the first half of 1992 was significant, the rise in share prices of the cement, banks, industry and service sectors was much higher. The index for the cement sector rose from 94.72 at the end of 1990 to 139.67 at the end of 1991, an increase of 47.4 per cent, and surged by a further 68.8 per cent in the first half of 1992. The index for the banking sector was up by 129.8 per cent in 1991 and an additional 44.7 per cent in the first half of 1992. The index

Exhibit 7.8

Official stock market index by sector, 1989 - 92

End of period	*Banking*	*Industry*	*Services*	*Agriculture*	*Electricity*[1]	*Cement*[1]	*Total*
1989							
	218.51	136.23	62.08	112.27	–	–	108.68
1990							
Q1	245.30	142.78	61.95	114.29	–	–	114.66
Q2	242.19	150.87	64.19	112.97	–	–	117.69
Q3	192.99	119.07	54.73	102.48	–	–	95.60
Q4	190.09	142.81	57.59	101.10	53.95	94.72	97.98
1991							
Q1	233.81	174.89	69.17	112.27	54.29	114.55	114.13
Q2	297.84	186.04	77.20	110.77	55.31	122.81	128.06
Q3	392.18	232.58	111.58	118.08	58.91	125.81	156.79
Q4	436.92	291.41	118.43	138.13	58.65	139.67	187.77
1992							
Q1	539.81	336.82	151.02	148.31	58.76	177.13	210.78
Q2	632.54	301.34	160.47	159.00	57.80	235.80	223.97
Q3	569.96	284.73	149.52	163.69	59.60	221.28	209.36
December 2	431.56	233.42	125.44	147.12	59.35	196.37	170.53

[1]The offical index for the electricity and cement sectors was introduced in the first quarter of 1991. Before that cement was considered part of industry, while electrity was part of services.

for the industrial sector was up by 104.1 per cent in 1991 and added a gain of 3.4 per cent in the first half of 1992, while the service sector's index rose by 105.6 per cent and 35.4 per cent in 1991 and the first half of 1992 respectively. The agricultural sector rose by 36.6 per cent in 1991 and 15.1 per cent in the first half 1992 and the electricity sector was up by 8.7 per cent in 1991 but lost 1.5 per cent in the first half of 1992.

Most of the decline in the overall index during the second half of 1992 was due to the 20 per cent loss recorded in share prices of the industrial sector. The banking sector index was down 1.3 per cent from the beginning of 1992, but its loss from the peak attained on 15 April was 33.7 per cent. The index for the cement sector was up 40.5 per cent during 1992, services up 5.9 per cent, agriculture up 6.5 per cent and electricity up 1.1 per cent.

The total value of shares traded in the banking sector in 1991 was SR3,446 million, making it the largest sector by turnover. It was followed by the industry sector with a total value of SR2,179 million, services (SR1,304 million), cement (SR890 million), agriculture (SR206 million) and electricity (SR156 million). In comparison with 1990, the value of shares traded recorded the highest increase in the services sector, up by 454.9 per cent, followed by industry (107.9 per cent), agriculture (98.1 per cent) and banking (50.8 per cent). Only the electricity sector recorded a drop (of 15 per cent) in turnover. The highest number of transactions and highest volume of shares traded were both recorded by the service sector, followed by industry, banking and agriculture. The lowest volume of shares traded and lowest number of transaction were in the electricity sector. In comparison with 1990, the total number of transactions for 1991 decreased for banking, cement, electricity and agriculture but rose for industry and services. Exhibit 7.9 gives a full breakdown.

Exhibit 7.9

Stock market activity by sector, 1989 - 91

Sector	*1989* Volume of shares traded (thousands)	*1989* Value of shares traded (SR millions)	*1989* Number of transactions	*1990* Volume of shares traded (thousands)	*1990* Value of shares traded (SR millions)	*1990* Number of transactions	*1991* Volume of shares traded (thousands)	*1991* Value of shares traded (SR millions)	*1991* Number of transactions	*Change 1990 to 1991 (%)* Volume of shares traded (thousands)	*Change 1990 to 1991 (%)* Value of shares traded (SR millions)	*Change 1990 to 1991 (%)* Number of transactions
Banking	2,523	1,552	55,065	2,478	2,285	30,680	3,079	3,446	23,156	24.3	50.8	-24.5
Industry	4,420	976	17,983	4,347	1,048	17,944	6,282	2,179	23,165	44.5	107.9	29.1
Cement	2,781	324	4,091	4,254	633	4,987	5,065	890	4,655	19.1	40.6	-6.7
Services	3,535	212	19,764	3,710	235	22,428	10,837	1,304	26,285	192.1	454.9	17.2
Electricity	1,005	122	1,199	1,561	173	1,173	1,327	156	1,068	-15.0	-9.8	-9.0
Agriculture	882	94	12,252	955	104	11,348	2,685	206	10,360	181.2	98.1	-8.7
Total	**15,147**	**3,281**	**110,354**	**17,307**	**4,478**	**88,560**	**29,275**	**8,181**	**88,689**	**69.2**	**82.7**	**0.1**

Stock market indicators

There are various popular measures used to check if share prices are overvalued or not. The most common are the price/earnings (P/E) ratio, dividend yield and price to book value. However, these measures reflect conditions in the market at a given point in time and cannot always be used as indicators of future trends. Saudi stocks may be overvalued in absolute terms but, when looked at from a dynamic perspective, taking into consideration economic growth prospects and overall liquidity in the Kingdom, as well as expected future earnings and the fact that there was virtually no increase in share prices from 1983 to 1990, several shares begin to seem less overpriced. The 110 per cent rise in share prices in 1991 and 1992 may be justified as being an upward movement of around 7 per cent annually over a 10-year period.

By December 1992, P/E ratios continued to show overvaluation for several Saudi shares. The P/E ratio estimates the payback period for an investor who has bought a given stock, ie the number of years needed for him to get his money back, based on the share's earnings for the previous year. The internationally accepted level for P/E ratios is about 15 (see Exhibit 7.10). Ratios for many Saudi shares, based on 1992 earnings and share prices early December 1992, can be seen from Exhibit 7.11 to be considerably higher.

It is important to note that measuring stock prices against past earnings may not be quite relevant. The market does not trade on what has already happened but on expectations of what may happen; whether these expectations are proved right or wrong is irrelevant. Looking ahead, the Saudi economy is expected to continue to grow in 1993 and 1994. The low levels of domestic interest rates, the expansionary fiscal policy being implemented, the additional impulse that the economy got from reductions in fees and charges on certain goods and services provided by the government (petrol, water, electricity, etc), as well as the general improvement in consumer and business confidence, all point towards better economic conditions ahead. Companies' earnings are expected to maintain their recent uptrend amid subdued inflation and solid economic growth.

Valuation should therefore be considered against the background of the overall economic environment. If corporate earnings are expected to rise by 10 per cent in 1993, then current share prices may be discounting such an improvement, pushing P/E ratios above historical standards. One way of assessing market valuation is to calculate P/E ratios using current share prices and projected earnings for the year ahead. Several stocks deemed overvalued using current P/E ratios look more acceptable when expected future earnings are factored in.

Dividend yields and share prices to book values, two other popular measures of the stock market, are also pointing to overvaluation in certain sectors of the Saudi market. Dividend yield measures current dividend per share (cash or stock payment distributed to the stock holder) as a percentage of the share's market price. When a share price rises so that dividends amount to less than 5 per cent of the share's market price, analysts regard the share as overvalued at current price levels. By December 1992, dividend yield for many Saudi shares was less than 5 per cent. Price to book value for various Saudi shares also showed that most bank shares were overvalued. The internationally acceptable ratio for share price to book value is 2.5.

P/E ratios and dividend yields provide investors with only partial information. The returns on stocks vary differently with changes in the entire market. The returns of some stocks are more sensitive to changes than those of others. To assist investors in determining the degree to

Exhibit 7.10
USA's Standard & Poors P/E ratio

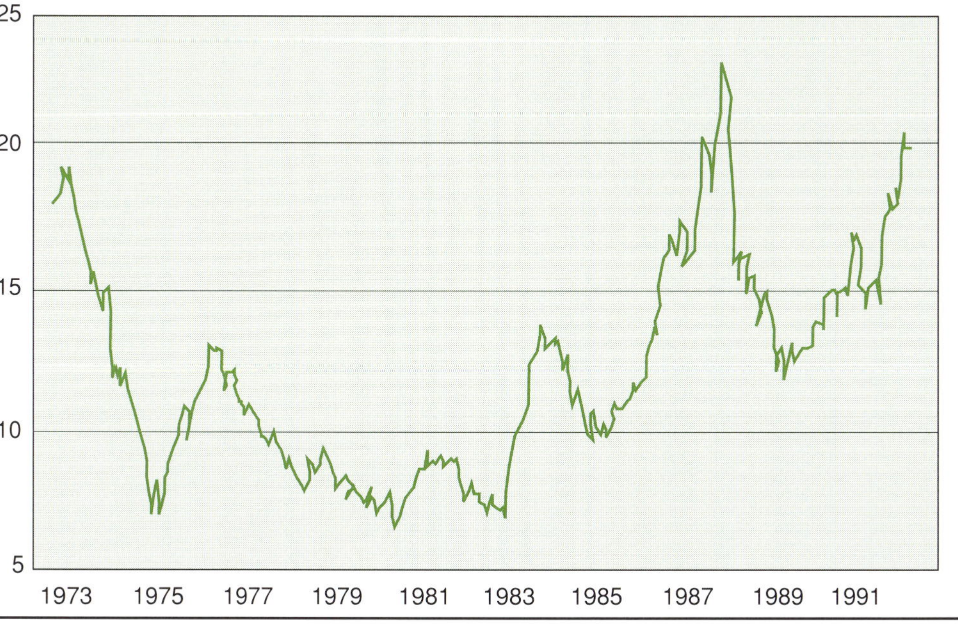

Exhibit 7.11

Financial measures for selected stocks, 1992

	Share price 10 December, 1992	*Dividend[1] per share, 1992*	*Earnings[1] per share, 1992*	*P/E ratio*	*Dividend yield (%)*	*Price to book value*
Banking sector						
Arab National Bank	1,470	34	48	30	2.3	3.6
SAMBA	2,900	87	114	25	3.0	5.6
Saudi British	1,225	22	50	25	1.7	4.1
Saudi Cairo	330	0	0	–	0	7.7
Al Saudi Al Hollandi	1,500	2	44	34	0.1	3.3
United Saudi Commercial	830	0	31	26	0	5.4
Riyad Bank	760	5	25	30	0.6	2.3
Saudi Investment Bank	840	0	46	18	0	2.5
Al Bank Al Saudi Al Fransi	1,120	21	42	27	1.8	3.8
Al Jazira	358	0	4	90	0	7.0
Al Rajhi	820	10	32	26	1.2	3.2
Industrial sector						
SABIC	334	10	15	22	2.9	1.8
Saudi Fertilisers (SAFCO)	1,290	15	84	15	1.1	1.7
Savola	650	20	31	21	3.0	2.6
National Industrialisation Corporation	126	3	6	21	2.3	1.1
Saudi Pharmaceutical	417	3	9	46	0.7	2.5
Saudi Ceramics Company	750	22	33	22	2.9	4.0
Saudi Cable Company	240	0	5	48	0	1.6
Cement sector						
Arab Cement	184	6	6	30	3.2	2.7
Saudi Cement	214	3	14	15	1.4	6.7
Yanbu Cement	290	11	20	15	3.7	2.4
Southern Cement	488	25	30	16	5.1	3.0
Saudi Kuwaiti Cement	300	11	21	14	3.6	2.4
Service sector						
Saudi Public Transport Company	131	10	4	33	7.6	1.1
Saudi Hotels & Resort Company	180	7	12	15	3.8	1.2
National Shipping Company	165	0	9	18	0	1.4
Saudi Real Estate Company	190	0	9	21	0	1.2
Tihama for Advertising Company	145	4	5	29	2.7	2.5
Saudi Automotive Service Company	80	0	15	11	0	1.1
Electricity sector						
Central Electricity	124	7	-5	–	5.6	1.2
Western Electricity	122	7	-7	–	5.7	1.3
Eastern Electricity	122	7	-4	–	5.7	1.5
Agriculture						
Al Qassim Agriculture	64	2	3	21	3.1	1.0
Hail Agricultural Development Company	265	20	12	22	7.6	1.6
Saudi Fisheries	500	15	35	14	3.0	1.8
Tabuk Agricultural Development Company	260	20	30	9	7.6	1.2

[1]First three quarters annualised.

which the returns on certain stocks vary with changes in the market, Exhibit 7.12 shows the beta values for selected stocks traded on the Saudi stock market. The beta value of a stock shows its responsiveness to market movements. Essentially, it measures the degree to which the percentage change in a stock's share price varies in relation to percentage changes in the entire market.

A beta value of 1.448 for the shares of Al Rajhi Investment and Banking Company, for example, indicates that, over a specific period of time in the past (in our analysis the 60 months to February 1992), for every 1 per cent rise in the market index the Al Rajhi stock recorded an increase of 1.448 per cent. Since the beta of Al Rajhi stock is positive, its share price movement is in the same direction as that of the market; the opposite is true for those shares with negative beta values. Stocks with beta values greater than 1 are considered aggressive stocks in the sense that investment in these stocks will subject the investor's returns to greater swings than those recorded by the market. The opposite is true for defensive stocks, ie those with beta values less than 1. Beta values can be used in a number of ways to help investors select the right stocks and in evaluating the performance of investment portfolios. If the investor is expecting a general price increase in the market, he should select stocks with beta values greater than 1 so that their returns increase at a greater rate than the market average.

Developing the Kingdom's capital markets

The drive towards industrialisation, greater private sector participation and the mobilisation of domestic resources shows the need for greater depth in the Kingdom's financial markets. The viability of domestic borrowing through the issuance of public debt instruments has already been tested. These markets now need developing; a greater volume of government bonds and bills should be issued, enabling a greater control of primary and secondary markets and finer pricing.

As the government bond market gains more depth, it will greatly facilitate the development of domestic futures and options markets. Corporations and banks may also be encouraged to issue their own debt instruments now that a benchmark on pricing of these issues has been established. The abundance of government bonds will help to acclimatise investors to the idea of buying fixed rate issues. However, to encourage the development of a private bond market, corporations need to be credit rated. Private and institutional investors will be reluctant to invest in unrated paper of other institutions, whether Saudi or otherwise. Credible rating agencies should be established to carry out periodic credit analysis of locally incorporated companies and to provide investors with reliable and up to date information on them. Capital Intelligence of Cyprus provides in-depth reports and ratings for most banks in the Gulf region. However, more should be done and other sectors need to be covered. A joint venture between a Saudi institution and an experienced international rating institution, operating in a similar fashion to local offices of international auditing firms, would go a long way towards satisfying this requirement.

To enhance the liquidity of debt instruments and increase investor demand an efficient secondary market needs to be established. Investment banking activities should be developed, either from within the existing commercial banking system or through the establishment of new institutions to provide brokerage services, trading and underwriting of securities. A major advantage of bonds and bills over bank deposits is

Exhibit 7.12

Beta values of selected stocks

Stock	*Beta value*
Aggressive stocks that move in the same direction as the market but outperform the index.	
Saudi American Bank	1.1725
National Shipping Company (New)	1.4373
Saudi Automotive Service Company	1.2317
Taiba Company for Investment & Development	1.6013
Makkah Construction Company	1.5446
Al Rajhi Investment & Banking Company	1.4485
Stocks that move in the opposite direction to the market.	
Tabuk Electricity Company	-0.2277
Tiema and Dhouhiya Electricity Company	-0.0343
Tihama for Advertising and PR	-0.0587
Stocks that are strongly influenced by swings in the overall market but underperform the index.	
Saudi British Bank	0.9066
United Saudi Commercial Bank	0.8390
Bank Al Saudi Al Fransi	0.8617
Al Jazira Bank	0.9435
National Industrialisation Company	0.8647
Saudi Pharmaceutical Industries	0.9049
Eastern Agricultural Company	0.8552
Stocks that are least influenced by swings in the overall market	
Saudi Refineries	0.0046
Southern Electricity Company	0.1928
Eastern Electricity Company	0.1390
National Gypsum	0.0847
Westerm Electricity Company	0.2026
Aseer for Trade and Industry	0.1552
National Gas and Industrialisation Company	0.2975
Tabuk Agricultural Development Company	0.2978

Beta values are calculated by regressing statistically R, the monthly returns of a stock (percentage change in its monthly average share price) as a function of the monthly returns of the market, M (percentage change in the average monthly value of the market index). The regression is based on data from February 1987 to February 1992. R=A+Beta M.

Source: Consulting Center for Finance and Investment (CCFI), Riyadh 1992.

their marketability. Subscribers to these issues should be able readily to liquidate their holdings whenever the need arises. A viable secondary market will also make it easier for SAMA to use its operations in these instruments more effectively to regulate liquidity.

The potential for secondary markets in debt instruments is clearly there. As a matter of fact, secondary markets in Saudi government debt issues have already surfaced but they still lack the versatility and depth needed to function efficiently. At present, participants in the bond markets are confined mainly to banks and autonomous government bodies, while the supply of debt instruments is limited. These bottlenecks may soon be relaxed. On the supply side, it is anticipated that a larger number of bonds will be issued in the next few years while, on the demand side, markets are expected to be opened directly to private sector investors. Market participants have identified a number of technical parameters that they advocate changing, including moving to physical securities, the development of a conventional repo market (facilitating the shorting of bonds outright), a move away from discrete issues every two weeks to making issues interchangeable and subject to reopening, the introduction of bearer registration and a more efficient redemption process.

An important incentive for banks to hold government bonds has to do with capital adequacy requirements; such bonds count as eligible assets for domestic liquidity ratio purposes. However, the most overwhelming element of support for the government bond programme has been drawn from the combination of a sharply positive yield curve and the declining interest rate cycle that has prevailed since its inception. Buyers have enjoyed an uninterrupted period of positive carry and capital appreciation and the same factors have induced the banks to be willing buyers in the secondary market. The behaviour of the Saudi bond market during a bear cycle has not yet been tested, however. Without a more developed capital market and a less rigid pricing mechanism, secondary market liquidity may dry up when the interest rate cycle turns round.

Retail products

Commercial banks have begun to build up an end-user market for Saudi bonds as a new investment product. A few banks have started to strip the bonds, selling them to customers for a period of three months, much like a CD, to be bought back by the bank at the end of this period. This gives the customer a higher return than with normal time deposits, with the spread reaching sometimes 25 basis points. The National Commercial Bank launched a medium- to long-term mutual fund in August 1988, investing mainly in Saudi government bonds. The fund is open to any investor, including foreigners interested in Saudi riyal-denominated assets. The success of this fund and others shows that it is possible to attract investment in the region at the longer end of the maturity spectrum.

Most Saudi banks have established in-house expertise in the field of unit trust management. Many are already providing their clients with a wide range of investment products denominated in international currencies, including money market funds, equity funds, bond funds, currency funds, real estate funds and combination funds. The marketing and investment expertise acquired should help these financial institutions to establish unit trusts for domestic debt instruments. The monetary authorities in the region should encourage this trend because it creates additional demand for debt and equity instruments in the secondary markets, opening up new investment opportunities for domestic investors, while keeping assets within the domestic markets.

An important prerequisite for deepening financial markets is the development of the Kingdom's legislative systems. In view of the globalisation of markets and the liberalisation of rules regarding financial transactions, Saudi Arabia's legal and regulatory framework should be in line with those of the rest of the world. This is an important issue, as Saudi financial markets and institutions will have to compete aggressively with the more advanced markets abroad. The next step is to ensure that Saudi companies meet formal accounting and disclosure requirements up to international standards. Ideally, any new legislative framework should be coordinated to apply evenly across the Gulf states. This would then open the national financial markets to crossborder trading, something to which the GCC states are publicly committed.

Deepening the Saudi stock market

The stock market is not a luxury but an essential prerequisite for the financial and economic development of any country, especially one where the private sector is being encouraged to take on additional economic responsibilities. The foundations for an efficient stock market in the Kingdom have already been laid. A substantial number of companies have gone public and, by the end of 1991, the market value of total Saudi shares traded had reached SR230 billion (US$61.3 billion). The number of shareholders has also been rising, reaching 20 per cent of the Saudi population in recent flotations, which is considered quite healthy. A large amount of private capital is still available and can be channelled into domestic investment opportunities. Some quite large and profitable public and private sector ventures have yet to go public. Overall, the political environment is stable, there is low inflation and good prospects of economic growth and the government is committed to encouraging greater private sector participation.

The challenges ahead are also quite significant. A number of changes have to be made to increase investor confidence in the stock market, to improve liquidity and to encourage greater participation by investors and companies. Some of the major issues to be tackled are discussed below.

Information

Steps have to be taken to improve both the quantity and the quality of information that is publicly available about Saudi companies. Companies are required to publish quarterly statements but the information provided is generally quite sketchy and it is difficult to analyse the performance of the companies and the quality of investments in them. The institution of formal credit analysis would be a great help in this respect.

Valuing companies

Despite the improvements in the level of share trading in Saudi Arabia, the stock market is still not geared towards those who wish to raise fresh capital or to take their private companies towards a public flotation. The authorities place considerable importance on companies' book value and, as fixed assets are gradually written down over the years, long-established companies can often be significantly undervalued. They are therefore reluctant to convert into joint stock companies by selling shares based on their book value, rather than on the far higher actual market value. To convert companies from private to public, the usual practice is to make a private placement and turn the shares into ordinary shares several years later. If the issue of properly evaluating existing capital is addressed, it may encourage a number of privately-owned companies to bring in new shareholders through public issues.

Commission

The commission structure for banks needs to be reconsidered. If banks are to be asked to play a major role in providing vitality to the stock market, it should be ensured that the returns to them are adequate to enable them to allocate the necessary quality of resources to share trading activity. Serious consideration should also be given to allowing banks to act as market makers, taking positions, underwriting shares and creating markets as either buyers or sellers of shares. This would undoubtedly give added depth to the market and would enhance the transparency of share trading in the Kingdom. Regulations could be enforced to ensure that banks carried out these activities according to prescribed forms. The extension of the duration of share trading to the full working hours of the banks would also increase the volume of shares traded.

Screen trading

SAMA recently upgraded the ESIS, a new system for share transactions whereby share ownership is transferred electronically from the seller to the buyer through the SSRC. The banks' central share trading rooms are now linked by a computer network with the SSRC. This will eliminate delays caused by the transfer of documents by mail and will help to make the market more efficient. The implementation of a computerised share registration system will be one of the first paperless securities trading systems in the world. Banks are now vying with one another to expand computerised share trading to their branches all over the Kingdom. Sooner rather than later all branches of Saudi banks will be linked to the SSRC and the central coordinating and clearing unit at SAMA by a computer network, thus ending the advantage of the central province especially Riyadh in quick trading of shares.

Boosting liquidity

The Saudi exchange is very limited and actual trading does not exceed 10 per cent of total shares issued. Most commercial banks have started unit trusts that invest in Saudi stocks and it is estimated that the overall capital of these funds could be as much as SR1.5 billion (US$400 million). If 70 per cent of this is invested in stocks, it will bring SR1.05 billion

Exhibit 7.13

Foreign and government ownership of listed Saudi stocks (1991 estimates)

Name of company	*Government ownership (%)*
Riyadh Bank	47
Saudi Cariro Bank	50
Saudi Investment Bank	8
National Agricultural Company	20
Saudi Fisheries Company	40
Tabuk Agricultural Development Company	8
Al Jouf Agricultural Company	11
Al Gassim Cement Company	39
Southern Cement Company	38
Saudi Kuwaiti Cement Company	30
National Gas and Industrialisation Company	14
Arab Cement Company	41
Saudi Basic Industrial Corp (SABIC)	70
Saudi Edible & Vegetable Oil (SAVOLA)	12
Eastern Electricity Company	49
Central Electricity Company	72
Southern Electricity Company	98
Western Electricity Company	84
Saudi Hotel and Resort Company	39
Saudi Real Estate Company	73
Saudi Public Transport Company	30
National Shipping Company	29
Taiba Company for Investment & Development	11
Makkah Construction Company	7

Name of company	*Foreign ownership (%)*
Al Jazira Bank (Pakistani)	35
Saudi Investment Bank (American, Japanese)	25
Saudi American Bank (American)	30
Arab National Bank (Jordanian)	40
Bank Al Saudi Al Hollandi (Dutch)	40
Saudi British Bank (British)	40
Bank Al Saudi Al Fransi (French)	40
Saudi Cairo Bank (Egyptian)	20
United Saudi Commercial Bank (Several nationalities)	30
Saudi Bahrani Cement (Bahraini)	15
Saudi Kuwaiti Cement Company (Kuwaiti)	54
Saudi Pharmaceutical Industries (Joint Arab)	25

Source: Annual reports and other published information.

(US$280 million) of additional capital to the market. The average volume of trading is put at around SR850 million (US$226.6 million) a month, so the new unit trusts will further contribute to the liquidity of shares traded in the Saudi stock market. The total amount collected through the nine share flotations that came to the market in 1991/92 exceeded SR40 billion compared to the targeted figure of SR9 billion. In other words, the shares were oversubscribed by more than four times. To counterbalance this, there should be a gradual increase in the supply of shares coming to the market. Several holding companies are planning to boost their capital by floating new shares. However, more is needed and the government should consider reducing gradually its shareholdings in the existing joint stock companies (where government ownership ranges between 7 per cent and 98 per cent), as well as starting a programme to privatise major public sector institutions such as SAMAREC, Saudi Telecommunications, Saudi Seaports Authority and Saudi Railways. Exhibit 7.13 lists major government-owned companies and those with substantial foreign ownership.

The authorities are seeking other means as well to widen the supply of shares by encouraging existing entities to make greater use of equity finance. For those sensitive about the sale of shares on the open market, there is the option of the closed joint stock company. This allows founding shareholders to buy and sell shares, and provides for the company to be converted automatically to an open joint stock company at a certain time in the future without the need for official approval. Arabian Chemical Investment Company, established in 1992 to back the Middle East's first private methyl-tertiary-butyl- ether (MTBE) plant, is one such example.

Conclusion

The leading international markets have made dramatic progress in recent years and now offer a more efficient and comprehensive service to investors than ever before. To have a chance to compete, the Kingdom's capital markets need to gain depth and versatility. The supply and the flow of stocks and debt instruments available for investment should be increased and a wider participation in secondary market activities needs to be encouraged. To make financial markets deeper requires a high degree of expertise among investors, borrowers and supervisory agencies. Underwriters, advisors, stockbrokers and fund managers need to be established. Credit rating agencies are needed to analyse domestic companies and to provide investors with reliable business information. More stringent reporting practices should also be implemented and an adequate legal system that recognises in full the rights of creditors and protects those of savers and investors needs to be put in place. This will eventually offer greater scope to Saudi investors, who are already active internationally and are familiar with the intricacies of financial instruments, to participate in the capital markets of the Kingdom. Expatriates should also be allowed to invest locally, if not directly, possibly through investment funds managed by Saudi banks.

Capital markets cannot be created or superimposed on a country; they evolve from a need. At present there is a need for diversified financial services and for intermediaries that can channel the savings of the private sector towards productive financial assets. The ability of the Kingdom to adapt to the new economic conditions and of Saudi financial institutions to live up to the challenge of new patterns of finance will determine the future shape of the Saudi capital markets.

8 Consumer markets: reaching the Saudi consumer in the 1990s

Introduction

Consumer markets in Saudi Arabia are becoming increasingly complex and competitive. They have evolved from being very basic in the 1960s to the highly sophisticated markets of the 1990s, with internationally known brand names, modern retail outlets and increasingly discerning consumers. The later 1990s could see a more mature market, as mass communication spreads similar tastes and wants across a wider spectrum of social and economic brackets. The demand for goods and services in the Kingdom will change dramatically over the next few years. This change will be largely driven by a growing national population, higher *per capita* income, the changing demographic profile of expatriates living in the Kingdom, a shifting of tastes and preferences, growth of local companies, the proliferation of supermarkets and more and better advertising. Manufacturers, distributors and retailers will therefore have to redefine their marketing strategies to compete and to preserve market share.

The Saudi consumer markets in the 1960s were in their infancy, with no emphasis on brand names and hence an absence of marketing. The head of the household usually did the shopping, purchasing a commodity or a product and not necessarily a specific brand. The corner grocery stores accounted for a large portion of retail food sales and small stores in the *souk* dominated the consumer goods market. Lower income households resisted going to the few supermarkets that were available then, assuming that the sophisticated atmosphere at these places would mean paying more. The best form of advertisement was by word of mouth, complemented by newspapers advertisements, rusty billboards on the side of the roads and neon signs.

The oil boom of the 1970s brought forth a richer, less price sensitive consumer. Modern retail outlets, such as supermarkets and other self service stores, sprang up and producers started paying more attention to the marketing of their products through advertising. Women increasingly assumed the role of the shopper and quality became associated with brand image. The products that enjoyed the lion's share of sales were often those that had arrived earliest. If they withstood the durability test and the after-sales service was good, they could establish a strong hold on the market. Market shares of over 50 per cent were not uncommon.

In the consumer goods market large numbers of products became known by their brand names (washing powder was often called *Tide*, toothpaste became *Kolynos*, cigarettes *Marlboro*, tissue paper *Kleenex* and vacuum cleaners *Hoover*). It was extremely difficult for a newcomer to break into the market. There was no television or radio advertising and, if a consumer could not read, he would have little contact with advertisements in the written media.

The process continued in the 1980s, with the consumer becoming ever more sophisticated. Then came the recession that brought with it an abrupt change in lifestyles and consumption habits. As spending power was cut, the consumer became more price sensitive. Increasing competition forced producers to develop more and better marketing techniques in order to preserve market share. The 1980s also saw the emergence of large commercial shopping malls and a gradual breakaway of retailers from the *souk*. The corner stores continued to attract a large proportion of retail sales, although supermarkets increased their share from 10 per cent share in 1980 to 30 per cent in 1990.

In 1986 the Saudi government allowed television advertising and since then other types of advertising have started to catch up. Higher quality billboards and neon signs, as well as more varied newspaper advertisements, began to appear. Importers and manufacturers also started conducting point-of-sale promotions to back up television campaigns. An interesting consequence of television advertising is that, during the recession period of 1986 to 1988 when it might be expected that cheaper, lower quality brands would have captured a larger market share, the brands that sold best were the well known, traditional, high quality ones, whose manufacturers and importers had the money to produce the most professional advertisements. However, the number of trading and industrial companies involved in advertising remained relatively small. Smart advertising, like planning, was something for the most sophisticated.

With the advent of the 1990s the pendulum has swung again. Economic activity has picked up after the end of the Gulf crisis and a new growth cycle has started, with higher disposable income and growing consumer markets. Total merchandise imports have been rising after the nadirs reached during the oil glut years of the mid-1980s, with an increase from US$17.1 billion in 1986 to around US$23 billion in 1991.

Characteristics of the Saudi consumer market

Saudi Arabia is a multiracial society with differing needs and tastes. It is a large country, which means that products can fail in one province and succeed in another. It is also an affluent, consumer-orientated society, with a *per capita* income of US$6,500 in 1990. The Saudi market is quality conscious and goods of every type find their way to the local market. People are now feeling more affluent after a period of strained economic conditions in the mid- and late 1980s. There are once again abundant cash resources and domestic markets are picking up quickly.

A survey completed in July 1991 by the Al Riyadh Development

Authority illustrates the effect of the high *per capita* income and the rising purchasing power on consumer markets. The survey shows that the total population of Riyadh rose by 49 per cent from 1986 to 1991, when it reached 2,073,800, of which 1,334,800 were Saudis and the remaining 739,000 foreigners. Overall income of households in Riyadh in 1991 was put at SR30 billion (US$8 billion), about 69 per cent of which was spent on personal consumption, while 31 per cent was saved. This means that Riyadh's total annual consumer market in 1991 was SR21 billion (US$5.6 billion), with the largest single block (US$1.8 billion) being spent on food. The demand for consumer goods generated by these high spending levels is partly met through imports. A large proportion of imported goods are

Exhibit 8.1

Expenditure distribution by income group (%)

Item	*Up to SR5,000*	*SR5,001-10,000*	*SR10,001-15,000*	*Over SR15,000*
Foodstuffs/toiletries	47	40	36	28
Furniture & consumer durables	11	13	13	22
Household supplies	22	25	27	27
Housing expenses	15	15	15	14
Motorcar expenses	5	7	9	9
Total	**100.0**	**100.0**	**100.0**	**100.0**

Source: Middle East Marketing Research Bureau household survey, 1987, published by *Business International*, London 1991.

Exhibit 8.2

Expenditure distribution by nationality (%)

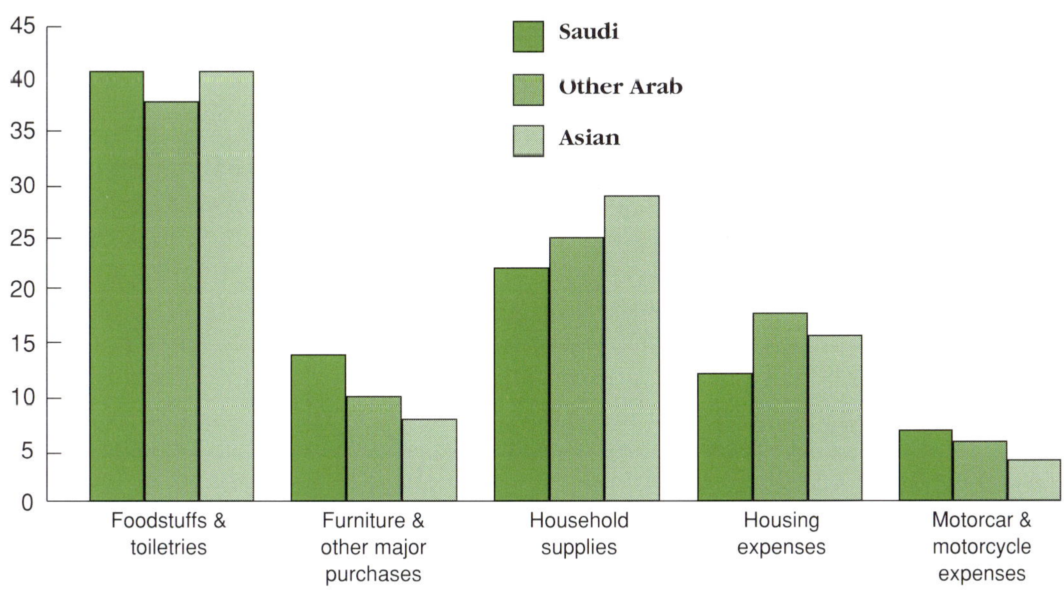

Source: MEMBR household survey, 1987, reported by *Saudi Arabia Monitor*, December 1990.

finished or intermediate products, with 80 per cent of the top 15 items being consumer products.

Expenditure profiles

According to the household survey carried out by the Middle East Research Bureau in 1987 and published by *Business International*, the percentage of total expenditure that went on foodstuffs and toiletries in Saudi Arabia ranged from 47 per cent for those in the income bracket up to SR5,000 (US$1,335) to 28 per cent for the income group over SR15,000 (US$4,005). Household supplies came next, with percentages varying between 22 per cent and 27 per cent, followed by furniture and other major purchases, housing expenses and expenses related to cars. These results are listed in full in Exhibit 8.1. Some important comparisons with spending patterns in the West need to be borne in mind. Not only is there no personal income tax in the Kingdom but also the government provides general subsidies to the population, both indigenous and expatriate, by supporting the prices of electricity, petrol, water, telephone and transport among others and by reduced charges for registering companies (see Chapter 2). Health and education are also provided free of charge, leaving a substantial portion of income to be spent on consumer goods and services.

There are significant differences in consumption habits between Saudis, Arab expatriates and Asian households (see Exhibit 8.2). The average Saudi household has 6.5 members while the average expatriate household has under five. Because immigrants are transitory, they tend to spend proportionately less on goods that they cannot take with them when they leave the country (eg electrical appliances and electronics) than on household supplies. The same household survey showed that 92 per cent of Saudi households have at least one car and 28 per cent have two or more. Almost every Saudi household has a television, refrigerator, cooker and washing machine. Two-thirds of all households have hi-fi and video equipment but there are few dishwashers, reflecting the availability of cheap home help (see Exhibit 8.3).

Saudi Arabian markets tend to be very volatile. The rapid growth of the indigenous population and the fairly sharp shifts in the size and composition of the expatriate population lead to constant changes in the retail environment in terms of the number and location of retail outlets. Another source of volatility is the decentralisation of retail activity away from *souks* and towards new residential areas. This involves changes in the nature of retail trade, with supermarkets and self service stores gradually gaining in importance. A report by the US Agricultural Trade Office in Riyadh (see Exhibit 8.4) says that there were almost 100 large (ie with more than 500 square metres of floor space) supermarkets in the Kingdom in 1990 and 875 smaller ones. The report quotes a 1990 market research survey as showing that roughly one-third of food shopping visits are to large supermarkets and one-third to grocery stores. Fewer visits are made to smaller supermarkets and wholesalers. The respondents quoted supermarkets' variety of products as the main reason for preference, followed by good quality, proximity to home and lower prices.

Exhibit 8.3

Ownership of consumer durables by nationality (%)

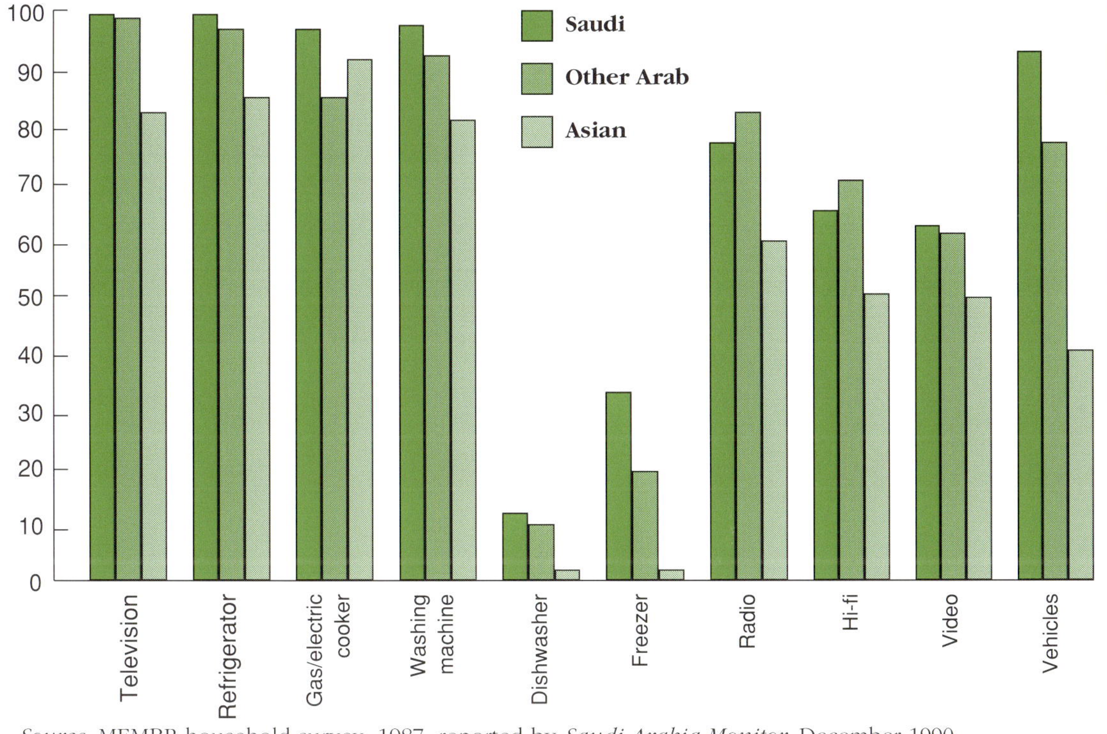

Source: MEMBR household survey, 1987, reported by *Saudi Arabia Monitor*, December 1990.

The annual market for imported vehicles in Saudi Arabia was estimated at around 200,000 units in 1991, with a total value of SR8.4 billion (US$2.24 billion). Japanese cars took almost 57 per cent of the market, with Toyota alone accounting for almost 45 per cent. The Kingdom is the seventh largest market for Japanese vehicles after the US, Germany, the UK, Australia, Canada and Thailand. American cars came next with a 30 per cent market share; European cars accounted for 10 per cent and 3 per cent was taken by Korean and other exporters. The total market for machines, electrical equipment and parts was estimated at SR1.6 billion (US$ 4.3 million) in 1991, for cosmetics and perfumes SR411 million (US$109.8 million), for clothing and textiles SR9 billion (US$2.4 billion) and for food products, including live animals, SR18.7 billion (US$5 billion).

The market for household products in Saudi Arabia is worth US$300 million a year at retail prices, according to a study published in 1992 by International Marketing & Economic Services (IMES) of the UK (see Exhibit 8.5). The study shows that the largest sector of the market is detergents, with a retail value of SR389 million (US$102 million), 86 per cent of which is supplied by local output. There is no local production of starch and ironing aids, furniture polish, metal polish or shoe polish. Unilever has mounted a serious challenge to market leaders Procter &

Exhibit 8.4

Retail outlets selling food in Saudi Arabia (1990)

Outlet	*Size (square metres)*	*Number in the Kingdom*
Supermarkets	Over 500	96
Self-service stores	100-500	875
Grocery stores	40-100	4,225
Small shops (*bakalas*)	Under 40	12,560

Source: Saudi Arabia – A Market for US Food Products, US Agricultural Trade Office, Riyadh, 1991.

Exhibit 8.5

The household products market, value and import penetration, 1991

Product	*Consumption (metric tons)*	*Market value (SR millions)*	*Local production (%)*
Detergents	53,000	389	86
Fabric softeners	3,800	34	5
Laundry aids	650	22	5
Starch/ironing aids	700	20	0
Bleach	50,000	130	98
Dishwashing liquid	11,500	80	87
General purpose cleaners	2,200	33	30
Glass cleaner	1,500	21	75
Oven cleaner	135	5	0
Carpet/upholstery care	580	9	50
Lavatory care	4,040	26	5
Drain openers	450	5	44
Air freshener	1,600	44	11
Insecticide	7,300	214	45
Disinfectant	4,400	65	35
Furniture polish	460	19	0
Metal polish	150	5	0
Shoe polish	130	7	0

Source: Household Products – Saudi Arabia 92, International Marketing & Economic Services, UK.

Gamble in the detergent market, using *Omo* and *Surf* imported from Malaysia and the UAE, and has plans to establish a production unit in the Kingdom. The Saudi household goods market is expected to grow at more than 12 per cent a year in inflation-adjusted terms until 1995.

There are different degrees of participation by Saudi husbands and wives in purchasing decisions. A recent study showed that approximately one-third of purchase decisions about foodstuff are made solely by Saudi husbands, one-third solely by wives and one-third jointly. There is a similar pattern for Arab immigrant families, while in Asian homes the husband makes more decisions. More husbands make the decisions when it comes to consumer durables, with about half of all husbands, irrespective of nationality, being the sole decision makers. They also make two-thirds of the actual purchases and only one in seven wives actually goes to the shop on her own to buy the goods. This is partly due to the fact that women are not allowed to drive in the Kingdom.

The changing structure of Saudi consumer markets

Five major trends will shape the Kingdom's consumer markets in the 1990s. One is the steady increase in the range of locally produced goods, especially through joint ventures between local and international producers; these will be favoured by government purchasers and protected from outside competition if necessary, particularly if exporters to the region are suspected of dumping. There is also a trend towards local processing of products from imported ingredients and in some cases enough is produced locally to meet all domestic needs. The government is helping this trend by providing concessionary finance to those setting up processing facilities and by protecting infant industries through a special 20 per cent tariff on competing imported products. Such items include iron and steel bars, furniture, soaps, detergents and cement among others.

The second trend is the rising number of supermarkets, commercial complexes and other self service outlets in the Kingdom, leaving the choice of brand in the hands of the purchaser. Not only is the number of supermarkets growing but the quality of the shops and of the services provided is also improving. The new commercial centres will continue to offer recreation and convenient shopping for the whole family. Competition will increase and advertising will undoubtedly become the cornerstone of marketing strategy.

Thirdly, socio-economic changes at the family level will also be significant. Multiple households belonging to one man and the extended family structure are gradually being replaced by smaller, cellular family units. Children are becoming economically independent at a much earlier age than before. Literacy rates are rising and are especially high for those under the age of 25. The Kingdom is also witnessing changes in use of leisure time, in attitudes, life styles, social values, education and income levels. As disposable income rises, spending on leisure goods will increase and individualism, luxury and quality will become more important. The fact that so many young women today are getting education at all levels from school to university must result over the coming decade in more women going out to work, especially in certain occupations. Women also have access to a wider public environment, in which they are more exposed to international consumer trends, and are developing purchasing patterns in which they are more free to make their own decisions; this should lead to substantial changes in product demand.

The expatriate population

The changing structure of the expatriate population, which constitutes a sizeable portion of the domestic market for food, household goods, consumer products and services, is the fourth trend that will affect spending patterns. In the 1990s a higher percentage of non-nationals will be born in the Kingdom than in the 1970s and 1980s. The process of demographic settling, whereby more dependants of expatriate workers move to the host country, will also become more entrenched in this decade. More foreign labour is being brought in to practice a trade, rather than being assigned to an individual project. Those planning to stay in the country for more than two years are naturally inclined to bring their families with them. This will transform the structure of the expatriate population, which was previously dominated by single males aged from 20 to 40, into a community more normally balanced by age and sex. According to the July 1991 survey of the city of Riyadh, 80 per cent of the foreign population was living in households that were nuclear or extended families, compared to only 69 per cent in 1986. On the other hand, the number of foreigners living in households formed of groups of unrelated individuals had decreased from nearly 30 per cent to 18 per cent. These changes make the composition of foreign households more similar to that of Saudi families.

It is apparent from the structure of the non-national population that any marketing strategy must take into account the highly differentiated national profiles which exist in the Kingdom. Purchasing methods and patterns of consumption vary greatly according to nationality, as well as according to age, sex, occupational level and educational attainment. A migrant worker from India, Bangladesh or the Philippines is unlikely to have a large disposable income, although at certain times, notably upon return visits to his home country, he may indulge in large purchases of durable goods. Many consumer items, such as electronics and household goods, gold, jewellery and toiletries, are up to 50 per cent cheaper in the Kingdom than elsewhere in Asia. Similarly, the presence of relatively settled patterns of living, for example among the Arab expatriates, is likely to result in different consumption trends from those prevailing for migrants working on a contract basis. Finally, the relatively higher income levels of the European and North American expatriate communities and their preference for shopping in integrated supermarkets and shopping malls also dictate a different marketing strategy from that directed at labourers from the Indian sub-continent, who tend to buy at local stores, many of which are run by their compatriots.

Changes in the population of Saudi nationals

Perhaps the most important trend is the changing demographic profile of the national population. Reliable figures for the Kingdom's population have not been available until now. The results of the first Saudi Census since 1974 have been released recently putting the Saudi population figure at around 16.9 million in 1992, with nationals accounting for close to 73 per cent of the population or 12.3 million.

The male population among the Saudi nationals is put at 6.2 million or 50.4 per cent of the total number of Saudis, while males were found constituting around 70.4 per cent of the total expatriate population in 1992. The annual population growth rate is expected to slow to 3.2 per cent during the remainder of the decade, reflecting higher levels of education and greater female participation in the labour force. The population is forecast to reach 23.1 million by the turn of the century and to double over the next 20 years. Given the current economic boom in the Kingdom, the number of expatriates is unlikely to decline in the next few years and the ratio of 73 to 27 between nationals and expatriates is expected to remain the same. Forecasts for population growth by age and race are given in Exhibit 8.6.

The Saudi national population is expected to reach 16.9 million by the year 2000. The high rate of population growth means that the Kingdom has a very youthful demographic profile, with around 50 per cent of the population, or 6.1 million, aged less than 15 years. By the year 2000 the number of children aged under 15 will have risen to 7.7 million but the percentage will have dropped to 46 per cent, reflecting slightly lower fertility rates over the decade. The baby boom generation of the 1960s and 1970s will enter the workforce, with the percentage of the population in the age bracket 18 to 59 reaching 46 per cent by the year 2000, compared with an estimated 43 per cent in 1992. The dependency ratio (the number of old and young divided by the number of working age) will, in turn, continue to fall during the 1990s and will have a significant positive effect on overall consumption levels in the Kingdom.

The recent household survey carried out by the High Commission for the Development of Riyadh found that most of the demographic change in the capital from 1986 to 1991 was a result of rapid growth in the Saudi population, which increased by 58 per cent over the period, compared with the 36 per cent growth registered by the foreign population. This took the Saudi share of the population from 61 per cent of the total in 1986 to 64 per cent in 1991. The increase in the foreign population was due mainly to a 76 per cent rise in the female population (the male population rose by only 26 per cent). The survey also found that in 1991 Egyptians formed the single largest group of foreign nationals, with 152,000 people, representing 21 per cent of the 739,000 total. The next largest foreign grouping, at 97,000, comprised Syrians, Jordanians, Lebanese and Iraqis. The remaining five major foreign groups consisted of nationals from Pakistan, Bangladesh and India (95,000), the Sudan (78,000) and Yemen (62,000).

There have been several important changes in the breakdown of Riyadh's population by age and sex, although the basic trends remain the same. There has been a heavy migration of young Saudi males, especially those aged 20 to 34, to Riyadh. Fertility remains high but its effects are being altered by migration. The percentage of those in the older age

Exhibit 8.6

The structure of the Saudi population (millions)

	1992	*2000*[1]
Total	**16.9**	**23.1**
Nationals	12.3	16.9
Expatriates	4.6	6.2
Nationals by age group		
Under 15	6.1	7.7
15 to 59	5.7	8.4
Over 60	0.5	0.8

[1]Forecasts.

Source: Based on the preliminary results of the official Saudi census, 1992.

group has increased, suggesting a decline in mortality for that group. The combined effect of these factors has been to increase the median age of the Saudi population from 16.5 in 1986 to 17.1 in 1991. The foreign population has a very different structure and has seen far more changes since 1986. In that year there were nearly two foreign males for every female in Riyadh. However, the heavy influx of foreign females, particularly those aged from 30 to 40, has brought down the ratio of males to females to 1.3 : 1. The large increase in the numbers of children since 1986 also suggests that increasing numbers of families are accompanying foreign workers who migrate to the capital city. The biggest increases in the foreign population since 1986 have been the addition of 22,000 males aged five to nine, 20,000 females aged 35 to 39 and 20,000 females aged 30 to 34. There has been a decline (by 13,000) of males aged between 29 and 34 and a small decline in the number of women aged over 65. Exhibit 8.7 gives full details.

The implications for consumer demand are significant. With such a young population, the market for children's clothing, soaps and detergents, baby food, nappies, toys, medicine and medical supplies and educational materials and services is large and growing rapidly in line with the general rise in population. Popular student fashions, whether in food, clothing or entertainment, will be a major influence on the overall consumer market. The formation of new households by young married couples over the next decade will increase the already large market for furniture and lighting fixtures, kitchenware, electrical appliances, textiles and carpets, linens, interior design and architectural services and passenger vehicles.

Exhibit 8.7

Population of Riyadh by age, sex and nationality

Age	*Total*	*Saudi total*	*Saudi male*	*Saudi female*	*Foreign total*	*Foreign male*	*Foreign female*
Under 1	49,472	33,197	18,887	14,310	16,275	7,039	9,236
1-4	250,572	168,645	81,819	86,826	81,927	41,300	40,627
5-9	293,330	203,793	101,402	102,391	89,537	47,279	42,258
10-14	220,679	167,094	86,240	80,854	53,585	26,829	26,756
15-19	193,426	154,940	76,329	78,611	38,486	18,151	20,335
20-24	178,212	140,980	81,112	59,868	37,232	17,155	20,077
25-29	192,676	111,736	59,128	52,608	80,940	48,874	32,066
30-34	176,744	69,598	39,295	30,303	107,146	59,449	47,697
35-39	148,819	53,299	25,749	27,550	95,520	58,672	36,848
40-44	103,012	36,717	17,315	19,402	66,295	44,942	21,353
45-49	64,660	35,303	19,088	16,215	29,357	23,243	6,114
50-54	51,028	33,164	19,195	13,969	17,864	13,691	4,173
55-59	26,238	19,482	11,231	8,251	6,756	5,381	1,375
60-64	21,244	17,955	11,626	6,329	3,289	1,862	1,427
65-69	9,216	8,623	4,757	3,866	593	277	316
70-74	10,596	9,861	5,654	4,207	735	636	99
Over 75	10,094	8,789	5,811	2,978	1,305	953	352
Total	**2,000,018**	**1,273,176**	**664,638**	**608,538**	**726,842**	**415,733**	**311,109**
Median age	**19.8**	**17.1**	**17.9**	**16.3**	**27.9**	**30.1**	**24.1**

Source: The High Commission for the Development of Riyadh, 1991 household survey as reported in *Saudi Arabia Monitor*, July/August 1992.

Spending on housing is also forecast to increase in importance and people's ambitions to live in and own bigger and better houses will become stronger.

The age structure of the national population also indicates that more citizens will be entering the labour force in the 1990s and it will rise to 7.7 million by the year 2000. However, Saudis will continue to be a minority in the age range from 20 to 39 years, as more than 70 per cent of the expatriates are in this bracket. In contrast, nine out of 10 of those under five years of age in the Kingdom will be nationals, as will almost all those over 65. The new Saudi arrivals in the labour force will have higher educational attainments and expectations than their parents. Their purchasing patterns are consequently expected to resemble more closely those in the West. Overall demand for sporting goods, financial services, luxury accessories, the latest cars, the newest and best consumer durables, medical equipment and services, pharmaceuticals, cosmetics and toiletries, as well as travel services, will also rise rapidly, not only because of the high birth rate but also because of the higher level of disposable income.

Reaching the Saudi consumer

Tomorrow's consumer will undoubtedly have different standards and values from those of his parents and certainly his grandparents. These young people have grown up with television and have seen role models other than those available in their homes. Saudi consumers of the 1990s will be more educated, with a higher level of sophistication and will be better informed of what is available in the market. Mass communications will spread similar tastes and wants across social and economic brackets. Manufacturers and retailers will have to respond by sharpening their marketing skills and advertising.

Unfortunately, the less sophisticated Saudi businessmen still consider marketing as an unnecessary overhead and continue to follow the "bedocratic" approach based on tradition and outmoded patterns of management. They are attuned to the boom years, when sales expanded as a natural consequence of the growth of the economy. Nobody spent money on market research and the odd newspaper and billboard advertisement cost little. Likewise, selling was regarded as a simple matter not worthy of special attention. Many industrial failures can be attributed to the simplistic belief by industrialists that, if there is a market for a certain quantity of an imported product and they can manufacture that quantity locally, they will automatically be able to take that market. Conversely, it is noticeable that many of the industries that are successful have grown out of good marketing operations; the entrepreneur has established a strong market base for an imported product and then integrated backwards into manufacturing it locally.

The need to maintain and increase market share in an increasingly competitive environment has recently pushed the importance of marketing to the forefront. Manufacturers, retailers, dealers and wholesalers are becoming more aware of the importance of marketing to augment sales

Exhibit 8.8
Advertising expenditure by type of medium, 1991

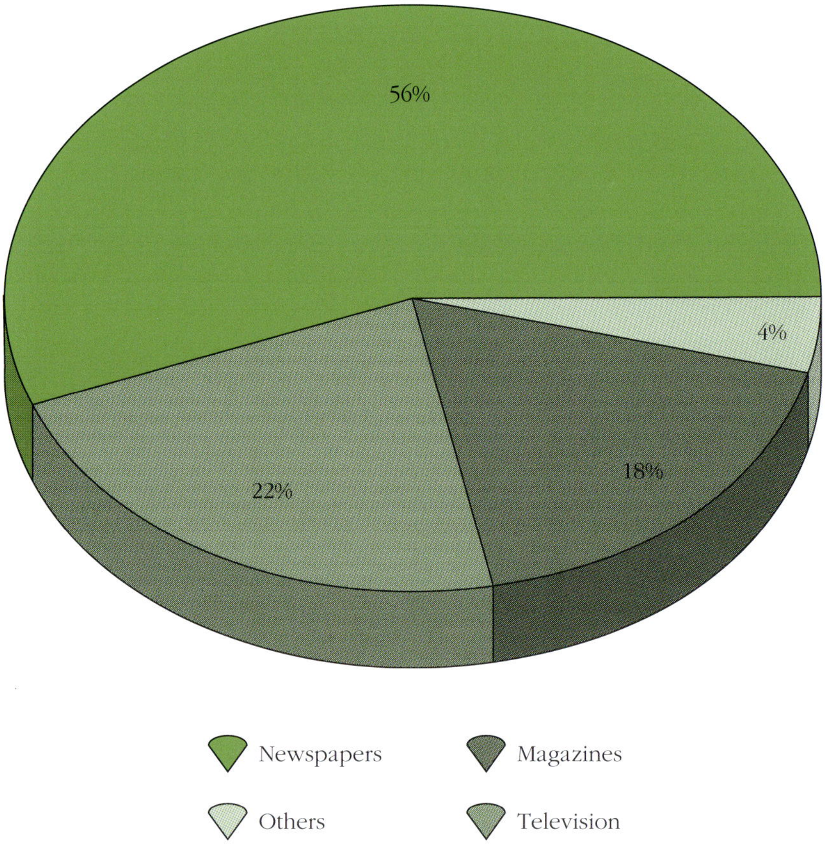

(Total: US$190 million)

and profitability. Advertising is the marketing industry's most important tool. The range of media available in the Kingdom is similar to that in the West. Essentially it consists of the print media (newspapers and magazines), the electronic media (mainly television) and the outdoor media. Direct mail to customers is little known. People in this part of the world regard direct mail as an invasion of privacy. The largest share of media advertising in the Kingdom goes to newspapers, which account for around 56 per cent of total advertising expenditure, followed by television advertising (22 per cent) magazines (18 per cent) and videos, billboards and others (4 per cent) (see Exhibit 8.8). With the rise in literacy, the print media can now reach a larger section of the population.

Expenditure on advertising in Saudi Arabia has been rising steadily over the past few years but still remains far below international levels. *Per capita* advertising spending is put at around US$13.50 a year, compared, for example, to US$55 in a small country such as Cyprus. Total advertising expenditure stood at around US$190 million in 1991 but is forecast to

Exhibit 8.9

Projected growth in advertising spending (US$ millions)

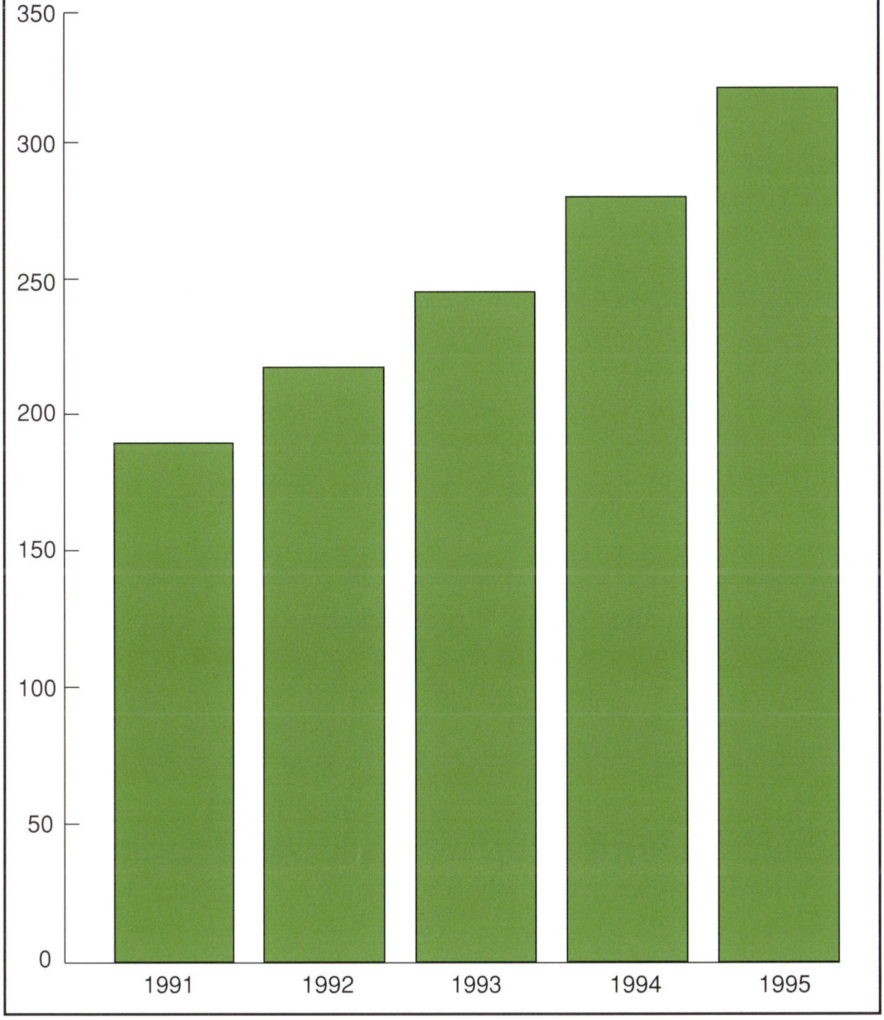

increase by around 15 per cent annually, reaching US$320 million in 1995 (see Exhibit 8.9).

Print media

The Kingdom has seven Arabic and three English daily newspapers, as well as four international (pan-Arab) papers published out of London. The most important two are *Asharq Al Awsat*, which is widely read in the Kingdom, and *Al-Hayat*. Most of the magazines are in the Arabic language and include regional and pan-regional publications. They cover a broad spectrum of subject matter, ranging from socio-political and business publications to women's magazines and family-orientated magazines. Most advertising expenditure for the print media passes through local or pan-Arab agencies, which act either directly, on behalf of a client or as an affiliate of one of the major international advertising firms. Commissions range from 15 to 20 per cent for major publications and can be up to 50 per cent for some pan-Arab publications with wide coverage. A full page advertisement in *Asharq Al Awsat* costs SR35,000 (US$9,333), while the cost averages around SR21,600 (US$5,760) for local newspapers.

Electronic media

This is generally taken to refer to television and video, since radio stations are government-owned and do not accept advertising. The greatest advantage of television as a marketing tool is its reach. More than 90 per cent of households have at least one television set. In Saudi Arabia a single showing on the Arabic channel of a 25- or 35-second commercial in prime time after the evening news costs SR12,000 (US$3,200) for imported products and SR8,400 (US$2,240) for locally manufactured products. For the English language channel, the advertising rates range from SR5,250 (US$1,400) for local products to SR7,500 (US$2,000) for imported products. This compares to around US$10,000 in major countries of the West. Home video advertising took off in the early 1970s but was later banned.

Although television is a very important advertising medium, it suffers from a number of drawbacks. The television network is owned by the government and does not market itself for advertisers. The amount of advertising time available is limited and the commercial breaks are few in number. Several commercials are often blocked together and then shown successively without a break. The widely spread local magazines, in both Arabic and English, are considered to be far better in terms of market penetration.

Other techniques

Another advertising medium prevalent in Saudi Arabia is the elevated billboard system. The modern network of roads, particularly the highways between major cities, will continue to provide effective outdoor advertising. However, the lack of media research remains a major drawback for firms advertising their products in the Kingdom, as no statistics are available on the effectiveness of media penetration. To be successful therefore, advertising campaigns should use a mixture of newspaper, magazines and television.

In a bid to attract the increasingly discerning and price conscious consumer, a number of companies and shops have got together to launch discount cards. Among the most successful is one issued by the International Saudi Business Center. Holders of the card have risen from 6,000 at its inception in 1986 to around 50,000 in 1991. The success of the card can be attributed largely to the discounts it offers on a wide range of consumer products and services. Expansion into the service sector by offering, for example, discounts on medical treatment is being considered. Judging from the large increase in the number of cardholders, discount cards should continue to be a useful marketing tool.

Exporters to this part of the world have for a long time appreciated the value of national, regional and international trade fairs, exhibitions and seminars. Such events are held regularly in the major cities of the Kingdom and often attract many visitors, including businessmen and representatives of purchasing organisations. They provide useful venues for market testing, for creating and developing business contacts and for introducing new products to the country.

Foreign principals are becoming more involved in marketing in the Kingdom. Where they are manufacturing locally in a joint venture, their participation in marketing stems naturally from their involvement in production. Where the foreign company is not manufacturing locally, or is manufacturing only one or two of the products it sells, it may select staff to help its agent's marketing efforts or to establish a liaison office to act as a link between the market and the planning operation at home. Some of the major consumer goods manufacturers already have all three types of presence. In a few cases foreign companies have taken over the management of part of their distributors' businesses on contract. A similar pattern is emerging among companies selling consumer durables and capital goods. Foreign principals are entering the country through the establishment of joint venture maintenance operations and at the same time are helping their distributors to market their products. A list of leading merchant families and wholesale trading houses in Saudi Arabia is given in Exhibit 8.10.

Besides promotions and discounts, manufacturers and retailers will have to continue to offer added incentives if they are to increase market share. Special offers, seasonal sales, free gifts and valuable prizes may help to lure additional customers. However, it is the availability of instalment schemes and good after-sales service that are more instrumental in increasing sales. Various popular car brands are now being sold in increased numbers in the Kingdom through instalment schemes. Such schemes are operated either directly by the distributors or in collaboration with finance companies. Today there are schemes that do not require any downpayment, with the whole amount payable in 48 instalments. Only one guarantor is needed and buyers must undertake to have instalments deducted directly from their salaries. Several companies in the Kingdom have also started to offer furniture, electronics and other consumer durables on an instalment basis. Saudi banks have jumped on the bandwagon of consumer finance and, as additional credit is made available in this field, it will greatly enhance demand in the Kingdom's consumer markets.

Conclusion

The drive for economic diversification in Saudi Arabia suggests that there will be a steady stream of locally manufactured products competing with imports for market share. Products such as cement, steel shapes, building materials, furniture, tyres, air conditioning units, lubricants, foodstuffs, dairy products, animal feeds, packaging materials, tissue paper, soap, edible oil, plastic bags, etc are being produced in the Kingdom; they are of high quality and competitively priced compared to imported products.

Exhibit 8.10

Leading merchant families and wholesale trading houses in Saudi Arabia

Name of family	*Major companies, establishments affiliates and subsidiaries*	*Selected agencies and activities*
Alireza	Haji Husein Alireza and Co Ltd; Kitchen World; Transcontinental Corporation; Rezatrade Marketing and Development; Husain Jamiland Rezatrade; NEC Saudi Arabia Ltd; Wexico Systems and Services; Xenel Industries Ltd; Dakhakhni Bookshops; Saudi Electronics and Trading Co; Rezayat Trading Co; ICI Trading and Rezatrade.	Mazda; Goodyear; Gerber; Lister; Arby's ICIT Pools; NEC; Westinghouse; Havana Cigars; Ford Mercury; Kia; Rolm; Fujitsu. Activities cover the entire range of commercial sectors in the Kingdom.
Binzagr	Abdullah & Said MO Binladen Co; Binzagr Co; Wahib S. Binzagr & Brothers; Arabian Stores Co; International Agencies Ltd; Binzagr International Trading Co.	Avon Products Inc; Advance Linen Services; Unilever Export; British American Tobacco; Brown & Williamson International Tobacco; Imperial Tobacco Lipton Export; HJ Heinz; Kelloggs; UB (Biscuits); Uncle Ben's; Royal Foods; Hershey International; Dr Pepper Co; Wilkinson Sword; Dunlop; General Tire.
Buqshan	Abdullah Said Buqshan & Bros; Buqshan Trading Co; Saudi Bazaar; Buqshan Pharmacy; Ahmad Sulaiman Buqshan & Co; Ali Abdullah Buqshan Showroom; Salim Ahmad Buqshan.	Perfumes:.Christian Dior, Georgio, Clarins, Muko, Kent; also clothing; jewellery; automobiles and spare parts; books; furniture; carpets; processed foods; shoes; household appliances; and electrical goods. One of the largest commercial companies in the Kingdom, but likes to keep a low profile.
Algosaibi	Abdulrehman Algosaibi General Trading Bureau; Ahmad Hamad Algosaibi & Bros; Algosaibi Grandmet Services Ltd; Algosaibi Hotel; Algosaibi Trading & Contracting Co; Khalifa A. Algosaibi Group of Companies.	Mitsui; White Westinghouse International Co; Sumitomo; Fiat; RC Cola; and a wide range of others from the US, UK, Germany, France, Italy, Belgium, Switzerland, Austria, Denmark, Sweden, Spain, Pakistan, Jordan and Japan.
Jamjoon	Jamjoon Group of Industries; Jamjoon Vehicles and Equipment; Chemtec Industries; Jamjoon General Agencies; Dar al-Shorouq Publication, Distribution & Printing; Yahya Jamjoon Establishment;	Widely diversified international range that has included: Pfizer; Ceiba-Geigy; Peugeot; Hino trucks; Kleber Tyres; Continental Pharma; Sans Souci; and Allercan.

Exhibit 8.10 *cont.*

Leading merchant families and wholesale trading houses in Saudi Arabia

Name of family	*Major companies, establishments affiliates and subsidiaries*	*Selected agencies and activities*
	Delicatessen Hanaa; Al Madina; Modern Commercial Establishment; Modern Vehicles and Equipment; Saudi Marketing Establishment; Radwa Trading Co; Al-Sharafiah Hotel; Trading and Construction World; Jamjoon Corporation for Commerce and Industry; Jamjoon Foremost Ltd.	
Juffali	The Juffali Group of Companies; National Electric & Products Co; Saudi Business Machines; EA Juffali & Bros.	Daimler-Benz; IBM; Kelvinator; Michelin; Siemens; Sulzer; York; Bosch. One of the oldest and most respected holding companies in the Kingdom and also includes a number of large industrial manufacturing concerns.
Kaki	Ahmad & Mohammad Saleh Kaki Group of Companies; Al Kaki Co; General Establishment for Trade & Contracts; Jiddah Kaki Hotel; National Printing Press.	Concentrates on: industry; contracting; banking; real estate; and technical services but buys in bulk for projects. Also runs large hotel and restaurant operations, including management services.
Kanoo	Yusuf B Ahmad Kanoo; Cable and Wireless Saudi Arabia.	Esso; Exxon; BASF. It has many branches and affiliates throughout the Gulf region.
Olayan	Arabian Automotive Co; General Trading Company; Olayan Saudi Holding Company; Olayan Saudi General Transportation Co.	Jaguar; Rover; Land Rover; General Foods; Kimberly-Clark; Rowntree Mackintosh; Chesebrough Ponds; Unigate; Tulip; Jacob Suchard; Tuborg; Löwenbräu; Borden; Waitaki; Campbells; Pillsbury; Overseas Trading (Lyons Tea); Beechnut; National Cheese; Société des Eaux Minérales (Sohat); Colgate Palmolive; Holland Canned Milk; Imperial Tobacco. Also huge international banking and financial interests, plus many local industries and joint ventures.
Pharaon	Saudi Research & Development Corporation; Redec Intertrade	Texas Instruments; Memorex; plus interests in:

Exhibit 8.10 *cont.*

Leading merchant families and wholesale trading houses in Saudi Arabia

Name of family	*Major companies, establishments affiliates and subsidiaries*	*Selected agencies and activities*
	Arinco; Saudi food Supplies & Supermarkets; Saudi Computer Services Co; Intermec; Arabian Homes.	BSN Gervais Danone; Industrie Buitoni Perugina; Montedison; Rosenthal Studio Line. Also large banking and financial interests in the US, local contracting and industrial trading.
Al Quraishi	Ali Zaid Al Quraishi & Bros; Saleh Zaid Al Quraishi Establishment for Trading and Contracting; Al Quraishi Distribution Services; Al Quraishi Leisure Services; Al Quraishi Furniture; Al Sabah Trading.	Samsonite; Canon; Sheaffer; AMF Bowling; Westinghouse; Reckitt & Colman; Tobacco Exporters International; Citizen; Swatch; Fabre-Leuba; Cussons; Fisher-Price; Mattel; Lego.
Shaker	Ibrahim Shaker Co Ltd; Shaker Trading Co.	General Electric; Electrolux.
Sharbatly	Saudi Arabian Marketing Corporation; Sharbatly Establishment for Trade & Development.	Importers and distributors of: foodstuffs; furniture; leisure and sporting goods; educational materials; paints; and toys.
Shobokshi	Ali and Fahd Shobokshi Group; Al Arousa Furniture Factory; Orient International Agencies; Orient Company for Trading & Marketing; Shobest Automotive Trading; Shobak Catering Group; Tihama Advertising; Shobokshi Commercial Enterprises; Public Relations and Marketing; General Agencies Corp; Alphatrans.	Thorn Lighting; Klein Philips BV; MAN; Magirus. The family founded the Arabic daily, *Okaz* and the English language *Saudi Gazette*.
Sudairi	Arabian Food Supplies.	Mars; Hero; Wellcome International; First Brands; Wrigleys; Green Giant; Ross; Pedigree Petfoods; Tate & Lyle.
Tamimi	Tamimi & Fouad; Tamimi & Fouad Foods Co Ltd.	Owns huge supermarkets in Riyadh, Dammam and Al Khobar. Originally set up with Safeway Stores of the US but now run independently. Imports, stores and distributes; foodstuffs; cosmetics; toiletries; and household goods.

Exhibit 8.10 *cont.*

Leading merchant families and wholesale trading houses in Saudi Arabia

Name of family	*Major companies, establishments affiliates and subsidiaries*	*Selected agencies and activities*
Zahid	Zahid Motors & Importers Co Ltd; Zahid Tractor & Heavy Machinery Co Ltd; Zahid Enterprises Co Ltd.	Renault; Volvo; Caterpillar; Mannesman Demag; Pirelli Tyres. Has also represented General Motors, Pignon and GMODC (Isuzu). Imports and sells: clothing; dairy foods; paints; and car care products.

As very few Saudi companies publish accounts or up to date lists of their agencies, it is advisable to check with the specific company to ascertain its present agencies and activities in detail.

Sources: JRL Carter, *Merchant Families of Saudi Arabia*, 2nd revised edition, London, 1984; Giselle C Bricault, ed; *Major Companies of the Arab World*, Graham & Trotman, London, 1988, and various other sources.

The trend towards import substitution in the field of basic food commodities and light consumer products will continue in the 1990s. It has become more evident that any leading product needs actually to be manufactured here in order to survive. Furthermore, the trend towards a common market in the Gulf by the year 2000 suggests that commodities produced domestically will soon have access to a Gulf-wide market.

The changing times ahead point to an ever greater need for firms to deliver a better, cheaper and more aggressively marketed product to the consumer. The increase in competition from local production should see established firms battling to maintain market share. This will be to the benefit of the Saudi consumer, who will ultimately enjoy good quality products and more competitive prices. The consumer, being more price sensitive, will opt for acceptable quality products with a cheaper price tag. The trend in the exchange markets, with the Saudi riyal pegged to the dollar, will play an important role in sales of consumer products. Exports from the newly industrialised countries of the Far East, considered to be dollar-based countries, will be seen competing more with established exporters from Europe and Japan.

It is critical that the distributors in the Kingdom be given every kind of support by their respective exporters. This includes advertising, exhibition participation, prompt deliveries, market-orientated product literature in Arabic, good after-sales support and training in product use. Because changing distributors may prove extremely difficult, great care should be taken when making the initial selection. A joint marketing effort between the supplier and the distributor is needed to help identify those who influence largescale purchasing (such as trade associations, public sector procurement committees, trade press editors, etc) and to keep them informed of the distinctive qualities of the product or service that is being promoted. Product and market research cannot be over-emphasised and market studies will be more useful if carried out by specialised institutions in the Kingdom who can better understand social habits and execute the surveys more effectively.

There is a pressing need for more media and product research. The limited availability of data relating to the effectiveness of media advertising on which millions of dollars may be spent makes the marketing task even more difficult. There is also a need for greater product research. Companies which have not already done so are increasingly adapting their products to the Saudi market. The future strategy should be to "make things they can sell" rather than to "sell things they already make". Instructions on most consumer products should be in both Arabic and English and equipment will need to be built to withstand the harsh climate of the Arabian peninsula.

The Saudi consumer in the 1990s will be wealthy, discerning and sophisticated. Though price will continue to be an important factor, the consumer will demand a certain quality and will require value for money. With the Kingdom experiencing one of the world's highest population growth rates and with large and rising disposable income, there will be a growing market for a whole range of consumer goods. In a bid to increase sales, manufacturers will be turning more and more towards the wholesalers and retailers of their products. Instead of aiming directly at the consumer, manufacturers will give incentives to the wholesaler to increase sales. Cash incentives may be given for volume sales based on sales history, so that the wholesaler's margin increases as sales increase. For products which move more slowly, manufacturers may give higher margins. The retailer/wholesaler will then push to increase sales of that particular product through discounts, promotion and advertising.

Domestic producers of consumer products are expected to face an uphill task against entrenched international brands. The label "made in Saudi Arabia" has already acquired a respectable image in the food processing and light consumer products industries. A more positive image has yet to be created for a wider range of consumer products manufactured domestically. This can be achieved through the execution of bold advertising and promotional campaigns. The following four-step strategy is recommended for effective market penetration in the 1990s: first, identify real consumer needs; secondly, develop products which meet those needs (this may involve altering the taste, colour or packaging of imported products); thirdly, create a demand for the product by advertising to reach the target consumers (by sex, age bracket, nationality etc); fourthly, continue improving the product since, once it succeeds, others will follow. Manufacturers need to progress constantly to create and maintain brand loyalty and to preserve market share.

Appendix

Sectors with the best sales prospects in the Saudi market

This information here is based on the Country Marketing Plan for Saudi Arabia for the fiscal year 1993, prepared by the US and foreign commercial services in Saudi Arabia.

Oil and gas field machinery and services

Market size: 1991 – US$5.65 billion, 1992 – US$6.25 billion; annual growth rate, 1992-95 – 9-10 per cent. *Total imports:* 1991 – US$4 billion, 1992 – US$5 billion; annual growth rate – 8 per cent. Expansion in the Saudi petroleum industry is expected to cost about US$33 billion, half of which will be spent in capital investment. *Most promising sub-sectors:* downhole and oil well head equipment, pipes and cases – US$2.5-US$3 billion; oil and gas field chemicals – US$200-US$300 million.

Operations and maintenance services

Market size: 1991 – US$4.5 billion, 1992 – US$5.15 billion; annual growth rate 1992-95 – 3 per cent. *Total sales by foreign-owned firms*: 1991 – US$3.5 billion, 1992 – US$4 billion; annual growth rate – 3 per cent. Market factors include high-tech sales of equipment and hardware, expansion plans in the oil and petrochemical sectors, and maintenance of infrastructure. *Most promising sub-sectors:* oil refineries maintenance – US$700-US$800 million; health care O&M services – US$2-US$2.5 billion; PTT O&M – US$200-US$250 million.

Building products

Market size: 1991 – US$3.2 billion, 1992 – US$3.37 billion; annual growth rate, 1992-95 – 8-9 per cent. *Total imports:* 1991 – US$1.8 billion, 1992 – US$1.85 billion; annual growth rate – 4-5 per cent. Construction work in the public and private sectors is on the upsurge again. Construction is currently the largest employer and the single largest investment sector. In the public sector, the oil industry will be spending about US$18 billion on expansion and upgrading works. *Most promising sub-sectors:* flooring systems – US$45-US$50 million; plumbing products – US$150-US$200 million; lighting products – US$25-US$30 million.

Automobiles and light trucks/vans

Market size: 1991 – US$1.65 billion, 1992 – US$1.73 billion; annual growth rate, 1992-95 – 4-5 per cent. *Total imports:* 1991 – US$1.65 billion, 1992 – US$1.73 billion; annual growth rate – 4-5 per cent. The Saudi population is growing at a rate – of 3.5 per cent annually. Demand for customised vans is growing rapidly and car rental companies are mushrooming. Japanese cars and trucks dominate the market even though American cars are benefiting from favourable exchange rates. *Most promising sub-sectors:* light trucks – US$225 million; customised cars and vans – US$80-US$90 million.

Automotive parts and service equipment

Market size: 1991 – US$1.4 billion, 1992 – US$1.5 billion; annual growth rate 1992-95 – 4-5 per cent. *Total imports:* 1991 – US$1.15 billion, 1992 – US$1.2 billion; annual growth rate – 4 per cent. Saudi Arabia is the fifth largest automobile market in the world. Limited off-the-shelf spare parts are manufactured locally under licence; the bulk of automotive parts are imported. More gas stations are being set up as full service centres offering wheel alignment and balancing, electrical and mechanical repairs, and include convenience stores and even pharmacies. A number of chains are already in operation across the country. *Most promising sub-sectors:* automotive accessories – US$50-US$60 million; wheel balancing equipment and accessories – US$75-US$100 million.

Chemical production machinery

Market size: 1991 – US$1.025 billion, 1992 – US$1.2 billion; annual growth rate, 1992-95 – 12-15 per cent. *Total imports:* 1991 – US$1.025 billion, 1992 – US$1.2 billion; annual growth rate – 12-15 per cent. The private sector is pushing ahead with many industrial ventures in the downstream petrochemical industry; there are also expansions at many major parastatal plants. *Most promising sub-sectors:* petrochemical production machinery – US$825 million (heat transfer equipment – US$300 million; mechanical equipment – US$275 million; electrical equipment – US$250 million).

Computer software

Market size: 1991 – US$650 million, 1992 – US$700 million; annual growth rate, 1992-95 – 7 per cent. *Total imports:* 1991 – US$420 million, 1992 – US$460 million; annual growth rate – 7 per cent. Imports of core software programs and database programs account for almost 60 per cent of the market. *Most promising sub-sectors:* database programs – US$100 million; business core programs – US$400-US$450 million.

Computers and peripherals

Market size: 1991 – US$400 million, 1992 – US$430 million; annual growth rate, 1992-95 – 5 per cent. *Total imports:* 1991 – US$400 million, 1992 – US$430 million; annual growth rate – 5 per cent. Computer utilisation is on the rise and the replacement market for upgraded and higher capacity computers is also growing. *Most promising sub-sector:* storage devices – US$50-US$60 million.

Architectural, construction and engineering services

Total sales: 1991 – US$600 million, 1992 – US$900 million; annual growth rate, 1992-95 – 5-6 per cent. *Total sales by foreign-owned firms:* 1991 – US$400 million, 1992 – US$700 million; annual growth rate – 4-5 per cent. Expansion in the oil and petrochemical sectors, the offset programme, utility expansion programmes and defence related projects offer opportunities for sub-contracting. (Saudi Arabia recently issued implementation rules for the Saudi Arabian Professional Partnerships Regulation, under which foreign professional firms may for the first time participate as firms in locally registered partnerships licensed to pursue one of the so-called "free professions", including consulting engineering). *Most promising sub-sectors:* road and bridge projects – US$200-US$250 million; public utility projects – US$350-US$400 million.

Air conditioning and refrigeration equipment

Market size: 1991 – US$750 million, 1992 – US$850 million; annual growth rate, 1992-95 – 12-14 per cent. *Total imports:* 1991 – US$450 million, 1992 – US$500 million; annual growth rate – 12 per cent. Harsh climatic conditions make the Kingdom a lucrative market for A/C equipment and parts. A resurgence in construction will also boost demand for these commodities. *Most promising sub-sector:* cold storage equipment – US$80-US$100 million.

Electrical power systems

Market size: 1991 – US$750 million, 1992 – US$850 million; annual growth rate, 1992-95 – 5-6 per cent. *Total imports:* 1991 – US$600 million, 1992 – US$675 million; annual growth rate – 5 per cent. A new power plant is being built in Riyadh. In addition, annual procurement of parts and materials for replacement and other expansion works will fuel demand. *Most promising sub-sector:* high-voltage substations – US$300-US$350 million.

Apparel

Market size: 1991 – US$835 million, 1992 – US$850 million; annual growth rate, 1992-95 – 4 per cent. *Total imports:* 1991 – US$820 million, 1992 – US$825 million; annual growth rate – 4.5 per cent. Higher per capita income and the increased number of expatriates will keep demand for apparel high. A favourable exchange rate – and the appeal of American brand names should help US product sales. *Most promising sub-sectors:* men's apparel – US$150-US$200 million; lingerie – US$80-US$90 million; women's and girls' apparel – US$150-US$200 million.

Education and manpower training services

Total sales: 1991 – US$500 million, 1992 – US$750 million; annual growth rate, 1992-95 – 8-9 per cent. *Total sales by foreign-owned firms:* 1991 – US$120 million; 1992 – US$200 million; annual growth rate – 7-8 per cent. Higher education and manpower training continue to have a high priority for Saudis. Each year, an increasing number of young Saudis enter the job market needing additional training to complement their educational backgrounds. *Most promising sub-sectors:* education abroad – US$80-US$90 million; technical training – US$50-US$55 million.

Household consumer goods

Market size: 1991 – US$670 million, 1992 – US$700 million; annual growth rate, 1992-95 – 4 per cent. *Total imports:* 1991 – US$600 million, 1992 – US$645 million; annual growth rate – 3-4 per cent. The buoyant housing market and higher disposable income level will boost sales in this area. *Most promising sub-sectors:* housewares US$160 million; electrical appliances – US$375 million.

Commercial vessels and equipment

Market size: 1991 – US$600 million, 1992 – US$660 million; annual growth rate, 1992-95 – 9 per cent. *Total imports:* 1991 – US$600 million, 1992 – US$650 million; annual growth rate – 9 per cent. Saudi Arabia is expanding its fleet of owned crude tankers and PLG carriers; it has several ships currently under construction and plans to buy more. Petrochemical carriers will also be purchased by various entities in line with the growth in petrochemical exports. *Most promising sub-sectors:* oil tankers – US$450 million; barges and tugboats – US$25-US$35 million.

Telecommunications equipment

Market size: 1991 – US$450 million, 1992 – US$500 million; annual growth rate, 1992-95 – 6 per cent. *Total imports:* 1991 – US$430 million, 1992 – US$470 million; annual growth rate – 6 per cent. The Kingdom is expanding and upgrading its telecommunications systems. Large investments are expected, especially in voice data communication, telephone network expansion, and possibly radio and TV coverage. *Most promising sub-sectors:* public pay telephones – US$45-US$50 million; data communications equipment – US$100-US$150 million.

Water resources equipment

Market size: 1991 – US$400 million, 1992 – US$420 million; annual growth rate, 1992-95 – 5 per cent. *Total imports:* 1991 – US$380 million, 1992 – US$400 million; annual growth rate – 5 per cent. With expansion of the Saudi agriculture sector, irrigation equipment is still a lucrative market sector. Saudi Arabia has the largest desalination volume in the world and is still expanding capacity. *Most promising sub-sector:* pumps – US$40-US$45 million; desalination equipment – US$250-US$300 million.

Textile products, made-up

Market size: 1991 – US$400 million, 1992 – US$425 million; annual growth rate 1992-95 – 6 per cent. *Total imports:* 1991 – US$380 million, 1992 – US$400 million; annual growth rate – 5 per cent. Well known brand names are in high demand. Rising disposable income levels will mean increase demand for top-of-the-range linens, towels and textiles in general. Sales will also get a boost from increased residential and office construction. *Most promising sub-sector:* wall-to-wall carpets – US$250 million.

Furniture

Market size: 1991 – US$400 million, 1992 – US$425 million; annual growth rate, 1992-95 – 4-5 per cent. *Total imports:* 1991 – US$300 million, 1992 – US$320 million; annual growth rate – 4-5 per cent. New housing developments are on the rise, which should generate – substantial new opportunities for furniture sales. *Most promising sub-sectors:* household furniture – US$225 million; office furniture – US$90-US$100 million; hospital furniture – US$75 million.

Drugs and pharmaceuticals

Market size: 1991 – US$385 million, 1992 – US$400 million; annual growth rate, 1992-95 – 5 per cent. *Total imports:* 1991 – US$275 million, 1992 – US$280 million; annual growth rate – 3-4 per cent. Switzerland and US are the largest suppliers of drugs and pharmaceuticals to Saudi Arabia. Local manufacturing under licensing arrangements is expanding. The market has opened to generic drugs, but there has not yet been a substantial influx of them. *Most promising sub-sectors:* generic drugs – US$25-US$35 million; veterinary preparations – US$50 million; vitamins and provitamins – US$70 million.

Construction equipment

Market size: 1991 – US$300 million, 1992 – US$350 million; annual growth rate, 1992-95 – 4-5 per cent. *Total imports:* 1991 – US$300 million, 1992 – US$350 million; annual growth rate – 4-5 per cent. Demand will be fueled by the oil and petrochemical expansions, utility and road projects, and the expansion and upgrading of various military and civilian installations. *Most promising sub-sectors:* earthmoving equipment – US$30-US$35 million; pile drivers – US$20-US$25 million; excavators – US$15-US$20 million; front-end loaders – US$30-US$35 million.

Computer services

Total sales: 1991 – US$300 million, 1992 – US$325 million; annual growth rate, 1992-95 – 7-8 per cent. *Total sales by foreign-owned firms:* 1991 – US$260 million, 1992 – US$265 million; annual growth rate – 7-8 per cent. Many businesses and institutions are becoming automated. The use of LAN and WAN is increasing as these entities integrate functions and systems. *Most promising sub-sector:* systems integration – US$300 million.

Printing and graphic art equipment

Market size: 1991 – US$250 million, 1992 – US$300 million; annual growth rate, 1992-95 – 5 per cent. *Total imports:* 1991 – US$245 million, 1992 – US$295 million; annual growth rate – 5 per cent. The Saudi printing industry is expanding. The replacement market is also good as Saudis replace outdated equipment with microprocessor-based equipment and state-of-the art machinery. *Most promising sub-sectors:* typesetting and typemaking machines – US$150 million; printing machines – US$100 million.

Franchising

Total sales: 1991 – US$170 million, 1992 – US$185 million; annual growth rate, 1992-95 – 9-10 per cent. *Total sales by foreign-owned firms:* 1991 – US$140 million, 1992 – US$155 million; annual growth rate – 10 per cent. There is excellent potential for this type of investment, especially for restaurants and fast-food outlets. *Most promising sub-sector:* fast-food outlets – US$150 million.

Materials handling machinery

Market size: 1991 – US$135 million, 1992 – US$150 million; annual growth rate, 1992-95 – 15-18 per cent. *Total imports:* 1991 – US$135 million, 1992 – US$150 million; annual growth rate – 15-18 per cent. The economic mini-boom reflected in increased investments in the industrial sector, a flourishing construction sector, accelerated development of the mining industry, and increased flows of goods and services at major Saudi entry ports will keep demand high in this sector. *Most promising sub-sectors:* forklifts – US$30 million; port handling equipment – US$75-US$80 million.

Food processing and packaging equipment

Market size: 1991 – US$90 million, 1992 – US$100 million; annual growth rate, 1992-95 – 9-10 per cent. *Total imports:* 1991 – US$90 million, 1992 – US$100 million; annual growth rate – 9-10 per cent. The food processing and packaging industry has tremendous growth potential because of the formation of new food-processing companies. *Most promising sub-sectors:* processing and packaging machinery for dates – US$13 million; for meat – US$20 million; for snack foods – US$20-US$25 million.

Travel and tourism services

Total sales: 1991 – US$75 million, 1992 – US$100 million; annual growth rate, 1992-95 – 6-7 per cent. *Total sales by foreign-owned firms:* 1991 – US$65 million, 1992 – US$80 million; annual growth rate – 6-7 per cent. Saudis tend to travel in large family groups and to make long stays. *Most promising sub-sector:* leisure travel – US$60 million.

Used/reconditioned equipment

Market size: 1991 – US$750 million, 1992 – US$800 million; annual growth rate 1992-95 – 6-7 per cent. *Total imports:* 1991 – US$490 million, 1992 – US$525 million; annual growth rate – 4 per cent. In the aftermath of the Gulf crisis, a lot of civilian and military hardware was auctioned for use by various local companies. In addition, many car showrooms have begun to establish liaison offices or persons overseas to procure second-hand vehicles, trucks, motor homes and vans. Finally, automotive spare parts dealers are increasingly stocking various rebuilt/reconditioned parts that appeal to budget conscious clients. *Most promising sub-sectors:* used automobiles – US$90 million; reconditioned automotive spare parts – US$125-US$150 million; used construction equipment – US$350-US$400 million.

Industrial chemicals

Market size: 1991 – US$520 million, 1992 – US$550 million; annual growth rate, 1992-95 – 6-7 per cent. *Total imports:* 1991 – US$450 million, 1992 – US$470 million; annual growth rate – 6 per cent. Oil and petrochemical projects and expansions will mean increased supplies of cleaning equipment and chemicals. Similar expansions of the water supply system will create opportunities for water treatment chemicals. *Most promising sub-sectors:* industrial cleaning agents – US$60-US$70 million; water treatment chemicals – US$80-US$90 million.

Paper and paperboard

Market size: 1991 – US$500 million, 1992 – US$550 million; annual growth rate, 1992-95 – 7 per cent. *Total imports:* 1991 – US$485 million, 1992 – US$525 million; annual growth rate – 6 per cent. Imports will increase substantially due to growth in the packaging industry, population growth and increased consumerism. *Most promising sub-sectors:* Kraft paper and paperboard – US$75 million; newsprint paper – US$125 million; toilet and facial tissue paper – US$175-US$200 million.

Industrial process controls

Market size: 1991 – US$120 million, 1992 – US$125 million; annual growth rate, 1992-95 – 4 per cent. *Total imports:* 1991 – US$115 million, 1992 – US$120 million; annual growth rate – 4-5 per cent. The expansion in the petroleum and petrochemical sectors and of the electric power grid and the replacement market, are expected to keep demand high in this area. *Most promising sub-sectors:* oil-related process control instrumentation – US$90-US$100 million; process controls for electric power – US$20-US$25 million.

Pollution control equipment

Market size: 1991 – US$112 million, 1992 – US$117 million; annual growth rate, 1992-95 – 4-5 per cent. *Total imports:* 1991 – US$107 million, 1992 – US$113 million; annual growth rate – 5 per cent. The government gives high priority to environmental protection and pollution control. During the fifth Five-year Plan, US$260 million has been allocated to environmental protection. Toxic and hazardous waste treatment and control are becoming increasingly important in industrial cities, especially Jubail and Yanbu'. *Most promising sub-sectors:* industrial filters – US$25-US$30 million; toxic and hazardous waste treatment – US$30-US$40 million; wastewater treatment – US$25-US$30 million.

Airport and ground support equipment

Market size: 1991 – US$110 million, 1992 – US$115 million; annual growth rate, 1992-95 – 8-10 per cent. *Total imports:* 1991 – US$110 million, 1992 – US$115 million; annual growth rate – 8-10 per cent. Existing domestic airport instrumentation and support equipment are being upgraded and new military airports are being built. *Most promising sub-sectors:* air traffic control equipment – US$40-45 million; airport support equipment – US$60-US$65 million.

Security and safety equipment

Market size: 1991 – US$80 million, 1992 – US$90 million; annual growth rate, 1992-95 – 10 per cent. *Total imports:* 1991 – US$72 million, 1992 – US$75 million; annual growth rate – 8-10 per cent. Concern for safety and security has increased since the Gulf War, and there is a growing interest in modern security and protection systems and installations. *Most promising sub-sectors:* industrial oil-related safety gear – US$30-US$35 million; airport security systems – US$50-US$55 million.

Sporting and recreation goods

Market size: 1991 – US$65 million, 1992 – US$68 million; annual growth rate, 1992-95 – 4 per cent. *Total imports:* 1991 – US$65 million, 1992 – US$68 million; annual growth rate – 4 per cent. Recent increases in the expatriate population will have a positive effect on demand for sporting goods. The government plans to build more recreation and amusement parks. Southeast Asian countries still dominate the sector. *Most promising sub-sectors:* outdoor playground equipment – US$15 million; amusement park equipment and rides – US$20 million; indoor health and fitness equipment – US$30-US$35 million.

Films, videos, recordings

Market size: 1991 – US$60 million, 1992 – US$65 million; annual growth rate, 1992-95 – 5 per cent. *Total imports:* 1991 – US$24 million, 1992 – US$28 million; annual growth rate – 5-6 per cent. Videotape rental shops are mushrooming. Satellite dishes have also become common and will pressure local TV stations to acquire better and more varied TV programmes in both English and Arabic. *Most promising sub-sectors:* TV programs – US$30-US$35 million; movie videos – US$25 million.

Machine tools and metal working equipment

Market size: 1991 – US$55 million, 1992 – US$60 million; annual growth rate, 1992-95 – 7 per cent. *Total imports:* 1991 – US$50 million, 1992 – US$54 million; annual growth rate – 7 per cent. New industrial estates are being developed in response to the industrial boom in the country. Non-oil industries are growing at 7.5 per cent annually and will account for a larger share of the Saudi GDP. *Most promising sub-sectors:* metal forming and finishing equipment – US$35 million; pipeline welding equipment – US$15-US$20 million.

Pumps, valves and compressors

Market size: 1991 – US$155 million, 1992 – US$60 million; annual growth rate, 1992-95 – 5-6 per cent. *Total imports:* 1991 – US$145 million, 1992 – US$150 million; annual growth rate – 5 per cent. Oil and petrochemical expansions will keep demand high in this product group. *Most promising sub-sector:* oil-related PVC – US$100 million.

Plastics production machinery

Market size: 1991 – US$17 million, 1992 – US$20 million; annual growth rate, 1992-95 – 7-8 per cent. *Total imports:* 1991 – US$17 million, 1992 –

Exhibit 8.11

Sectors with the best sales prospects in the Saudi market, 1993 - 95

Sector	*Market size (US$ millions)*	*Annual growth rate (%)*	*Total imports (US$ millions)*
Oil & Gas field Machinery & Services	6,250	9-10	5,000
Operation & maintenance services	5,200	3	4,000
Building products	3,400	8-9	1,900
Automobiles & light trucks/vans	1,730	4-5	1,730
Automotive parts & service equipment	1,500	4-5	1,200
Chemical production machinery	1,200	12-15	1,200
Computers & computer software	1,150	4-7	850
Architectural, construction & engineering	900	5-6	700
Air conditioning & refrigeration equipment	850	12-14	450
Electrical power systems	850	5-6	645
Apparel	850	4-5	825
Education & manpower training services	750	8-9	200
Household consumer goods	700	4	645
Commercial vessels & equipment	660	9	650
Telecommunications equipment	500	6	460
Agricultural sector & water desalination	450	5	400
Textile products, made-up	425	6	400
Furniture	425	4-5	320
Drugs & pharmaceuticals	400	5	280
Construction equipment	350	4-5	350
Computer services	325	7-8	265
Printing & graphic art equipment	300	5	295
Franchising	185	8-9	155
Materials handling machinery	150	15	150
Food processing & packaging equipment	100	9-10	90

Source: Based on the Country Marketing Plan for Saudi Arabia for the fiscal year 1993, prepared by the US and foreign commercial services in Saudi Arabia.

US$20 million; annual growth rate – 7-8 per cent. The private sector is spearheading development of the plastics industry. Nine capital-rich joint stock companies were established to invest in petrochemical and plastics related industries. European machinery manufacturers have kept a dominant share of the market. *Most promising sub-sectors:* extrusion equipment – US$8-US$9 million; plastic packaging machinery – US$10-US$11 million.

Dental equipment

Market size: 1991 – US$12 million, 1992 – US$14 million; annual growth rate, 1992-95 – 8-9 per cent. *Total imports:* 1991 – US$12 million, 1992 – US$14 million; annual growth rate – 8-9 per cent. Providing better medical services to the Saudi population is a government priority. More full-service dental clinics are being set up every year by the private sector. *Most promising sub-sectors:* dental materials and supplies – US$4-US$5 million; surgical equipment – US$9 million.

9 External sectors: trade flows and balance of payments structure

Introduction

Saudi Arabia is among the 20 largest economies in the world, with a total GDP of US$107 billion in 1991. The Kingdom is the largest market for foreign goods and services in the Middle East and one of the top 15 importers in the world. In 1991 Saudi Arabia imported close to SR108.9 billion (US$29 billion) worth of goods from the rest of the world and paid close to SR143 billion (US$38 billion) for services rendered by foreign companies working in the Kingdom. Compared with industrialised countries, Saudi Arabia imported more goods than Greece, Portugal, Turkey, Ireland or New Zealand. The Kingdom is also a larger market than Australia and Thailand if imports of services are included. After dropping from a peak of SR139 billion (US$37 billion) in 1982 to a low of SR70 billion (US$18.6 billion) in 1986, Saudi merchandise imports began to rise once more, reaching SR108.9 billion (US$29.04 billion) in 1991 (see Exhibit 9.1).

Exhibit 9.1

Saudi Arabian exports and imports, 1982 - 91 (SR billions)

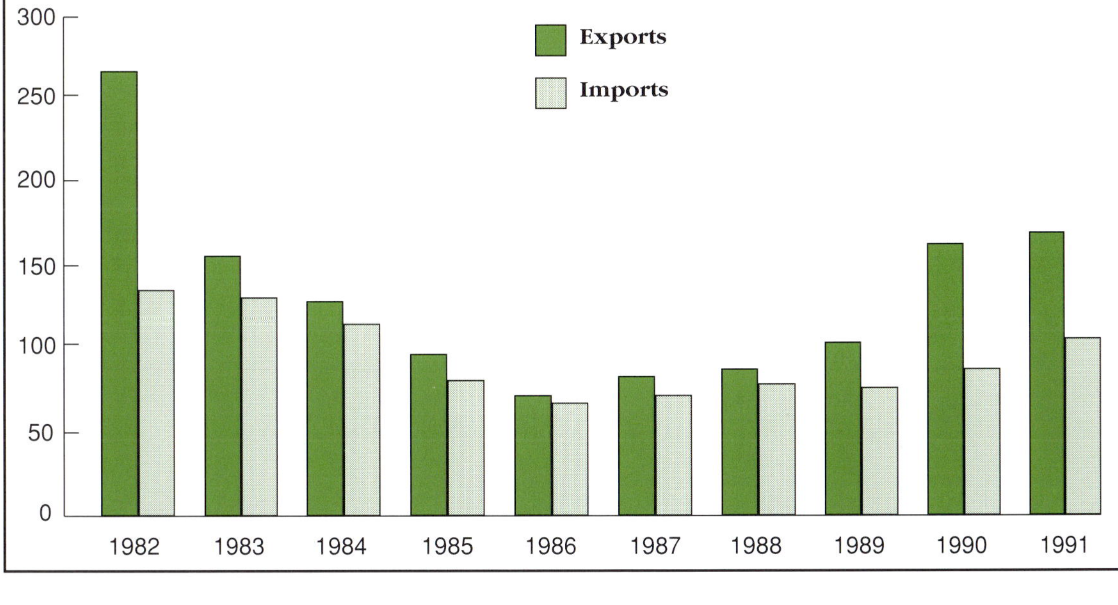

Saudi Arabia maintains no exchange controls and does not impose trade restrictions for balance of payments reasons, although a few items are banned for religious reasons. Commercial policy, including incentives and measures aimed at influencing capital flows, are used to promote domestic economic activity. Most imports are subject to tariffs at the rate of 12 per cent, with a 30 per cent duty on tobacco. However, in order to promote import-substituting industries, a limited number of manufactured imports are subject to protective tariffs of 20 per cent (detergents and soap, plastic products, marble and cement tiles, macaroni, confectionery, furniture, cement and iron bars, among others). On the other hand, certain raw material inputs and essential foodstuffs (sugar, rice, tea, meat, barley, etc) are allowed to be imported free of tariffs. Foreign contractors are required to sub-contract 30 per cent of government contracts to Saudi Arabian firms when domestic contractors are in a position to fulfil such sub-contracts. Similarly, machinery, equipment and services needed for the implementation of government projects have to be procured through domestic firms.

The Saudi riyal, while officially pegged to the SDR, has in effect been linked to the US dollar (the intervention currency) for several years. The Kingdom's exchange rate policy aims at maintaining stable exchange rates with other members of the GCC, at minimising exchange risks for the private sector (who consider themselves as dollar-based), at ensuring competitiveness of Saudi manufactured products and at curtailing inflation. Accordingly, the exchange rate of SR3.75 to the US dollar is likely to be sustained for the foreseeable future.

Saudi exports

Oil exports

Total exports by Saudi Arabia were SR179 billion (US$47.7 billion) in 1991, up by 7.5 per cent from their 1990 level of SR166.3 billion (US$44.3 billion) and almost double their 1988 value of SR91.3 billion (US$24.3 billion). Exhibit 9.2 gives details of each sector's contribution to these totals.

Crude oil constitutes the bulk of Saudi exports, accounting for 78.1 per cent of the total; petrochemical products account for 13.3 per cent, refined oil products 5 per cent and other commodities 3.6 per cent (see Exhibit 9.3).

The major markets for Saudi Arabia's exports are Asia (mainly Japan and other South East Asian countries), which accounts for 34 per cent of total exports, followed by North America (24 per cent), western Europe (21.2 per cent) and the GCC countries (6.7 per cent). Around half of total Saudi exports to the GCC countries was in the form of crude oil to Bahrain for processing at the Island refinery. Saudi industrial exports to other GCC states did not exceed SR5 billion (US$1.33 billion) out of total exports to the five Gulf states of SR12 billion (US$3.2 billion). Exports to other Arab and Islamic countries have been rising in the last few years, accounting in 1991 for 8.5 per cent of total Saudi exports. Complete figures are given in Exhibit 9.4.

Exhibit 9.2

Saudi Arabian exports by sector, 1988 - 91 (SR millions)

	1991	*1990*	*1989*	*1988*
Oil & other mineral products	164,102	150,837	90,839	75,995
Chemicals	5,615	5,720	5,737	6,386
Resins, plastics & rubber	3,465	3,819	4,236	3,897
Base metals	1,179	1,537	1,419	971
Transport equipment	833	1,066	705	866
Machinery & electrical appliances	804	728	652	638
Vegetable products	670	835	1,141	1,001
Live animals & animal products	543	337	231	237
Paper & products	327	325	311	270
Textiles	310	250	275	209
Miscellaneous manufactured items	299	54	66	50
Stone, plaster, ceramic & glass	190	127	111	147
Fats & oil	93	54	33	7
Processed food & drink	65	220	179	136
Leather products	65	111	120	214
Wood & products	31	54	45	51
Instruments & equipment	17	88	47	42
Footwear & accessories	14	9	12	16
Jewellery	11	231	135	156
Total	**178,974**	**166,339**	**106,294**	**91,289**

Source: Central Department of Statistics, foreign trade statistics 1991.

The value of Saudi Arabia's oil exports, including crude oil, refined oil products and natural gas liquids (NGLs), fell steeply from a peak of US$111 billion in 1981 to a low of US$18 billion in 1986, before recovering to about US$20 billion in 1987 and 1988 and US$24 billion in 1989. Saudi Arabia responded to the Gulf crisis and the loss of Iraqi and Kuwaiti output by boosting its production and exports of crude oil. This, together with firmer oil prices, helped to raise total oil exports to US$40 billion in 1990, US$43.7 billion in 1991 and an estimated US$44.2 billion in 1992. Implicitly included in these revenues are oil grants to selected countries and the countertrade agreements established by the government to support special projects (eg the 500,000 b/d allocated to the British Al-Yamamah arms sale programme and special construction projects in the Kingdom for which an estimated 340,000 b/d of oil has been reserved).

The geographical distribution of Saudi Arabia's crude oil exports has changed dramatically over the past decade from a focus on the Far East towards a more balanced distribution among major markets in the US, western Europe and the Far East. During the early 1980s Saudi Arabia shipped more than half its annual crude oil exports to customers in the Far East (especially Japan), 25 per cent to Europe and less than 10 per cent to North America, whereas in 1991 almost 30 per cent of total exports were directed to North America, 30 per cent to the Far East and 25 per cent to Europe.

Several factors contributed to this change. In the US a continuing decline in domestic production, rising demand for oil imports and the development of Saudi Arabia's joint venture with Texaco provided a base demand for Saudi crude which had not been there previously. In addition,

Exhibit 9.3

Export by sector, 1991

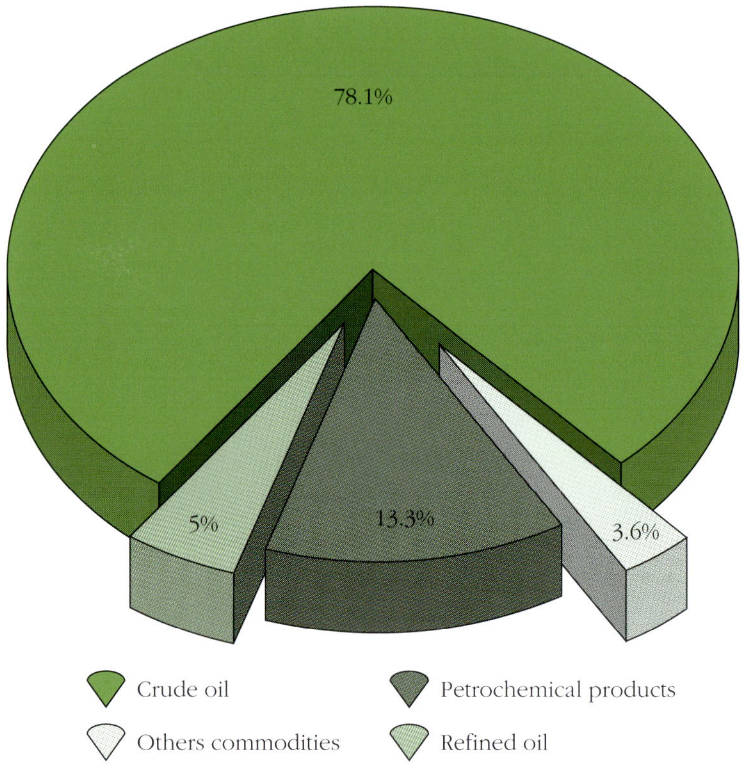

more flexible Saudi pricing arrangements and more generous allowances for transport costs helped to attract North American customers who had shied away from Saudi crude during the days of high, fixed official selling prices. As a result, Saudi Arabia has become the single largest supplier of oil and oil products to the US, with supplies of approximately 1.64 million b/d in the first half of 1992 accounting for 55 per cent of US oil imports from OPEC and over 30 per cent of total US imports of 5.4 million b/d.

In contrast, Saudi crude exports to the Far East declined during the 1980s, as Japan and South Korea adopted policies intended to limit their dependence on oil from the Gulf. As a result, Saudi crude and product exports to the Far East dropped from approximately 2.3 million b/d in 1983 to only about 1.1 million b/d in 1986, before recovering to about 2 million b/d in 1991. In the first half of 1992 Saudi Arabia once more became Japan's leading crude supplier, with oil exports reaching 1.12 million b/d. Looking ahead, this recovery in Japan and other Far Eastern markets will almost certainly continue. The Far East is the fastest growing market in the world for crude oil and oil products. Moreover, Japan and South Korea have both come to the conclusion in recent years that there is no alternative to a growing dependence on Gulf oil and have revised their approaches to energy security by focusing on enhancing trade flows with the Kingdom and with other Gulf states, rather than reducing them as had been the case in the past.

Saudi Arabia is a major factor in the world liquified petroleum gas (LPG) markets. It accounts for 7 to 10 per cent of world output of NGLs,

Exhibit 9.4

Exports and imports by region, 1991 (SR millions)

Region	*Exports*	*% of total*	*Imports*	*% of total*	*Imports as a % of exports*
Asian (non Islamic, non Arab)	60,568	33.8	26,669	24.5	44.0
North America	42,525	23.7	23,018	21.1	54.1
Western Europe	37,968	21.2	45,462	41.7	119.1
Gulf Cooperation Council	12,043	6.7	1,527	1.4	12.7
Islamic, non arab countries	10,117	5.6	4,041	3.7	39.9
Other Arab League countries	5,198	2.9	2,908	2.7	55.9
South America	4,992	2.8	2,155	2.0	43.2
Australia & Oceania	2,284	1.3	1,385	1.3	60.6
African (non-Arabic or Islamic)	1,766	0.98	276	0.3	15.6
Eastern Europe	1,249	0.69	1,096	1.0	87.7
Not defined	262	0.14	342	0.3	130.1
Total	**178,974**	**100.0**	**108,881**	**100.0**	**60.8**

Source: Central Department of Statistics, foreign trade statistics, 1991.

such as propane, butane and natural gasoline, and, with 30 per cent of the world seaborne trade in LPGs (propane and butane), it is the world's largest exporter of these products. ARAMCO has the capacity to produce about 600,000 b/d of NGLs, including approximately 315,000 b/d of propane, 165,000 b/d of butane and 120,000 b/d of natural gasoline. In addition, Saudi Arabia's refineries can contribute up to 40,000 b/d of LPGs when operating at full capacity.

Saudi Arabia's refining industry plays a role out of proportion to its size in the world trade in refined products. While its 1.6 million b/d capacity accounts for only about 2 per cent of world totals, annual exports of around 765,000 b/d account for about 10 per cent of total free world trade in oil products. Saudi refined product exports peaked in 1988 at about 819,000 b/d but declined in the following years in response to the rationalisation of SAMAREC's refinery operations (cutting production from the least sophisticated refineries), surging domestic military demand during 1990 and 1991 and a recovering national economy, which should itself add 50,000 b/d *per annum* to domestic demand. As a result, Saudi product exports have totalled no more than 765,000 b/d in 1991 and are estimated to have reached 785,000 b/d in 1992.

Non-oil exports

After having remained virtually unchanged at a low level in the early 1980s, the value of Saudi Arabia's non-oil exports increased substantially from SR3.75 billion (US$1 billion) in 1983 to SR6.2 billion (US$1.66 billion) in 1986 and SR16.87 billion (US$4.5 billion) in 1991. The annual rate of growth of non-oil exports during the period from 1986 to 1991 period exceeded 22 per cent (see Exhibit 9.5). With the sharp fall in oil exports, the contribution of non-oil exports to total export value rose from less than 1 per cent in 1981 to around 17 per cent in 1991. The strong growth

Exhibit 9.5

Saudi Arabia's non-oil exports (SR millions)

	1986	*1991*	*Annual growth (%)*
Petrochemicals	4,238	9,080	18
Vegetable products	173	670	30
Base Metal products	88	1,179	54
Processed food & oil	65	158	16
Paper products	18	327	85
Stone articles, cement & ceramics	24	280	65
Machinery & electrical appliances	28	821	98
Others	1,612	4,360	23
Total	**6,246**	**16,875**	**22**

Source: Ministry of Trade, 1992.

in non-oil exports since 1983 was associated with the commencement of exports of petrochemical products from the plants constructed at Jubail and Yanbu' and reflected both a gradual expansion of capacity and rising world market prices. However, prices of basic petrochemical products declined by between 10 per cent and 30 per cent in 1991 and 1992 because of the economic slowdown in the major industrial countries. This was partially offset by higher Saudi production of petrochemical products but the value of total exports of chemicals, resins, plastics and rubber dropped by 4.9 per cent in 1991.

Accounting for 5 per cent of world petrochemical capacity at the end of 1991, SABIC is a major exporter of chemicals, fertilisers, metals, plastics and gases. Total 1991 production at all SABIC affiliates was 13.14 million metric tons, up from the 13.07 million in 1990. Exports stood at 10.11 million metric tons (equivalent to almost 80 per cent of total production), compared with 10.54 million the previous year. By far the leading category of production and exports was chemicals, of which 7 million metric tons were produced and 4.6 million exported. Representing a rapidly growing business area at SABIC, fertiliser production reached 2.3 million metric tons, 56 per cent of which was exported. Output of metals, including steel and aluminium co-produced with Bahrain at the Aluminium Bahrain (Alba) facility, was 1.7 million metric tons, all of which was exported. Plastics production reached 1.4 million metric tons, all of which was exported, while output of industrial gases totalled 600,000 metric tons, of which 500,000 metric tons was sold abroad.

Underscoring the role of SABIC in the diversification of Saudi exports, overseas sales accounted for 63 per cent of deliveries in 1991. The share of exports in these deliveries would have been even higher if it were not for the fact that 50 per cent of the company's fertiliser output is consumed domestically. The leading foreign destination of SABIC products was the Far East, accounting for 24 per cent of total shipments. Southeast Asia took 14 per cent, while Europe accounted for 13 per cent. North America and Latin America took 6 per cent and 4 per cent of shipments, respectively, while Africa took 2 per cent. A major marketing focus in the future will be on eastern Europe and the former USSR.

Other non-oil exports remained low until 1986, as the emphasis in domestic production was mainly on import-substituting activities. In the past four years, however, exports of non-petrochemical manufactured goods have increased substantially, in response partly to the real effective depreciation of the riyal against non-dollar currencies but also owing to various export promotion measures and the huge private sector investments in industry. While exports of agricultural products (mainly wheat) have also increased sharply in the past few years (up 30 per cent during the period from 1986 to 1991), they accounted for less than 16 per cent of non-oil export value in 1991.

Exports of manufactured goods (other than petrochemicals) continued to grow rapidly, reaching a total of SR5.79 billion (US$1.54 billion) in 1991 from SR5.01 billion (US$1.34 billion) in 1988. The most important items exported are base metals (steel, copper, cable, wires, etc), transport equipment, machinery and electrical appliances (especially air conditioners), wheat and other vegetable products, paper products and animal products.

Saudi imports

Following rapid growth from the mid-1970s to 1982, the value of merchandise imports declined by more than 50 per cent in the four years

Exhibit 9.6

Imports by broad economic category, 1991

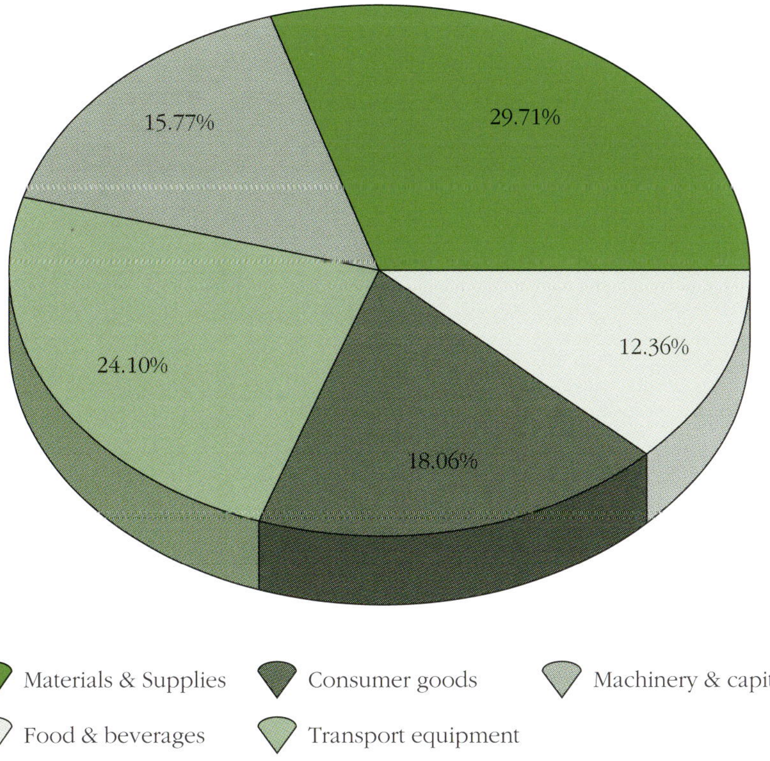

ended 1986. This sharp decline resulted largely from the substantial reduction in domestic consumption associated with the drop in government spending and the related stagnation in private sector economic activity during that period. The fall in imports was particularly pronounced for capital goods, construction material and transport equipment. Imports rose by about US$2.7 billion in 1987 and 1988 before declining by US$0.6 billion in 1989, owing to the much smaller increase in import prices than in the two preceding years. In real terms, however, imports are estimated to have continued to decline (by a total of about 6 per cent in this three-year period), despite the resumption of growth in the non-oil sectors. This is explained mainly by the rise in import-substituting domestic production, the sharp reduction in government spending on infrastructure and other projects and the reduced level of domestic demand during that period.

Imports surged in 1990 and 1991, reflecting the upturn in domestic economic activity and the additional expenditure associated with the Gulf crisis. Merchandise imports reached SR90 billion (US$24 billion) in 1990 and were up by 20 per cent in 1991 to SR108.9 billion (US$29.04 billion). A breakdown of imports by broad economic category is given in Exhibit 9.6.

Around 50 per cent of total imports enter the Kingdom through Jeddah seaport. Dammam seaport comes next with around 16.9 per cent of the total, followed by Jeddah, Riyadh and Dhahran airports with 9.4 per cent, 9 per cent and 7.5 per cent respectively.

A breakdown into more specific categories is given in Exhibit 9.7. This shows transport equipment and parts accounting for SR22.9 billion

Exhibit 9.7

Saudi Arabian imports by sector, 1988 - 91 (SR millions)

	1991	*1990*	*1989*	*1988*
Transport equipment & parts	22,868	18,471	14,640	11,930
Machinery & applicances	21,115	14,777	14,557	15,527
Base metals	9,931	7,830	6,476	8,133
Textiles	9,169	7,947	7,754	8,665
Chemicals	8,065	7,232	5,274	6,470
Live animals & animal products	5,613	4,838	4,392	4,278
Jewellery & gold	5,531	6,213	3,848	1,970
Processed food & drink	4,446	3,639	3,461	3,768
Resins, plastics, rubber	4,213	3,518	2,943	3,302
Vegetable products	3,610	3,737	4,499	4,789
Instruments & equipment	3,072	2,836	2,927	3,110
Miscellaneous manufactured items	2,648	1,751	1,773	2,034
Paper & products	1,879	1,736	1,349	1,600
Stone, plaster, ceramic & glass	1,848	1,677	1,666	1,965
Wood & products	1,564	1,249	1,088	1,403
Footwear & accessories	1,194	895	975	932
Minerals	844	760	727	711
Fats & oils	490	403	212	267
Leather products	435	358	374	393
Art	303	244	265	311
Arms & ammunition	45	28	21	24
Total	**108,881**	**90,139**	**79,219**	**81,582**

Source: Central Department of Statistics, foreign trade statistics, 1991.

(US$6.1 billion) in 1991, up 23.8 per cent on the level the year before, followed by machinery and appliances at SR21.1 billion (US$5.6 billion), up 42.8 per cent on the year before, base metals at SR9.3 billion (US$2.5 billion), up 26.8 per cent on the 1990 level and textiles at SR9.2 billion (US$2.4 billion), up 15 per cent on the year before. The value of chemicals imported rose by 11 per cent to SR8.06 billion (US$2.15 billion) in 1991, while foodstuffs imported rose by 12 per cent to SR13.6 billion (US$3.6 billion). Gold and jewellery where among the few imported items whose import value dropped in 1991, with an 11 per cent fall to SR5.53 billion (US$1.47 billion).

Exhibit 9.8 shows the 15 major exporting countries to Saudi Arabia and Exhibit 9.9 lists their chief exports to the Kingdom.

Since 1988 the US has maintained its position as the largest exporter to the Kingdom. In 1991 total US exports to Saudi Arabia rose to SR22 billion (US$5.87 billion) or 20.2 per cent of the market, compared to SR15.06 billion (US$4 billion), a market share of 16.7 per cent, in 1990. The main US products imported were aircraft parts, military equipment, cars, machinery parts, cigarettes, household appliances, furniture, computers, electrical generators and foodstuffs. Japan slipped to second position in 1988 and has held it ever since. Its exports of SR14.9 billion (US$3.97 billion) represented 13.7 per cent of the total Saudi import market in 1991, down from 15.3 per cent in 1990. Japanese exports to the Kingdom were dominated by cars and trucks, vehicle parts, tyres, electronics and electrical appliances. The UK remained in third place for the fifth consecutive year, although its market share has moved up from 7 per cent in 1988 to 11.3 per cent in 1991. Its exports of SR12.2 billion (US$3.25 billion) were dominated by aircraft parts, military products, medicines, gold ingots and cigarettes. Germany, with SR8.52 billion (US$2.27 billion), increased its share of the market from 7.4 per cent in 1990 to 7.8 per cent in 1991. Its main exports were vehicles, machinery and equipment, iron and aluminium structures and spare parts. These four countries between them account for more than 50 per cent of total Saudi imports.

The other top exporters to the Kingdom were Switzerland at SR5.28 billion (US$1.41 billion), with gold accounting for 80 per cent of its exports, Italy at SR5 billion (US$1.34 billion), a 4.6 per cent market share, France at SR4.36 billion (US$1.16 billion), a 4 per cent market share, South Korea at SR3.2 billion, China at SR2.3 billion, Taiwan at SR2.12 billion and the Netherlands at SR2.1 billion. China made substantial gains in the late 1980s and held 8th position in 1991, with synthetic clothes and textiles as its main exports. Saudi imports from the top 15 countries together reached SR88.47 billion (US$23.6 billion) in 1991 81.2 per cent of total imports.

Imports from all major industrial countries, except Switzerland, recorded notable growth rates in 1991. US exports to the Kingdom had the highest growth rate of 46 per cent, following a rise of 5 per cent in 1990 and 9 per cent in 1989. Imports from Germany were up by 28 per cent after increases of 34 per cent and 16 per cent in the preceding two years. Imports from France rose by 22 per cent, compared to 5 per cent growth in 1990 and a decline of 20 per cent in 1989. Imports from the UK grew by 21 per cent in 1991, following 26 per cent growth in 1990 and 36 per cent in 1989, as the UK became an important source of military imports.

Exhibit 9.8

Saudi Arabian imports by country, 1990 - 91 (SR millions)

	1990		***1991***	
	Value	*% of total*	*Value*	*% of total*
US	15,062	16.7	22,003	20.2
Japan	13,815	15.3	14,915	13.7
UK	10,182	11.3	12,267	11.3
Germany	6,645	7.4	8,520	7.8
Switzerland	5,929	6.6	5,282	4.9
Italy	4,181	4.6	5,028	4.6
France	3,573	4.0	4,366	4.0
South Korea	2,960	3.3	3,220	2.9
China	1,668	1.8	2,345	2.2
Taiwan	1,969	2.2	2,127	2.0
Netherlands	2,036	2.3	2,100	1.9
Belgium	1,558	1.7	2,044	1.8
Brazil	1,116	1.4	1,434	1.3
Sweden	1,169	1.3	1,432	1.3
Spain	984	1.0	1,384	1.2
Top 15	**72,847**	**80.9**	**88,467**	**81.2**
Grand total	**90,139**	**100.0**	**108,881**	**100.0**

Sources: Ministry of Finance & National Economy; Central Department of Statistics, foreign trade statistics, 1991.

Exhibit 9.9

Principal goods imported by country, 1991

US	Aircraft, military equipment, machinery, cars, generators, cigarettes, household appliances, furniture, computers, agricultural products.
Japan	Cars, trucks, tyres, vehicles parts, electronics, electrical applicances.
UK	Aircraft and military parts, medicines, cigarettes, gold ingots.
Germany	Machinery and equipment, vehicles, iron and aluminium structures, parts.
Switzerland	Gold, medicines, chemicals, watches.
Italy	Wood furniture, marble paving stones, leather footwear, clothes.
France	Frozen chicken, electrical circuit equipment, cheese, clothes.
South Korea	Clothes (synthetic), tyres, iron and steel sheets and plates.
China	Clothes (synthetic), textiles.
Taiwan	Clothes (synthetic), plastic trunks and suitcases.
Netherlands	Medicines, milk solids, preserved milks.
Belgium	Moquette carpets and rugs, medicines, shovel loaders.
Brazil	Frozen chicken, iron ore and concentrates.
Sweden	Telecommunications equipment, gold, agricultural engines, paperboard.
Spain	Military propellers, tyres, ceramic tiles.

Source: Central Department of Statistics, foreign trade statistics, 1991.

Japan's exports to the Kingdom were up by 7.9 per cent in 1991, after rising by 13 per cent in 1990 and dropping by 13 per cent in 1989.

The breakdown of imports by region shows that western Europe is the largest exporter to the Kingdom, with a market share of 41.7 per cent, amounting to SR45.5 billion (US$12.1 billion) in 1991. Asia was the second largest at SR26.7 billion (7.1 billion), a 24.5 per cent market share, followed by North America (mainly the US) with 21.1 per cent market share. The three regions combined amounted to SR95.1 billion (US$25.4 billion) or 87.3 per cent of the total. The remaining 12.7 per cent of the market was shared by other Arab and Islamic countries. The Kingdom continued to record surpluses in its merchandise trade balance with its major regional trading partners, with the exception of western Europe where Saudi imports exceeded its exports by 19.7 per cent in 1991. Exhibit 9.10 shows balance of trade by region.

Imports from other GCC countries amounted to SR1.5 billion (US$400 million) in 1991, slightly down on the previous year's figure of SR1.6 billion (US$436 million) and representing just 1.4 per cent of the total. The UAE maintained its position as the largest exporter to the Kingdom among GCC member states, with 55 per cent of the total, followed by Bahrain with a share of 17 per cent, Kuwait with 15 per cent, Oman with 8 per cent and Qatar with 5 per cent. Saudi Arabia's imports from other Arab countries were SR2.9 billion (US$773 million) or 2.7 per cent of the total, compared to SR2.6 billion (US$687 million) in 1990.

Private sector imports financed by commercial banks recorded a 30.4 per cent increase from SR55 billion (US$14.7 billion) in 1990 to

Exhibit 9.10

Balance of trade by country groups, 1991 (SR billions)

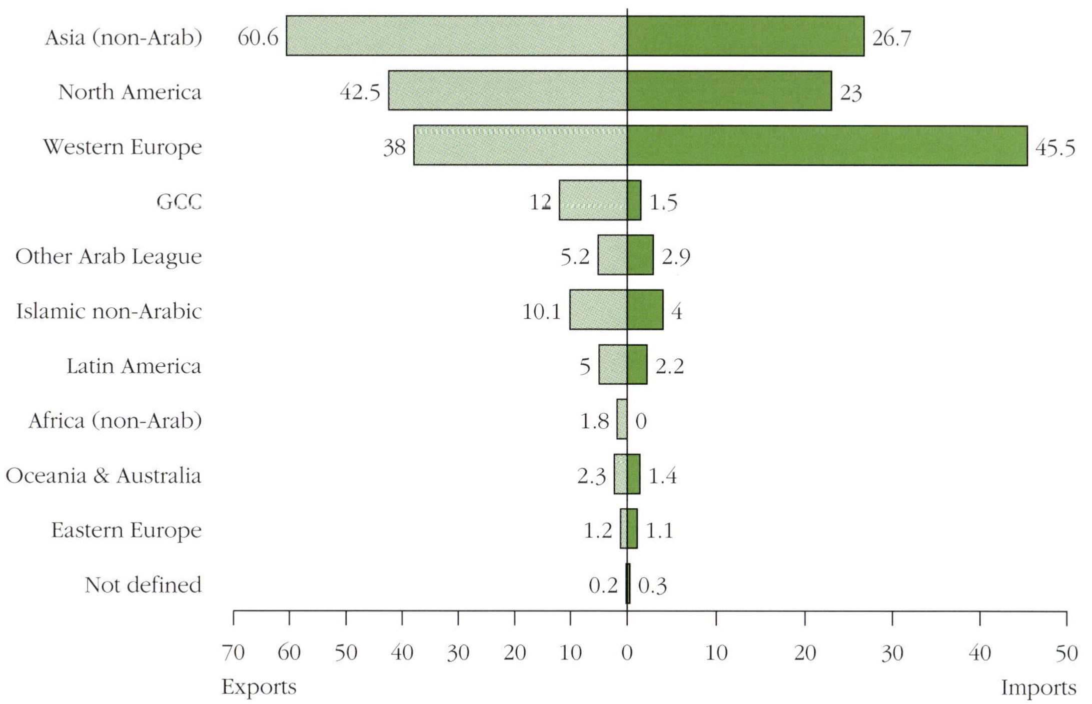

Exhibit 9.11

Private sector imports financed by commercial banks, 1988 - 92 (SR millions)

	1988	*1989*	*1990*	*1991*	*% change 1990-91*	*1992*[1]	*% change 1991-92*[2]
Foodstuffs	7,294	7,379	7,580	8,232	8.6	2,495	26.0
Textiles & clothing	5,910	5,984	6,005	7,366	22.6	1,864	84.3
Building materials	3,737	4,196	3,678	4,371	18.8	1,326	59.6
Motor vehicles	7,972	8,270	9,373	13,908	48.3	4,362	70.9
Machinery & applicances	7,323	7,580	8,242	9,501	15.2	2,527	38.8
Other	17,615	19,037	20,078	28,303	40.9	6,664	22.9
Total	**49,851**	**52,446**	**54,956**	**71,681**	**30.4**	**19,238**	**41.3**

[1]First quarter figures.

[2]First quarter 1992 compared to the same period in 1991.

Source: Saudi Arabian Monetary Agency, *Quarterly Bulletin*, 2nd quarter 1992.

SR71.7 billion (US$19.1 billion) in 1991. This followed a 4.8 per cent increase in 1990 and a 5.2 per cent increase in 1989 (see Exhibit 9.11). The uptrend continued in 1992, with an increase of 41.3 per cent in the first quarter over the same period in 1991. Total imports rose by only 20.7 per cent, so private sector imports financed by commercial banks rose as a proportion of total imports by around 10 per cent to 70 per cent.

Data on the composition of imports financed by commercial banks show that motor vehicle imports maintained their lead, accounting for 19.4 per cent of the total in 1991, compared to 17 per cent in 1990. Machinery and appliances imports held the second position for the fourth consecutive year, with 13.2 per cent of the total, followed by foodstuffs (11.4 per cent), textiles and clothing (10.2 per cent) and building materials (6 per cent). Imports of vehicles financed by commercial banks jumped by 48.3 per cent in 1991 after growing by 13 per cent in 1990. The second highest growth rate of 22.6 per cent was recorded by imports of textiles and clothing, while imports of building materials increased by 15 per cent owing to the upturn in the activities of the construction sector in the last two years.

Balance of payments

For many years Saudi Arabia has maintained a surplus on merchandise trade and a deficit on services and private transfers. Both the trade surplus and the deficit on invisible transactions have increased sharply in the last two years in response mainly to the rise in oil export earnings and in service payments. The trade surplus fell to a low of only US$3 billion in 1986 but recovered over the following years to about US$22 billion in 1991. The deficit on services and private transfers, after declining from US$35 billion in 1981 to US$12 billion in 1988, increased to about US$47.8 billion in 1991, mainly owing to expenditures associated with the Gulf crisis. This increase more than accounted for the rise in the current account deficit in that year to an unprecedented US$25.7 billion (see Exhibit 9.12). The merchandise trade surplus is estimated to have increased to US$20.3 billion in 1992 which, together with the decline in the services and transfers deficit (after the completion of the emergency payments), is believed to have led to a much smaller current account deficit of US$8.8 billion in 1992 and a small surplus on the Kingdom's balance of payments.

The surge in export earnings in 1990 was in a large part offset by higher imports and, more importantly, by the rise in external payments for services and transfers associated with the Gulf crisis. The latter reflected increased defence expenditure, contributions to the multinational military operations, increased foreign aid, rise in freight and insurance expenses and larger outward remittances by expatriate workers, especially those who had left the country. However, the rise in both oil export earnings and other exports had a more immediate effect on the balance of payments than the increase in services and transfers payments, with the result that the current account deficit in 1990 (US$4.3 billion) was less than half its level in the preceding year.

Balance of payments figures for 1991 show an increase of about 50 per cent in invisible payments to around US$59 billion, reflecting financing of the multinational military force and payment for other services (US$38.6 billion compared to US$22.4 billion the year before) and further increases in transfers by foreign workers (to US$13.7 billion from US$11.6 billion) and in foreign aid disbursements (to US$6.5 billion from US$4.4 billion). A sizeable trade surplus, and a small decline in investment income (the main source of invisible receipts) could not prevent the large rise in the current account deficit. The greater part of the current account deficit was financed through net capital inflows. This is reflected by external government borrowing from a consortium of foreign commercial banks of US$4.5 billion and foreign currency borrowing of US$2.5 billion from domestic banks. Autonomous capital inflows also increased, reflecting a restoration of confidence in the private sector and buoyant business conditions in the Kingdom.

Exhibit 9.12

Saudi Arabia's trade and current account balances, 1987 - 91 (US$ billions)

	1987	*1988*	*1989*	*1990*	*1991*	*1992*[1]
1. Merchandise trade	4.8	4.5	9.1	22.8	22.1	20.3
Exports	23.1	24.3	28.3	44.3	48.2	49.0
Imports	-18.3	-19.8	-19.2	-21.5	-26.1	-28.7
2. Services & transfers	-14.5	-11.8	-18.3	-27.1	-47.8	-29.1
Receipts	12.5	12.1	12.3	11.3	11.0	10.9
Investment income (net)	(9.9)	(9.7)	(9.7)	(8.3)	(8.0)	(7.7)
Other receipts	(2.6)	(2.4)	(2.6)	(3.0)	(3.0)	(3.2)
Payments	-27.0	-23.9	-30.6	-38.4	-58.8	-40.0
Services	(-18.8)	(-14.9)	(-20.1)	(-22.4)	(-38.6)	(-26.0)
Private transfers	(-4.9)	(-6.5)	(-8.3)	(-11.6)	(-13.7)	(-10.0)
Official transfers	(-3.3)	(-2.5)	(-2.2)	(-4.4)	(-6.5)	(-4.0)
3. Current account balance (1+2)	-9.7	-7.3	-9.2	-4.3	-25.7	-8.8

[1]Forecasts.

Source: IMF, *International Financial Statistics*, October 1992.

Continuing improvements in the current account are expected to generate a small surplus in the balance of payments position during the period 1992 to 1996. This, together with rising capital inflows by Saudi commercial banks and non-bank private sector entities, should help to boost the Kingdom's foreign assets. According to the Bank of International Settlement (BIS), the Saudi banking sector withdrew US$6.42 billion from banks in the industrialised countries during the first quarter of 1992. BIS reporting banks in 18 industrialised countries and major offshore centres had liabilities to the Saudi banking sector of US$46.38 billion at the end of March 1992, while liabilities to the non-bank sector stood at US$30.29 billion. Placement of funds abroad by Saudi private sector entities was put at US$76.7 billion at the end of the first quarter of 1992.

Oil exports should rise to US$44.8 billion in 1992, compared to US$43.7 billion the year before, while non-oil exports are likely to stay around US$4.5 billion, depressed by lower prices of petrochemical products. Imports are believed to have surged in line with the strong growth of the Saudi economy and generally higher import prices in dollar terms. The emergency expenditures associated with the Gulf crisis that boosted 1990 and 1991 import figures have been removed. Total imports for 1992 are expected to be 10 per cent higher than the 1991 level.

In the services and transfer balance a much smaller deficit is recorded, as receipts (mainly investment income) are only slightly below the previous year's level, owing to lower dollar interest rates in 1992, while service payments and transfers are 32 per cent below the corresponding 1991 figures. Private transfers by foreign workers and payments for freight and insurance, interest on foreign debt and private sector services (eg consulting, contracting, banking and money spent by nationals travelling abroad) all resumed their historic trend after being swollen by the crisis of 1990 and 1991. Official transfers and foreign aid dropped from the unusually high level of 1991 and the deficit in the services and transfers balance is estimated at US$29.1 billion in 1992, down from US$47.8 billion the year before. The smaller current account deficit is expected to be financed through a net capital inflow of around US$15 billion, resulting in an external surplus in the balance of payments of about US$6 billion in 1992.

Balance of payments projections for 1993 to 1996 envisage annual external current account deficits of no more than US$5 billion. Net capital inflows from commercial banks and private sector entities are expected to continue, helping to finance the current account deficit and bringing a small surplus in the overall balance of payments during the period, leading also to a cumulative increase in SAMA's foreign reserves.

Conclusion

Changes in the size and nature of the Saudi market in recent years have had important consequences for foreign suppliers. Shifts have taken place in the balance between demand for capital and intermediate goods and that for finished consumer goods, largely owing to the policy of industrialisation and import substitution implemented by the Kingdom. With the establishment

Exhibit 9.13
Imports by utilisation of items, 1991

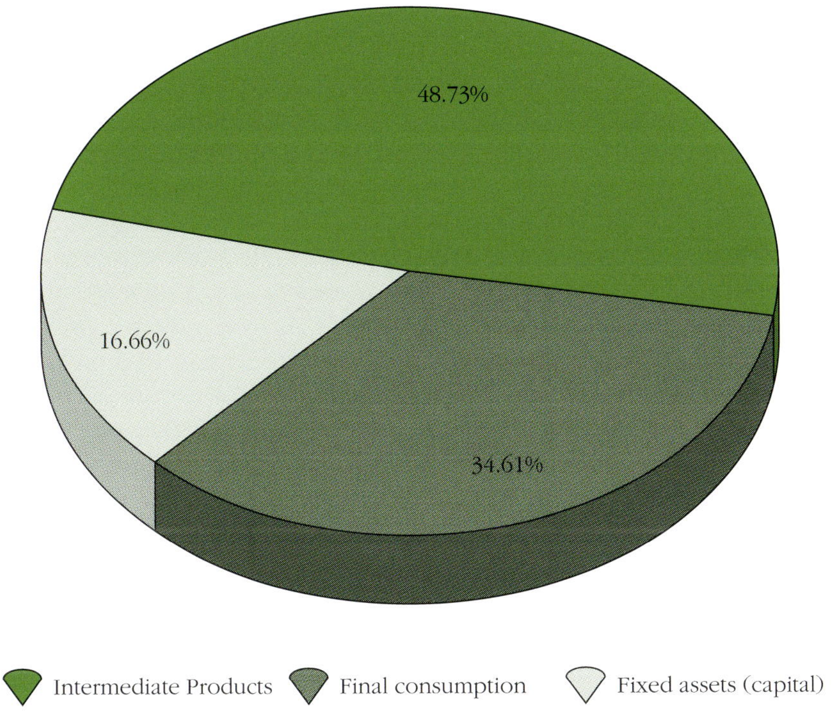

of new industries, demand for machinery and equipment, fixed assets and intermediate products has risen to 65 per cent of total imports in 1991, compared with less than 50 per cent in the 1980s, while the percentage of products imported for final consumption has dropped to 35 per cent (see Exhibit 9.13). At the same time, demand is growing for replacement items because of the need to maintain the new industries and basic infrastructure. Since such items are required for existing projects, issues such as compatibility have become much more crucial.

The Saudi economy is quite open to trade and has fewer import restrictions, in the form of either tariffs or quotas, than many developing countries. Export earnings have comfortably covered all import payments during the last decade and, although there are some balance of payments pressures, there is a reluctance to restrict imports through the imposition of controls. Saudi openness to trade has deep-seated cultural roots, as well as being necessitated by the nature of the Kingdom's resource base. For example, there is no need for protection to safeguard employment, as the Kingdom continues to depend on a large amount of expatriate labour. There are a few infant industries that need to be protected but the loss of opportunity to exporters owing to import substitution is very small compared to overall Saudi imports. Furthermore, tariffs would raise prices for consumers and, in a society where the interests of consumers are paramount, such rises would be extremely unwelcome.

Growing emphasis is being put on promoting Saudi exports of

manufactured products. The Kingdom's non-oil exports have surged in the past few years, with the private sector playing an increasingly significant role in this domain. Saudi Arabia is strategically located for industries exporting to surrounding markets. The GCC states offer a market of 18 million consumers with *per capita* income and consumption among the highest in the world. The Kingdom also has established bilateral trade agreements with other Arab and Islamic countries. In other countries tariffs on Saudi products are virtually non-existent, increasing the Kingdom's effective export market to more than 100 million consumers. One way to boost exports of manufactured Saudi products is to tie the implementation of projects abroad financed by Saudi development loans and grants to purchasing of Saudi products, as other aid agencies do. The establishment of a specialised institution that provides export finance and guarantees to the private sector will go a long way towards promoting Saudi exports of manufactured products. In the meantime, Saudi exporters could draw more heavily on regional financial institutions with export credit programmes such as the Islamic Development Bank, the Arab Monetary Fund and the Inter-Arab Investment Guarantee Corporation. In turn these institutions should try to increase their credit ceiling to Saudi exporters and reduce their costs of operation.

The very high taxation on oil and oil products in foreign markets has had a negative impact on Saudi Arabia's export potential. In this respect the proposed energy tax by the European Community (EC) is viewed with great concern. Access for Saudi Arabia's non-oil exports, mainly petrochemicals, to overseas markets, especially the EC, continues to be constrained by barriers. The EC imposes 13 to 15 per cent tariffs on Saudi petrochemical exports, in order to protect the European chemical industry. Without these protective measures, the Kingdom's trade deficit with the EC of around SR7.5 billion (US$2 billion) in 1991 would be at least partially corrected.

10 Investment climate and joint venture opportunities

Introduction

In the past few years a new development strategy has been unfolding in Saudi Arabia, with the main emphasis being on industrialisation and economic diversification. Growth led by the public sector and an overdependence on oil are gradually giving way to private sector initiatives and the building up of a diversified production base. While the Kingdom is still one of the most important import markets in the world, the local market has nevertheless become highly competitive. Several well known brands, mainly in light consumer products and food, have begun to be manufactured domestically. Dealing with Saudi Arabia as simply a residual market for foreign exports of goods and services is less viable now than it used to be. Foreign companies involved in export trade to Saudi Arabia are gradually realising that the best way for them to maintain, and possibly expand, their share of the market is to establish a presence in the Kingdom.

The government is trying to attract importers to manufacture in the country with a range of incentives, including exemption from import taxes on materials and equipment required for local production, exemption from taxes on profits, the provision of industrial sites, low energy cost, abundance of inexpensive feedstocks, capital loans and grants, freedom of capital movement and repatriation of profits, full convertibility of the Saudi riyal and preferential purchasing of local products and services by the government. There is also selective use of tariffs to protect locally manufactured products.

Saudi Arabia is ideally located for exporting to the surrounding Arab states, Turkey, the Indian sub-continent, East Africa, Southeast Asia, China and the Central Asian states of the former Soviet Union. Many of these countries are in the early stages of development and offer potentially huge new markets, particularly for basic commodities. There is a market of 350 million people in the Middle East and Muslim Africa alone, to which Saudi Arabia has favourable access through various national and regional organisations and their aid programmes.

Investment opportunities in Saudi Arabia can be made more commercially viable if both local and international investors understand the Kingdom's new development strategy, take a long-term view of the potential available and are prepared to commit themselves to establishing a base for future market growth. The country does not need simply the establishment of production units on a turnkey basis but the transfer, adaptation and acquisition of know-how technology. Even though domestic financial resources are readily available, foreign investors are, nevertheless, encouraged to hold some equity participation in projects to ensure their long-term commitment to the country.

Saudi Arabia is distinguished from other developing countries by the quality of its facilities for investors, including first class infrastructure and modern amenities which do not generally exist in other developing countries. In fact, where such facilities are lacking in other countries, their provision is frequently included in the cost of investment projects. Furthermore, the kind of bureaucratic bottlenecks that have hampered investments in many third world countries are far less of a constraint here. The Kingdom's high *per capita* income and purchasing power, the abundance of capital, oil and gas and cheap petrochemical feedstock undoubtedly increase the chances of achieving a reasonable return on investment.

The treatment of joint venture projects on an equal basis with projects financed fully by national capital allows the foreign investor to benefit from the provision of export credits, for which a number of regulations have been issued on the Arab and Islamic levels. On the Arab level use can be made of financial guarantees against commercial and non-commercial risks from the Kuwait-based Inter-Arab Investment Guarantee Corporation. On the level of trade exchanges between Islamic countries the foreign investor can enjoy the benefits of the Longer-Term Trade Financing Scheme of the Islamic Development Bank which specialises in financing the trading of non-traditional commodities between Islamic countries.

Regulations governing foreign investment

Tax issues

Foreign capital enjoys free movement; there are no restrictions on the repatriation of profits or on foreign currency transactions and no personal income tax on expatriate staff. Industrial licences are generally granted only to nationals; however, foreign capital can be invested without the participation of Saudi Arabian nationals, although it does not benefit from the various incentives offered to foreign investment under the provisions of the Foreign Capital Investment Law (the Investment Law).

This law offers various benefits to foreign capital invested in industry, including exemption from all income and company taxes for five years (10 years in the case of manufacturing or agricultural joint ventures). The tax holiday begins after production has commenced and, at the end of the exemption period, projects will be subject to the Saudi rules for the taxation of foreign investments, while Saudi joint venture partners will be subject to *Zakat* (a religious tax) at the rate of 2.5 per cent of income. Corporate rates of tax to non-Saudis (excluding GCC citizens) range from 25 per cent on the first SR100,000 (US$26,666) to 45 per cent on amounts over SR1 million (US$266,666). Foreign employees are not taxed on their wages or salaries but self-employed individuals are taxed at the rate of 5 per cent if their income ranges between SR6,000 (US$1,600) and SR16,000 (US$4,266) and up to 30 per cent if their income exceeds SR66,000 (US$17,600). There is no sales or value added tax, no estate tax and no gift tax in the Kingdom.

The Investment Law stipulates that foreign participation must not exceed 75 per cent of the joint venture capital. Industrial projects licensed under the Investment Law enjoy the same privileges granted to national capital under the National Industries Protection and Encouragement Regulations. They also benefit from existing bilateral agreements between Saudi Arabia and other Arab countries. However, in order to be eligible for the advantages of the Investment Law, foreign capital must be invested in economic development projects (excluding the extraction of oil) which fall within the priorities of the country's development plan, must include an element of foreign technical expertise and know-how and must contribute to the training of Saudi personnel, for which subsidies are provided by the government.

Raw and semi-manufactured materials, machinery, equipment and spare parts imported to the country for newly established projects or for the expansion of existing ones are exempt from customs duties. There are no export taxes and certain local industries are afforded a protective duty of up to 20 per cent on competing imported goods. This protection is more readily given when the product is of a high quality and can meet a major portion of local demand. Few items, mainly food products, medicine, gold and books are imported duty free, while the standard rate of customs duty on most other items is 12 per cent.

Other incentives

Other incentives available for joint ventures include the extension of loans on favourable terms, primarily through the SIDF. Loans amounting to up to 50 per cent of the project cost are granted at an initial fee of 2.5 per cent and service charges of about 1 per cent per annum. Loans normally extend for ten years with a maximum redemption period of 15 years and a grace period of up to two years from the beginning of production. The remaining 50 per cent of funding is usually divided equally between commercial bank loans and equity. Utilities are provided at low and subsidised prices (among the lowest in the world), while factory sites are available for rent in the Kingdom's large industrial estates for as little as US$0.02 per square metre annually for a period of 25 years. These areas also provide local services, including health centres, schools, a fire fighting service and recreational facilities. In addition, industrial service back-up, whether in maintenance, distribution, telecommunications, banking or advertising, has improved so that it can be compared favourably with that of many competing economies.

Non-tariff protection usually takes the form of preferential government purchasing of national products and government subsidies for the training of Saudi employees. The legislation dealing with preferential purchasing stipulates that governments and governmental institutions give preference in their purchases to tenders for national industrial products, even when prices exceed those of their imported counterparts by up to 10 per cent. This policy of preferential purchasing applies only if the locally produced items meet standard specifications for kind and quality.

To qualify for this privilege, a company must have a minimum Saudi participation in equity of 51 per cent. Joint ventures are also encouraged by the provision of technical and other support services, including market research and feasibility studies provided by government institutions to help identify viable investment opportunities. The SIDF and other credit agencies have developed expertise in evaluating feasibility studies submitted by investors and providing financial and technical assistance to projects. Other benefits enjoyed by joint venture industries include reduction of port service fees on exports and other advantages applicable to domestic companies.

Licensing

The Ministry of Industry and Electricity licences direct foreign investment, except in the case of mineral concessions, which are governed by separate concessionary agreements. Otherwise, all proposals for new investments, reinvestments, mergers or acquisitions must go through the Ministry's licensing process. For ventures with government participation, the process is usually nothing more than a formality. On the other hand, for purely private ventures, the process can involve a considerable amount of time and effort.

Operating under the Foreign Capital Investment Code (see the Appendix to this chapter on page 206), the Ministry of Industry and Electricity's "Foreign Capital Investment Review Board" screens all licence applications and counsels prospective investors. Licence applications must be accompanied by several documents, including a feasibility study, an outline of the venture's proposed capital structure and legal form, its partnership agreement, its plans for training Saudi nationals for technical and managerial positions, and its plans for the procurement of machinery and other equipment. Permits to use the necessary industrial patents, the foreign partner's foreign certificate of registration, and authorisation from the foreign partner's board of directors must also be submitted.

Following the initial screening, applications go to the Foreign Capital Investment Committee for evaluation. The Committee is chaired by the Deputy Ministry of Industry and Electricity and includes representatives from other relevant ministries, including the Ministries of Commerce, Finance, Agriculture, Planning and Petroleum. Licence applications approved by the Committee go to the Minister of Industry and Electricity for his approval, following which the new joint venture must apply for a commercial registration number from the Ministry of Commerce. Depending on the type of business, additional approvals may be needed, such as from the Ministry of Health in the case of a health care business.

The Foreign Capital Investment Committee considers a variety of factors in making its evaluations. Foremost is the project's compatibility with Saudi Arabia's basic economic goals: economic diversification, access to modern technology, and the development of a trained Saudi labour force to reduce dependence on foreign labour. The committee looks with special favour on projects involving the transfer of high technology to Saudi Arabia, and prefers firms with experience in the field of the proposed investment. The Committee carefully evaluates royalty arrangements and prices of equipment to be supplied by the foreign partner. In addition, while there is no minimum foreign equity requirement for joint ventures, more than nominal investment is encouraged. Intangible property is not counted towards this investment and a Saudi accountant must evaluate the monetary worth of any contributions in kind.

For foreign firms seeking to establish joint ventures, it is important to note that the Foreign Capital Investment Committee reportedly will not issue a second licence for any given type of new venture until the previously licensed venture has been established. However, the Committee usually agrees to extend the duration of licences whenever difficulties arise in implementation. While this has been beneficial to initial licences, it has also allowed individual companies to tie up industrial and commercial opportunities for extended periods, while they mobilise support for their own ventures.

Professionals, including architects, consultants and consulting engineers, are required to register with and be certified by the Ministry of Commerce, in accordance with the requirements defined in the Ministry of Commerce's Resolution 264, published in 1982. These regulations, in theory, permit the registration of Saudi/foreign joint ventures, but have never fully been implemented. As a result, most foreign consulting firms now work as adjuncts to established Saudi firms.

Corporate organisation and liability

While company law in Saudi Arabia permits a variety of corporate structures, joint ventures almost always take the form of limited liability partnerships. This form of organisation does confer limited liability, there is a price attached. Foreign partners in service and contracting ventures organised as limited liability partnerships must pay in the full amount of their contribution to authorised capital in cash or kind before the start of operations. For industrial projects, the required amount is normally 25 per cent, although it may be higher for some industries. In addition, 10 per cent of profits must be set aside each year in a statutory reserve until it equals 50 per cent of the venture's authorised capital.

Investment dispute settlement

The Saudi commercial law system is still developing as new institutions are slowly established to simplify and modernise settlement of commercial disputes. While some progress was made toward regularising dispute resolution mechanisms, dispute settlement in Saudi Arabia continues to be time consuming. Moreover, even after a decision is reached in a dispute, effective enforcement of the judgement can take time to effect. In general, Saudi litigants have an advantage over foreign parties in any investment dispute, because of their first-hand knowledge of Saudi law

Exhibit 10.1

Joint ventures between Saudi Arabia and selected foreign countries, 1992

Country	*Activity*	*Number of projects*	*Capital (SR millions)*	*Contribution by foreign partners (SR millions)*	*(%)*
US	Industrial	62	8,907	4,850	54
	Non-industrial	124	1,704	981	57
	Total	**186**	**10,611**	**5,831**	**55**
Panama	Industrial	4	8,521	4,223	50
	Non-industrial	22	51	22	43
	Total	**26**	**8,572**	**4,245**	**50**
Germany	Industrial	28	4,929	496	10
	Non-industrial	55	212	100	47
	Total	**83**	**5,141**	**596**	**12**
Kuwait	Industrial	24	3,437	112	3
	Non-industrial	7	73	14	19
	Total	**31**	**3,510**	**1,126**	**32**
Lebanon	Industrial	88	2,454	807	33
	Non-industrial	73	677	150	22
	Total	**161**	**3,131**	**957**	**31**
Japan	Industrial	8	2,560	1,306	51
	Non-industrial	32	252	75	30
	Total	**40**	**2,812**	**1,381**	**49**
Bermuda	Industrial	9	2,643	1,313	50
	Non-industrial	19	37	18	49
	Total	**28**	**2,680**	**1,331**	**50**
UK	Industrial	36	1,173	396	34
	Non-industrial	91	919	351	38
	Total	**127**	**2,092**	**747**	**36**
South Korea	Industrial	7	1,810	326	18
	Non-industrial	39	218	114	52
	Total	**46**	**2,028**	**440**	**22**
Switzerland	Industrial	37	1,640	631	38
	Non-industrial	35	125	56	45
	Total	**72**	**1,765**	**687**	**39**
France	Industrial	20	944	252	27
	Non-industrial	44	516	220	43
	Total	**64**	**1,460**	**472**	**32**
Jordan	Industrial	58	1,022	474	46
	Non-industrial	17	343	137	40
	Total	**75**	**1,365**	**611**	**45**
Italy	Industrial	12	1,203	237	20
	Non-industrial	33	129	70	54
	Total	**45**	**1,332**	**307**	**23**
Netherlands	Industrial	16	618	257	42
	Non-industrial	30	217	100	46
	Total	**46**	**835**	**359**	**43**
UAE	Industrial	11	493	52	11
	Non-industrial	8	128	1	1
	Total	**19**	**621**	**53**	**9**

Exhibit 10.1 *cont.*

Joint ventures between Saudi Arabia and selected foreign countries, 1992

Country	*Activity*	*Number of projects*	*Capital (SR millions)*	*Contribution by foreign partners (SR millions)*	*(%)*
Egypt	Industrial	5	58	16	28
	Non-industrial	9	389	157	40
	Total	**14**	**447**	**173**	**39**

Source: Saudi Arabian Ministry of Industry and Electricity, published in the *Arab News*, 22 May 1990.

and culture and the relatively amorphous dispute settlement processes. As a result, most foreign partners involved in a dispute find it advisable to hire local attorneys with knowledge of Saudi legal practices. It remains, therefore, vitally important that a foreign investor take steps to protect himself, by thoroughly researching the business record of his proposed Saudi partner, retaining legal counsel, complying with all legal steps in the investment process, and securing a well-drafted agreement.

The Saudi Arabian legal system is derived from the legal norms of Islam, known as the Shariah. The Ministry of Justice oversees the Shariah-based judicial system, but most ministries have committees to rule on matters under their jurisdiction. Of principal interest to investors who have disputes with private individuals are the Committees for Labour Disputes under the Ministry of Labour, the Committee for Tax Matters under the Ministry of Finance and National Economy, and the Negotiable Instruments Committee (also called the Commercial Paper Committee), also under the Ministry of Finance, which has jurisdiction over disputes involving letters of credit and cheques. In additional, the Banking Disputes Committee of the Saudi Arabian Monetary Agency (SAMA) adjudicates disputes between bankers and their clients.

More often, disputes are settled privately between the parties involved. However, if this is impossible, the investor can pursue either local arbitration by one or more arbitrators chosen by the disputants. Decisions should be signed by the local Governor and are then enforceable by the police if necessary. The arbitral award also must be approved by the local courts. Alternatively, offshore arbitration could be followed, whereby parties to a commercial agency or distributorship contract may stipulate the arbitration law or regulations of any state as applicable to the contract. Arbitration by a committee chosen by the local Chambers of Commerce and Industry is also an option. In the case of foreigners, the foreign Chamber of Commerce (for instance, the Arab-British or the Arab American Chambers of Commerce) acts on behalf of its member.

Existing foreign investment in the Kingdom

The major overseas investors

While the trend so far has been to go for the big international companies as potential partners for joint ventures in the Kingdom, it is likely that the international companies have now exploited most of the areas in which they are interested. Small and medium-sized overseas companies are thus likely to be much more interested in exploring joint venture opportunities in the future. However, it is these companies in particular which require advice and support, as they frequently lack the resources to carry out the preliminary work necessary for setting up an overseas manufacturing operation.

According to the Ministry of Industry and Electricity the total number of joint venture projects between the Kingdom and other countries was 1,462 in 1990, with 115 additional projects in the process of being implemented. The total capital invested in these projects amounted to SR75 billion (US$20 billion), of which SR53 billion (US$14.6 billion) was in industrial projects and SR8.3 billion (US$2.2 billion) in the contracting sector. The US is the Kingdom's leading joint venture partner among the industrialised countries and was involved in projects with a total capital of SR10,611 million (US$2,829 million) in 62 industrial and 124 non-industrial projects. Allocated by sector, 36 per cent of US investments were in the petroleum sector (mainly refining and downstream applications), followed by 28 per cent in finance and insurance, 12 per cent in manufacturing and the balance in other services. Exhibit 10.1 lists the countries with the most joint ventures in Saudi Arabia in 1990.

The US was followed by Panama with projects capitalised at SR8,572 million (US$2.29 billion), Germany at SR5,141 million (US$1,371 million) and Bermuda at SR2,680 million (US$715 million). The strong showing by Panama and Bermuda may be attributed to the fact that a number of multinational companies are registered there to benefit from less restrictive business regulations and taxation. Excluding its share in the AOC, which operates in the Neutral Zone, Japan participated in 40 joint venture projects, with a total investment of SR2,812 million (US$750 million), only eight of which were industrial. Joint ventures participated in by the UK had a total capitalisation of SR2,092 million (US$558 million), by South Korea SR2,028 million (US$541 million), by Switzerland SR1,765 million (US$471 million), by France SR1,460 million (US$389 million) and by Italy SR1,332 million (US$355 million). American, British and to a lesser extent French investments are believed to have increased considerably in the last two years as the offset investment programmes with these countries have started to be implemented.

By 1990 the various Arab countries had 430 joint venture projects in the Kingdom. Kuwait came top and was involved in projects with a total capitalisation of SR3,510 million (US$936 million), followed by Lebanon with SR3,131 million (US$835 million), Jordan with SR1,365 million (US$364 million), the UAE with SR621 million (US$166 million) and Egypt with SR447 million (US$119 million). Most of the other Arab countries had little or no participation in joint venture projects in the Kingdom.

Principal target industries for investors

Foreign investment in the Kingdom is concentrated in the chemical industry (including petrochemicals and fertilisers), building materials and minerals, which together contributed more than 96 per cent of total foreign investment in non-oil manufacturing up to the end of 1988; the

Exhibit 10.2

Share of non-Saudi partners in total joint industrial investment up to the end of 1988

Industrial activity	*Total joint industrial investment (US$ millions)*	*Number of projects*	*Investment by foreign partners (US$ millions)*	*Share of foreign partners in total investment (%)*
Foodstuffs	292.0	30	91.1	31.2
Clothing & textiles	35.2	7	13.4	38.2
Wood Products	27.5	12	13.7	49.9
Paper products, printing & publishing	219.5	18	95.7	43.6
Chemicals	14,451.0	91	6,950.9	48.1
Glass & ceramics	74.2	3	11.2	15.1
Building materials	1,146.0	61	327.7	28.6
Minerals	1,511.0	150	258.4	17.1
Other	60.0	8	30.9	51.6
Total	**17,817.0**	**380**	**7,590.0**	**42.6**

Source: Methods of Attracting Foreign Investments in Joint Projects in Saudi Arabia, paper presented by Jeddah Chamber of Commerce and Industry to Saudi Businessmen's Fourth Conference held on 1 June 1989.

Exhibit 10.3

Major joint venture projects in Saudi Arabia with SIDF funding, 1988

Countries involved	*Engineering products*	*Chemicals*	*Consumer products*	*Building materials*	*Other*	*Total*
Germany	6	4	3	8	1	22
France	9	3	1	4	–	17
Netherlands	7	2	–	1	–	10
Belgium	2	1	–	1	–	4
Luxembourg	–	–	–	1	–	1
Italy	4	1	2	4		11
UK	7	4	7	10	–	28
Denmark	1	1	6	–	–	8
Greece	–	1	–	–	1	2
Total EC	**36**	**17**	**19**	**29**	**2**	**103**
US	27	14	4	10	–	55
Japan	4	1	1	–	1	7
Switzerland	6	11	–	6	1	24
Total	**97**	**60**	**54**	**63**	**6**	**280**

Source: Saudi Industrial Development Fund, *Guide to Saudi Arabian Manufactured Products*, 1989.

chemical industry alone accounted for 92 per cent or US$6.95 billion. Foreign investment accounted for 42.6 per cent of total capital invested in non-oil manufacturing in 1988. Industries with the highest concentration of foreign capital were wood products (49.9 per cent of total capital investment), chemicals (48 per cent), paper products (43.6 per cent), ready-made clothes (38.2 per cent) and building materials (28.6 per cent). Exhibit 10.2 sets out the proportion of foreign investment in a number of industries in 1988.

The EC countries were most heavily involved in engineering products and building materials (35 per cent and 28.2 per cent of total EC commitments respectively). The UK, Germany and France were the most active EC countries, with totals of 28, 22 and 17 projects respectively. The US had 27 of its 55 joint venture projects in the engineering products sector, 14 in chemicals and 10 in building materials. Denmark had six out of its eight joint venture projects in the consumer goods sector (all in dairy product and fruit juice projects). Exhibit 10.3 gives the details.

Defence offset programmes

An offset investment programme was introduced in Saudi Arabia to ensure that the Kingdom benefited more substantially from the large, mainly defence-related contracts it awarded to foreign suppliers and contractors. These foreign counterparties are expected to offset the cost to the Saudi government by investing 35 per cent of the contract value in joint ventures in the Kingdom. Since developing the concept in 1985, the Saudis have concluded major offset agreements with military suppliers from the US (Peace Shield) and the UK (Al-Yamamah) and are finalising one with the French (SWARY II). Joint ventures under the Kingdom's offset programme are expected to generate more than US$4 billion in new industrial projects by the end of this decade. The offset concept is relatively new in the Kingdom and the pace of new investment under the programme has generally been slow.

The policy was first put into practice with agreement on the US$4 billion Peace Shield early warning radar package. The main contractor, Boeing, on behalf of itself and its US sub-contractors, came up with nine potential projects with a combined investment of US$700 million. Five of these are being implemented:

- Al-Salam Aircraft Company: a high technology aircraft, repair, overhaul and modification centre, capitalised at US$80 million. Construction of facilities is well underway at an industrial estate adjacent to Riyadh's King Khaled International Airport;

- Aircraft Accessories and Components Company (AACC): capitalised at US$11 million, this facility will manufacture accessories and components to be used by the Al-Salam Aircraft Company;

- Advanced Electronics Company Limited (AEC): capitalised at US$47 million, this company is already operating at a temporary facility next to King Khaled Airport. It manufactures, assembles and services electronic devices for sectors including communications, integrated logistics support and systems integration;

- International Systems Engineering Company (ISE): this computer software development firm is also already operating. Capitalised at

Exhibit 10.4

Existing and planned projects under the Al-Yamamah programme

Initial proposal number	*Private sector involvement*	*Project*	*Initial approval by the Saudi Economic Offset Committee*
1	BAe/Dowty/Hughes Military Industries Corporation (MIC)	Missile engineering facility	8 November 1989
2	BAe	Investment in Alusa aluminum smelter	Under consideration
3	Royal Ordinance /General Dynamics/MIC	Military equipment manufacture	Under consideration
4	BAe/YBA Kanoo/MPRC	Technical training centres, capitalised at US$21 million	8 July 1990
5	Fryma Fabrics/Nafa Enterprises	Polyethylene yarn and netting manufacturer, capitalised at US$27 million	22 January 1990
6	Rolls Royce/Middle East Propulsion Center	Entry into Middle East Propulsion Center	8 November 1989
7	BAe	Acrylic sheet manufacturing and forming, capitalised at US$53 million	22 January 1990
8	BAe/Dansk	Bioprotein production, capitalised at US$53 million	Under consideration
9	BAe/DAF/MIC	Specialised vehicle production	29 July 1990
10	Cooperheat/Al Hajery Est	Heat-treatment engineering	20 October 1990
11	Booker Tate/Savola	Oilseed processing plant, capitalised at US$99 million	1 May 1991
12	Glaxo Group/Saudi Import Company	Pharmaceutical plant, capitalised at US$25 million	23 October 1991
13	Vanderlande/BAe Natel/Almabani Systems	Materials handling, capitalised at US$30 million	23 October 1991
14	BAe/Technomaiera	Special processing of marble/granite, capitalised at US$80 million	13 April 1992
15	Bibby Sterilin/BAe	Medical plastic disposables	Under consideration

US$16.3 million, the company works in systems engineering associated with computer, communications and information systems and their various applications;

• Middle East Propulsion Center (MEPC): this is a proposed project for the maintenance, repair and overhaul of gas turbine engines.

In January 1991 the Boeing contract was officially terminated and

Hughes Aircraft Systems took over as the prime contractor to finish the command, control and communications systems, now known as Peace Shield II. Investment proposals under the new offset programme are in the preliminary stages and the projects could involve a space technology venture for satellite communications, a packet-switching plant for private and public applications, a mobile digital telephone assembly plant, a software development company for management, logistics and security applications and an automotive battery plant.

The UK offset programme (Al-Yamamah) is expected to stimulate at least US$2 billion in joint venture investment. Several projects have been approved and some are still under consideration (see Exhibit 10.4).

Under a memorandum of understanding signed by the French and Saudi governments in June 1990, Thomson-CSF is to reinvest 35 per cent of the value of military contracts into economically viable projects in the Kingdom. If the deal is formalised, it could generate contracts worth US$2.7 billion. Thomson-CSF is moving ahead on some investment proposals. One proposal already underway is a gold-refining venture between Thomson-CSF and Shairco, involving a total investment of US$48 million. Other French proposals include a potato-processing plant capitalised at US$36 million, an alkyd resins plant capitalised at US$48 million and a steel sheet plant capitalised at US$116 million.

Opportunities for profitable joint ventures

There are many niches in the Saudi market that have not yet been filled and where joint ventures with foreign institutions may prove quite profitable. A number of joint venture projects have been identified under the various offset programmes mentioned above. In the manufacturing sector there are projects in areas such as tertiary petrochemicals, primary metals and fabrication, high technology, defence-related industries, agro-industry, high value-added agriculture and agricultural products, building materials, food and beverages, plastic and chemical products, fabricated metal products, pharmaceuticals and drug packaging, aluminium containers, competitive import substitution projects such as components and supplies, natural resources development and new industries in the consumer products field.

There are also opportunities for joint venture investments in the services sector, which contributes about one-third of the country's GDP. Saudi Arabia is a major consumer of foreign services, with roughly one-fifth of total consumption being spent on imported services. Operations and maintenance represent undoubtedly the biggest growth area, with a market estimated to be worth more than US$8 billion a year. Other promising opportunities in the services sector include projects that focus on business services, efficiency and productivity improvement, financial industry diversification (leasing companies, venture capital firms, insurance companies, export banking etc), manpower training systems, business, financial and economic information services, contract services, domestic tourism development and private sector collaboration in communications, health care, transportation and education.

Food processing provides an important outlet for joint venture opportunities. There are many fast food restaurants being set up in the Kingdom but there are no convenience food preparations in the stores in spite of the many local chicken, dairy, wheat, dates, and other farms that provide abundant produce which could be processed locally. There are many opportunities in the fast moving goods sector as well, particularly those which are attractive to the young, especially toiletries and toys. There are many developments in the industrialised countries that could find an attractive and growing market in these services.

Consumer durables are gaining increasing importance in the market – particularly for households. By the year 2000, approximately 100,000 new homes will be build every year. In addition, the replacement market is very active – approximately 250,000 households are re-furbished every year. White and brown goods are purchased in large volumes in the Kingdom. Some argue that economies of scale prohibit these goods from being manufactured locally and yet there are example of successful companies that have replaced imports and are competing in the export markets.

The spare parts market is also becoming increasingly important, there are nearly 3 million vehicles licensed in Saudi Arabia. The time is coming when a number of the components that are replaced during servicing will be available from local facilities. The Kingdom has started to exploit its mineral wealth. The mining and refining of gold deposits is one example and there are also marble and granite quarries as well as bauxite deposits that have not yet been fully exploited.

There is also a major development in the retail trade, through establishing high quality chain stores. At present only around 20 per cent of merchandise is sold through large retail stores or supermarkets. There are good opportunities for the more prestigious chain stores in Europe, US and Japan to set up in Saudi Arabia.

There are also opportunities in travel and tourism. The Kingdom is host to more than a million pilgrims every year. In addition families and relatives of expatriates living in the Kingdom visit the country regularly. Foreign residents and Saudis are also great travellers. There are many opportunities to improve the quality of services in these areas and the population here is willing to pay for better services.

Finally health care and education is an area of major importance. The commitment to train the Saudi youth for the new challenges of the 21st century suggests that more training expertise will be needed. Life expectancy rates among nationals have increased considerably. This trend is likely to continue and more and better health services are required.

The successful implementation of joint ventures

For a joint venture to succeed needs a great amount of effort by the parties involved. It is a partnership that involves more than the agreement to subscribe capital, technology, manufacturing expertise, marketing and sales know-how. The partnership is concerned with the handling of a long-term relationship. It involves sharing common management philosophies, strategic vision and understanding, as well as the division of risk and reward. It is worth noting that Saudi investors are generally not interested in participating as passive partners, ceding control to another party; they seek equitable division of responsibility and of revenue.

The ingredients for a successful venture in the Kingdom are essentially common to enterprises anywhere in the world: strategy, cost-effectiveness, superior production, technology, product competitiveness etc. However, there are certain aspects of strategy and management peculiar to Saudi Arabia which it might be useful to emphasise.

Planning

Solid business planning is required, with emphasis on marketing and distribution. The marketing part of the feasibility study is particularly critical and partners should agree on the objectives before starting out on the venture. The goals should be realistic and the new enterprise should be given sufficient time to become operational.

Competitive advantage

Achievement of an internationally competitive position is essential and joint ventures need to concentrate on those projects which have identifiable competitive advantage. Projects that need government support and tariff protection to survive should not be considered.

Local sources of supply

The joint venture should take full advantage of, and seek to develop, local sources of supply. It should encourage local sub-contracting whenever economically feasible. Because of the infancy of the industrial infrastructure in the Kingdom, the trend so far has been to carry out all processes and operations in-house, very often at considerable cost, because there has been no opportunity to contract out to specialised firms.

Organisation and training

The venture should listen to the local partner on organisational and personnel matters. It should establish from the outset a framework for a progression towards local management, with seconded management being phased out. Effective training programmes for local employees must also be developed.

Quality of management

High calibre managers have to be recruited to establish the venture. Employment in the Kingdom must be regarded as providing the same degree of career progression as a job in a developed country. The undeniable challenges of doing business in this part of the world should be viewed as valuable experience.

Agreement with the local partner

Full agreement on sources of supply and methods of funding for equipment, supplies and services is essential; the local partner may have his own interests in trading, construction or transport. The degree of technical support and input required from the foreign partner must also be established (eg technical sales, servicing facilities, etc). Local ownership should be at least 51 per cent to enable the venture to enjoy benefits denied to foreign-controlled joint ventures. The interests of the foreign partners can be protected by structuring the voting rights so that their permission is needed for any major policy decision.

Existing constraints on profitable joint ventures

Rates of return on investments in the Kingdom have declined from the highs of the 1970s and early 1980s and are close to those common elsewhere in the world. International companies are beginning to examine their options, given that their capital resources are limited and there are other markets in the world that may provide an equally competitive risk/return profile. However, the risk of doing business in Saudi Arabia tends sometimes to be exaggerated by foreign companies and there are many misconceptions that require clarification.

Uncertainties in the world oil market and its impact on public sector expenditure, duplication and surplus capacity in several areas of business, the risk associated with choosing the right partner, high unit costs of production and the lack of skilled manpower, genuine business risks associated with new markets and new products, the relatively small size of the domestic market, the less developed legal environment and concern about the future stability of the region are perhaps the main risks facing foreign investment in this part of the world.

The importance of the region's security and stability has come to the forefront following the Iraqi invasion of Kuwait. Even though Saudi Arabia is itself stable, the country lies in a high risk area and this increases the non-commercial risk element of any investment project. However, the recent crisis clearly demonstrated that the world is committed to the sovereignty, physical security and territorial integrity of the Gulf states. The Kingdom's internal stability over the past two decades has confounded doubters and remains far greater than that of most other developing countries.

Developments in the oil market are of vital concern to international companies planning to invest in joint venture projects in Saudi Arabia. The Kingdom's dependence on oil is worrying because it leaves the Saudi economy exposed to the vagaries of the world oil market. However, Saudi Arabia has been following a policy of economic diversification, the outcome of which will become more visible in the 1990s. The Kingdom has huge oil reserves that will keep it prosperous for many years to come and is the fortunate possessor of some of the cheapest oil in the world, which enables it to draw a large "economic rent" from oil sales. Annual oil revenues of around US$40 billion are undoubtedly more than sufficient to maintain healthy economic conditions for the 14 million people living in the Kingdom.

The Saudi market is among the most open and easily accessible in the world. The competition is intense and there is therefore a genuine market risk to be addressed by investors from abroad before embarking on a joint venture project. Managing for profitability is the key to success. A comprehensive feasibility study, based on realistic assumptions concerning market size, economic growth prospects, government expenditure, regional competition and trading patterns and the availability and costs of raw materials, labour and services in the light of the incentives available, is essential. If a joint venture project does not prove to be commercially viable over a specified period, it should not be considered. Future tariff or quota imposition should not be included as one of the criteria for the success of a project.

Another area of concern to the international investor has to do with choosing, and working with, a local joint venture partner. It is a more difficult decision here than elsewhere because people's real wealth and power are often disguised and companies' results are not fully disclosed. Choosing the right Saudi partner is essential, as it will be relied upon to provide local knowledge and contacts, assistance with marketing and a contribution to the establishment and operation of the business. Because it can prove difficult to identify the right joint venture partner, cooperation should ideally be developed on a satisfactory previous trading relationship, whereby trading partners evolve to become industrial partners. A sleeping partner should not be contemplated, as interest in, and enthusiasm for, the development of the project are vital for its success.

The Saudi consumer markets are characterised by high *per capita* purchasing power but the volume of sales is not so large as one would find in more densely populated countries. In addition, duplication and lack of coordination have resulted in excess capacity in certain industries. However, investors can look to all six GCC countries as a potential market. The overwhelming similarities between Gulf countries are gradually creating regional cooperation and more complementary arrangements between them. It is a declared policy that economic integration in the region will proceed more rapidly. The limited size of the domestic market is no longer a constraint when the size of the entire GCC is taken into account, with further potential for exporting to surrounding Arab states, Turkey, the Indian sub-continent, Central Asia and part of East Africa.

With respect to the high unit costs of production, it is true that the Kingdom does not yet have a large pool of trained Saudi workers who can man an expanding industrial sector. However, the country has no problem attracting the required skills from abroad. Besides, the cost of doing business has been falling recently. Wages and the prices of utilities and government services have dropped considerably and the country continues to record low inflation rates. The financial and tax incentives and the low energy costs also reduce any potential increase in unit costs of production. Of more specific interest to industry, the implicit price deflator for gross fixed investment in Saudi Arabia, which may be taken as a proxy for capital goods prices, is estimated to have grown at the modest average rate of 1.6 per cent annually between 1985 and 1991. Furthermore, those foreign firms who have invested in the country are finding their entry into export markets eased by the sharp depreciation of the Saudi riyal (pegged to the US dollar) against the currencies of Europe and Japan.

Another limitation to joint venture investment is the relatively undeveloped legal environment in the country. Resolution of legal disputes, even though it is improving, is still procedurally cumbersome and there is not a large body of published judicial precedent. In general, the legal system has not evolved at the same pace as the modernisation process. The absence of a well defined legal infrastructure to fall back on may have discouraged international business from taking longer-term positions in the country. However, comprehensive regulatory measures are being introduced, aimed at strengthening and simplifying the rules governing contracts and related disputes, and bureaucratic procedures are being streamlined to help create a more attractive industrial environment.

Conclusion

The nature of joint ventures in the Kingdom is changing: the early joint ventures were mainly in the construction sector, while recent collaborations have been more in the area of heavy industry (mainly petrochemicals, steel and refining). A third phase is now beginning, with future joint ventures likely to be in downstream industries, high technology, consumer goods, the food industry and services.

International companies are looking at their worldwide operations and questioning whether it is an opportune time for them to invest in the Kingdom. A short-term view of the country may prove deceptive. Long range strategic planning is required and those who do not make a decision now will find themselves at a disadvantage because of the initiative of others in the same line of business. Foreign companies who are interested in a quick profit will not find it now; the Saudi economy, in common with others, will have its ups and downs and foreign investors should be prepared to weather the occasional storm. Only those with a long-term commitment will be able to reap the benefits of their investment.

The failure rate of joint ventures worldwide is generally high. To succeed, planning and cooperation between the foreign and local partners are needed; compatibility, commitment and trust are the characteristics of a successful and enduring alliance. The foreign party is expected to provide technical and managerial expertise, while the local partner will reciprocate with his knowledge of the domestic market, his contacts with government agencies and his thorough understanding of the legal system.

Thorough market and cost research should be carried out in order to ensure the viability of an investment decision. Joint ventures in the Kingdom, just as elsewhere, have commercial risks that need to be managed and coped with. Even though ample financial and non-financial incentives are available for these projects, the government is not ready to underwrite their success. It is a pure business decision, with profitability as the key indicator. The Kingdom has become a normal market and no longer promises abnormal returns on investment. Foreign companies need to adjust their expectations accordingly and concentrate on those projects that have identifiable comparative advantages.

In a much tighter business environment the advantages of being on the spot increase. A foreign company with a formal joint venture presence, a proven management and marketing team and an effective distribution network can develop its business and promote its interests better than competitors who lack a Saudi base. Those on the spot will have easier access to the whole GCC market and will probably be eligible for GCC incentives. With the implementation of the Unified Economic Agreement among the six GCC states, a large number of manufacturing projects become viable on a regional basis. The Agreement specifies that local manufacturing within the GCC will be protected by a common tariff applied by all the member states once reasonable capacity has been reached. Investment decisions should, therefore, capitalise on the opportunities provided by the existing cooperative schemes among the GCC states; this will enable investors to reap the benefits of a market extending throughout the Gulf and with prospects for exports to other Middle Eastern, North African and Central Asian countries.

Appendix

Foreign Capital Investment Law

Promulgated by Royal Decree No M/4 of 2/2/1399 AH

Article 1

For the purposes of this Law, Foreign Capital shall mean any coins, currency notes, securities, machinery, equipment, spare parts, raw materials, products, transportation facilities, and intangible rights, such as patents, trademarks, and similar assets, where such capital is owned either by a natural person who is not of Saudi Arabian nationality or by a corporate person whose capital shareholders are not all of Saudi Arabian nationality.

Article 2

Without violation to the provisions of other laws in force, Foreign Capital investment requires a licence issued by the Minister of Industry and Electricity following the recommendation of the Foreign Investment Committee, provided that the following two conditions are fulfilled:

- the Foreign Capital shall be invested in development projects which, for the purposes of this Law, do not include petroleum and mineral extraction projects; and
- the investment shall be accompanied by foreign technical know-how and expertise.

Article 3

Development projects shall be determined by a resolution from the Minister of Industry and Electricity following the recommendations of the Foreign Investment Committee within the guidelines of the development plan.

Article 4

A committee called the "Foreign Capital Committee" shall be set up in the Ministry of Industry and Electricity. The committee shall be composed of the following members:

- the Deputy Minister of Industry and Electricity, or his substitute (in the event of his absence), to act as Chairman;
- a representative from the Ministry of Planning;
- a representative from the Ministry of Finance and National Economy;
- a representative from the Ministry of Agriculture and Water;
- a representative from the Ministry of Petroleum and Mineral Resources; and
- a representative from the Ministry of Commerce.

None of the representatives for the membership of the committee shall rank lower than the tenth grade. The Director of the Foreign Investment Bureau at the Ministry of Industry and Electricity shall act as Secretary to the Committee and the Minister of Industry and Electricity shall appoint a legal advisor for the committee. The committee may, at its own discretion, call on certain experts during the discussion of certain subjects, but these experts shall have no voting right. The meetings of the committee shall be valid only if attended by at least four members including the Chairman; and the committee's deliberations shall be confidential. The resolutions of the committee shall be adopted by a majority of attending votes. In case of a tie, the Chairman shall have the casting vote. However, the committee's resolutions shall not become final unless approved and ratified by the Minister of Industry and Electricity.

Article 5

The Committee, referred to in Article 4, shall have the following tasks:

- to propose the projects that will be classified as development projects;
- to consider Foreign Investment applications;
- to examine any complaints or claims submitted by foreign investors or other parties concerned arising out of questions governed by this Law; and to submit its recommendations on these matters to the competent authorities;
- to recommend penalties which, in the opinion of the committee, should be imposed on any project violating the provisions of this Law;

- to draft rules of procedures for the implementation of this Law; and
- to consider matters, referred to the Committee by the Minister of Industry and Electricity, concerning the provisions of this Law.

Article 6

The Foreign Capital Investment Bureau of the Ministry of Industry and Electricity shall supply all necessary information, clarifications, and statistical data to any foreign applicant who desires to invest capital in the Kingdom. The bureau shall also facilitate and complete necessary formalities pertaining to licensed Foreign Investments. The Ministry of Foreign Affairs and the Ministry of Interior shall grant to investors licensed in accordance with this Law, their employees and workers entry and exit visas and residence permits.

Article 7

Foreign Capital which has fulfilled the conditions provided for in this Law shall have the following privileges:

- privileges enjoyed by national capital under the Law for the Protection and Promotion of National Industries in respect to industrial projects only;
- exemption from Income Tax and Company Tax for a period of ten years to any industrial or agricultural projects having Foreign Capital. Other projects shall be exempted from such taxes for a period of five years.

The projects which enjoy exemption at the time of the implementation of this Law shall benefit from the provisions of exemption mentioned in this sub-clause.

The prerequisite for a tax exemption is that Saudi capital shall not be less than twenty five per cent of the total capital of the project and that such a percentage shall be maintained throughout the period of exemption.

For industrial projects the period of exemption shall start as of the date of the commencement of production and for other projects from the start of activities.

This last sub-clause may be amended by a resolution by the Council of Minsters; and

- ownership of any real estate required by Foreign Investment projects in accordance with the Law for Non-Saudi Ownership of Real Estate.

Article 8

Without violation to the provisions herein, projects benefiting from the provisions of this Law shall be subject to the Labour Law, the Law for Social Insurance, and other Laws in force in the Kingdom.

Article 9

The provisions of this Law shall not apply to the projects in which Foreign Capital is invested in the following cases:

• if the project was legally in existence prior to the implementation of this Law. However, the operation of such projects or any increase in their capital shall be subject to the provisions of this Law; and

• if the project is authorised to operate in the Kingdom by virtue of special laws or agreements.

Article 10

Any project licensed under this Law, violating the provisions herein, shall be warned by the Minister of Industry and Electricity to abide by these provisions within a period to be specified by the Minister. Should such project not comply with the said warning, the Minister may, following a recommendation by the Foreign Investment Committee, withdraw the licence granted to that project or order its final liquidation and closure.

Following a recommendation by the said committee, the Minister may, in lieu of withdrawing the licence, deprive such project of all or part of the privileges provided under this Law.

However, parties concerned may appeal to the Board of Grievances, against the Minister's decision imposing such penalty, within thirty days as of the date on which the decision has been officially notified.

The verdict of the Board of Grievances shall be final and binding.

Article 11

The rules of procedure for the implementation of this Law shall be issued by the Minister of Industry and Electricity and shall be published in the *Official Gazette.*

Article 12

This Law shall be published in the *Official Gazette* and shall become effective thirty days after the date of its publication. The Foreign Capital Investment Law promulgated by the Royal Decree No. 35 dated 11/10/1383 AH shall be superseded as of the date this Law is put into effect.

Procedure for establishing projects

(1) The prospective investor should write to the Ministry of Industry and Electricity for permission of the Ministry to initiate a feasibility study on the proposed project.

The latter should contain the following information:

• type of industrial activity proposed;
• approximate output capacity of the project;
• location of the project; and
• name and address of the investor, including telephone/telex number, if available.

(2) The above letter of the prospective investor will be studied by the Grace-Period Section of the Industrial Licensing Department to judge the supply and demand position for both the product proposed and

substitute products. If the study shows a need for the establishment of the proposed industrial project, the prospective investor will receive from the Ministry permission for a grace period of six months, within which (subject to No. 3 below), he will submit to the Ministry the following:

- projects with proposed capital investment between one and ten millions Saudi riyals. The prescribed "Licence Application Form" should be completed, wherein the capital investment should consist of the fixed capital plus the quarterly cost of raw materials, salaries and wages, and running costs; and
- projects with proposed capital investment of more than ten million Saudi riyals. In addition to the above, the following items are required: economic study of the project (market, investment required, production cost, break-even point, return on investment, and cash flow); and technical study of the project (method of production, types of equipment, raw materials, etc).

(3) If the prospective investor finds that the grace period of six months is not sufficient to complete the feasibility study he may, at the end of this period, be granted upon his request an extension of period not more than three months. The extension is granted to him if he provides reasonable justification to the Ministry.

(4) At the end of the grace period, or when the study is finalised, an application for Licence should be made on the prescribed Licence Application Form, which is available at the Foreign Capital Investment Bureau. The completed application form and the relevant studies should be submitted to the Foreign Capital Investment Bureau. These documents should be submitted under a covering letter showing the date and number of Ministry's permission referred to in (2) or (3) above.

(5) Grace periods are granted only to businessmen and investors in general. The Ministry does not grant grace periods to consulting firms or any intermediaries.

(6) Expansions of licensed projects do not require the application for grace periods. But the owner of the licensed project will have to submit an Expansion Application Form together with a written justification showing increased market demands and potentialities.

(7) Incomplete applications will not be accepted by the Foreign Investment Bureau.

(8) The Foreign Investment Bureau will forward the Licence application/ documents to the Industrial Licensing Department for evaluation. On receipt of the evaluation Report, the documents would be placed before the Foreign Investment Committee which will, in turn, submit its recommendation to the Minister of Industry and Electricity.